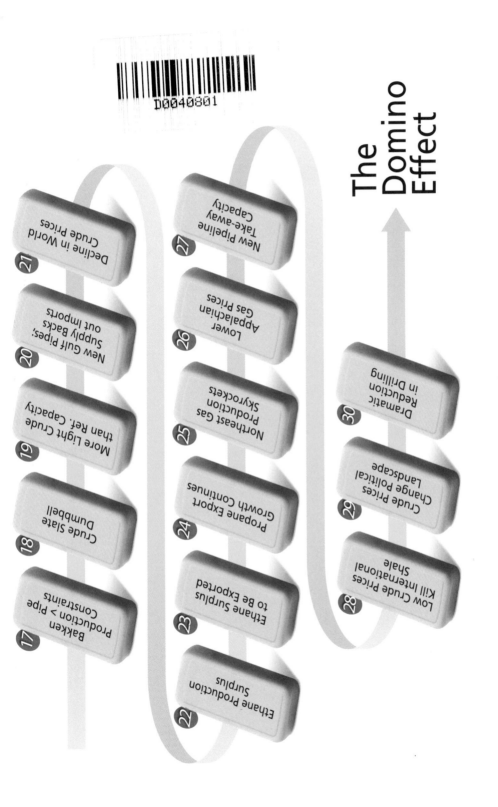

The Domino Effect

21 Decline in World Crude Prices

20 New Gulf pipes; Supply Backs out imports

19 More Light Crude than Ref. Capacity

18 Crude Slate Dumbbell

17 Bakken Production > Pipe Constraints

22 Ethane Production Surplus

23 Ethane Surplus to Be Exported

24 Propane Export Growth Continues

25 Northeast Gas Production Skyrockets

26 Lower Appalachian Gas Prices

27 New pipeline Take-away Capacity

28 Low Crude Prices Kill International Shale

29 Crude Prices Change Political Landscape

30 Dramatic Reduction in Drilling

The Domino Effect

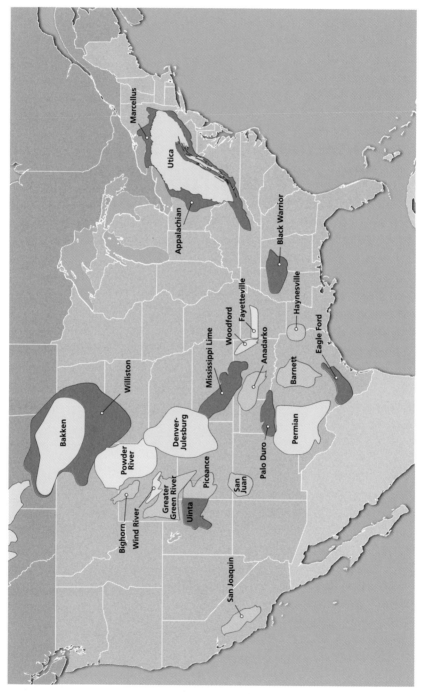

U.S. Drill-Bit-Hydrocarbon-Producing Basins

The Domino Effect

How the Shale Revolution Is Transforming Energy Markets, Industries, and Economies

E. Russell Braziel

**NTA
PRESS**

For information regarding bulk purchases [and discounts], please write sales@dominoeffect.com.

Cover Design by Roger Ibanez
Book Design and Production by CWL Publishing Enterprises, Inc., Madison, Wisconsin, www.cwlpub.com.
Manufacturing by Thomson-Shore, Dexter, Michigan

Photo Credits:
Picture of E. Russell Braziel, back cover, Michael Carr and Associates, Houston, TX, www.michaelcarrphotography.com
Figure 4.2. Fishtail Bits and Roughnecks © Story Sloane, http://www.sloane-gallery.com
Figure 4.3. Sharp-Hughes Rock Bit (http://aoghs.org/this-week-in-petroleum-history/oil-history-august-5)
Figure 12.3. © Abdelmajidfahim | Dreamstime.com - Pipeline Pig Cleaner Photo

The author wishes to thank the following for permission to use their copyrighted material:
"The Times They Are A-Changin'" by Bob Dylan. Copyright © 1963, 1964 by Warner Bros. Inc.; renewed 1991, 1992 by Special Rider Music.
Quotation from Albert Einstein, Cosmic Religion: With Other Opinions and Aphorisms (2009: Dover Publications, ISBN 978-0486470108), page 97.
Words and Music by John Lennon and Paul McCartney, Copyright © 1968 Sony/ATV Music Publishing LLC. Copyright Renewed. All Rights Administered by Sony/ATV Music Publishing LLC, 424 Church Street, Suite 1200, Nashville, TN 37219. International Copyright Secured. All Rights Reserved. Reprinted by Permission of Hal Leonard Corporation.

To my wife, Teresa
our children, Heather, TJ, and David
and our grandchildren, Jane, Lawson, and Alice

Contents

The Domino Effect:
An Introduction

T HIS BOOK IS ABOUT UNDERSTANDING ENERGY MARKETS: PRICES, FLOWS, *infrastructure, value, and economics. It is a critical examination of the responses of those markets since the advent of the shale revolution, a framework for understanding what happens next, and an explanation of how shale will continue to drive the energy industry in the coming decades in the United States and throughout the world.*

The shale revolution has run roughshod over U.S. energy markets, transforming an era characterized by shortage into one of abundance. It came first to natural gas—then to the markets for natural gas liquids. And finally, it landed like a ton of bricks on crude oil. The revolution has spurred billions of dollars in infrastructure investment, reversed the direction of pipeline flows, and radically disrupted energy prices. It has been said that this is just another cycle in an industry with a long history of boom-bust cycles. But could something completely new be reshaping the dynamics of energy markets?

The answer to that question is a resounding yes! The shale revolution has unleashed forces that not only disrupt and realign energy markets but that have dramatic political, economic, and national defense implications. To say that these developments have been a surprise is the energy market understatement of the twenty-first century.

In fact, there have been a lot of surprises: U.S. petrochemicals have seen a renaissance and are planning huge capacity increases. Coal companies are turning out the lights as natural gas takes power generation market share. Natural gas pipelines that moved gas from the Gulf Coast to the Northeast for decades are reversing and flowing gas the other way. The fastest growing markets for U.S. energy supplies are exports. Railroads have assumed a major role in moving crude from producers to refineries. Crude oil prices dropped by 50% in late 2014. And there have been many more seemingly unrelated developments in the energy markets that did not make the headlines. But should they really have been that surprising?

All these developments may seem to have happened randomly, but not so. There is a pattern here. It is a pattern that not only ties these seemingly disparate events together but reveals why this is much more than just another boom-bust cycle. This pattern not only helps explain why the shale revolution has evolved the way it has but also provides a framework for understanding how it is likely to play out in the future.

But this pattern is not just hanging out there for anyone to see. Otherwise, this whole thing would not have been such a surprise to so many people. The pattern is obscured by the rush of market noise, misinformation, and general ignorance about what really makes energy markets tick.

This pattern is the *domino effect*.

The domino effect is a way of understanding what is going on in today's energy markets. It is defined by a sequence of market events, but it is explained by a set of principles that drive these events. It applies across the markets for natural gas, natural gas liquids (NGLs), and crude oil. In fact, it is the interrelationship across these three energy commodity groups that enables the chain of events which defines the domino effect.

The catalyst for launching the domino effect has been technology—more specifically the pace of technological innovation in drilling and completion technologies that has shifted the supply curve—changing the economics of oil and gas production in a certain geological formation.

Shale.

It's a rock. More specifically, shale is a sedimentary rock that, millions of years ago, was mud and other organic materials at the bottom of some marsh or bog, eventually buried under thousands of feet of more rock and dirt that compressed and cooked it into solid rock. It is that organic material—the remains of plants and animals—that eventually became the oil and gas we use today.

Almost all of the organic materials beneath the earth's surface were originally deposited in shales and other sedimentary rocks called mudstones. The organic materials make up only a very small percentage of this rock, but there is a lot of this source rock deposited in locations around the world. It is the cradle of all the oil and gas that has been, or ever will be, produced.

Until very recently, it was not economically feasible to extract oil and gas directly from the shale. Shale has a fine grain and is highly compacted, so the hydrocarbons are imprisoned inside the rock. Fortunately for modern civilization, over millions of years some of these hydrocarbons percolated up and out of the shales into much more permeable and porous rock, locked below other geologic formations which captured the escaping hydrocarbons in underground reservoirs or traps. It is these traps that oil and gas producers have been tapping since the inception of oil and gas drilling. These formations, called conventional reservoirs, were sometimes hard to find. But once found, they could be expected to yield economically producible quantities of oil and gas. Such reservoirs were the source of essentially all oil and gas production up until the onset of the shale revolution.

Unfortunately, over time, conventional reservoirs became increasingly tapped out and new ones were hard to find, a fact that supported the notion that the United States was depleting its oil and gas production and would someday run out. Pundits pointed toward the decline of U.S. production from the mid-1980s through the 1990s as conclusive evidence that this must be true. As the world entered a new millennium, the U.S. energy industry was in full swing with investments to accommodate a world of energy shortage. Multi-billion-dollar outlays for liquefied natural gas (LNG) import terminals were underway. Refineries were gearing up to run far greater quantities of imported crude oil because U.S. oil was running out. Power generation companies were scrambling to bring on coal, wind, solar, and even nuclear generation to avoid being caught by declining supplies of natural gas.

But then, seemingly overnight, evidence started to emerge that something had changed. In the mid-2000s, natural gas prices declined and stayed low. Defying conventional wisdom, gas production started to ramp up toward all-time historical highs. It was not supposed to happen like that. Lower prices are supposed to result in fewer working drill rigs, which cuts back drilling activity. And less drilling is, in turn, supposed to result in lower production volumes. But this time, in the natural gas markets of the late 2000s, that relationship did not hold true.

Over time it became apparent that this transformation in the relationship between price, rig counts, drilling, and production was not confined to natural gas. By 2012, NGL prices succumbed to oversupply. And then, in late 2014, the full brunt of oversupply hit global crude oil markets.

Driving this shift in market relationships is technology—more specifically the application of technologies that have made oil and gas drilling much more productive than in the past. A single rig can drill more wells and produce more hydrocarbons at a much lower per-unit cost than was possible in the pre-shale era. In other words, the production of each barrel of oil and each cubic foot of natural gas from shale is cheaper than from conventional reservoirs using traditional production techniques. It is this improvement in productivity that has changed the landscape of energy markets.

Of course, like all overnight success stories, this one did not really happen overnight. Horizontal drilling and hydraulic fracturing technologies have been around for many decades. It was just that producers had not figured out how to use these technologies to extract oil and gas directly out of shale. That revelation happened in the late 1990s, but the significance of the shift was below the radar of most of the energy market.

The signs started to become visible in the mid-2000s. But few were paying attention. Even when some of the independent producers proclaimed giant discoveries that would provide 100 years and more of natural gas supply, it was written off as hype and self-promotion. Not this time. The giant discoveries were real. As the months and years rolled by and production statistics accumulated, so did the evidence. Eventually, even the hard-core nonbelievers had to admit something had changed.

But exactly what changed, whether it will last and how it will play out in the decades ahead, was and still remains the subject of robust debate. Why did the whole shale thing seem to come out of the blue? How can much more expensive wells be more profitable? They have steep decline curves, so won't the revolution just sputter out in a wave of failed companies and investment portfolios? Could shale just be a big Ponzi scheme? And why does shale development seem to be confined to the United States? How do you separate the truth from fiction? On what basis do you reach your conclusions? And how do you translate those conclusions into an understanding of the opportunities presented by this remarkable sea change in energy markets?

These are big questions. The key to the answers lies in a clear, unbiased understanding of what is going on in the new reality of hydrocarbon energy markets. Providing that understanding is the intent of *The Domino Effect*.

A total of 30 dominoes have toppled since the late 1990s through the present, representing a chain reaction of tightly linked market events that have shaped today's energy industry. In the decades to come, many more dominoes will fall. These dominoes are not simply random occurrences. Instead, the domino sequence is driven by six principles that underlie energy commodity markets. Understanding these principles and the individual dominoes provides the context for how we got here and holds the keys for understanding what will happen next.

Omnia Causa Fiunt

Everything Happens for a Reason

How *The Domino Effect* Is Organized

This book is organized into five parts, outlined below. Even if you are an expert in energy markets, the concepts presented in this book will make much more sense if you read each part sequentially. Later chapters refer back to concepts described in the earlier chapters, concepts that may not always track with generally accepted thinking on the topic.

Part I. The Times They Are A-Changin': The Domino Effect

The four chapters in Part I explain how the domino effect developed and how it reshaped energy markets in the early years of the shale revolution. Chapter 1 is an overview of the domino effect concept. Chapters 2 and 3 show how the first 16 dominoes fell and what happened when they did. Then, Chapter 4 introduces the six domino effect principles and explains the concept of the drill-bit hydrocarbons, the three energy commodities that define the shale revolution.

Part II. The Three Amigos: Natural Gas, NGLs, and Crude Oil

To understand energy commodity markets today, it is necessary to have a sense of their history, the way they trade, and what has been happening to each of the drill-bit hydrocarbon markets since the shale revolution began. Chapter 5 gets into the details of natural gas markets. Then, Chapter 6 examines natural gas liquids (NGLs). Finally we wrap up Part II with crude oil, certainly the highest-profile member of the drill-bit hydrocarbon family.

Part III. Takin' Care of Business: How Things Work in the Energy Markets

Part III explains how energy markets work. Chapters 8 and 9 provide a foundation in production economics: why the production of shale oil and gas can be so lucrative, even when prices are down. Chapters 10 and 11 review how those economics impact markets and why shale changes everything about the interrelationships between energy commodities. Chapters 12, 13, and 14 uncover the secrets of energy market behavior: how supply, demand, and infrastructure interact to drive prices, and how prices drive infrastructure development.

Part IV. What's Goin' On: How the Energy Markets Are Changing and Why

Far from slowing down, the pace of change in energy markets is speeding up. Building upon the early dominoes and the foundation of energy fundamentals presented in Parts II and III, Part IV picks up with the most recent dominoes to topple, those that continue to demonstrate the incredible pace of change brought on by the shale revolution. Chapter 15 considers huge shifts in the crude oil and refining sectors, including the impact of changing crude quality, new export rules, infrastructure investments, and dramatic price declines. Chapter 16 looks at natural gas liquids and how increasing production is driving a petrochemical renaissance and a transition to an export-driven market. Chapter 17 describes the most significant developments in the natural gas markets, including huge production increases from the Marcellus/Utica region, new demand from gas-fired power generation and exports.

Part V: Break on Through to the Other Side: The New World of Energy Abundance

Part V addresses the broader implications of the shale revolution and what is likely to happen next. Chapter 18 examines the potential for shale development outside the borders of North America. Chapter 19 explores the political, economic, and national defense implications of the domino effect, particularly the impact of exporting all three drill-bit hydrocarbons or their derivatives. Chapter 20 weaves the six principles from Chapter 4 together with the sum total of the 30 fallen dominoes into a road map that enables you to recognize the dominoes which are likely to fall in the future. Finally, Chapter 21 wraps up with a high-level assessment of the opportunities—investment, trade, and career—that have been opened by the shale revolution and the domino effect.

Chapter 18. Does the United States Have a Monopoly on Shale?
Chapter 19. The Big Picture: Economic and Political Fallout
Chapter 20. You Ain't Seen Nothin' Yet: The Next Dominoes to Fall
Chapter 21. Over the Horizon: Assessment of the Opportunities

The Bottom Line

Technology has transformed energy markets. Production growth has been astronomical. Billions of dollars in infrastructure investment to get energy commodities to market has been made or is currently underway. At the same time, the shifting sources of supply will make some existing assets obsolete. The U.S. will become a major energy supplier to the world. Opportunities to build huge value are abundant. It is a great time to be involved in the energy industry.

To the Reader

THIS BOOK IS ABOUT ENERGY MARKETS. I'VE WRITTEN IT FOR THREE reasons. First, because energy matters. It is a driving force behind industrial progress, from the first fire lit by a caveman to the shale revolution of the twenty-first century. Since I began my career in this business, just a few months after the 1973 oil crisis, energy markets have been characterized mostly by long-term production declines and the expectation that energy prices would march steadily upward. Shale is changing that perception, shifting the fundamental dynamics of how the oil and gas industry works. Shale has created a game-changing disruption, touching every aspect of the energy business, from where we drill a hole in the ground to where that energy is used and for what. With this book, my intent is to explain what has changed, why and how it has changed, and what it means for the future of energy markets.

Which brings me to my second reason: a multi-commodity perspective. Over my forty-odd-year career, I have worked in the markets for all three of the energy commodity families at the heart of the shale revolution: natural gas, natural gas liquids, and crude oil. You might well ask, "What's so exceptional about that?" Surely energy companies rotate employees through different products and markets to give them a breadth of experience, right?

Wrong. Or at least not usually right. In the past, it was pretty rare to work in a commercial role in more than one of these hydrocarbon markets, even if your company was involved in all three. That was the old way the energy business operated, but no longer. Today, cross-commodity relationships are driving change through energy markets and are disrupting conventional thinking about how these markets behave. In my opinion, having the opportunity to work in natural gas, NGL, and crude oil trading organizations has given me a unique perspective from which to explain the relationships between these three commodity groups.

This leads me to the third reason for writing this book: the need for an understandable, usable, and (mostly) unbiased explanation of what the shale revolution really means. Presumably, since you are reading these pages, you are part of a growing audience eager to learn more about energy markets. You might be a market wonk or industry insider with whom I frequently debate these issues in the course of the RBN Energy blog dialogue. You might be an investment banker or hedge fund manager who is keen to understand the incredibly disruptive energy market events and translate them into investment opportunities. You might be an industry executive who needs to know the long-term implications of the shale hydrocarbon energy resource. You might be a concerned citizen, interested in understanding one of the most important and significant economic developments in decades.

Regardless of your motivation, it probably has something to do with the onslaught of the shale revolution and the paucity of nontechnical, apolitical information on the topic. It seems there is a gap in the written material: either it is confined to the domain of geophysicists and engineers, or else it is propaganda supporting one side or the other in the energy-versus-environment debate.

The intent of *The Domino Effect* is to fill this gap with a reasoned, relatively unbiased assessment of the factors driving today's energy market developments. I say "relatively unbiased" because, having spent my entire career in this industry, it would be somewhat implausible to assert that I am truly unbiased. However, it is my erstwhile intention to cover these developments from the most unbiased, apolitical, and open-minded perspective possible. I will not be discussing the political debates surrounding fracking or anti-fracking, global warming versus clean energy, or any other issue that pits energy production against the environment. It's not that I don't care about these issues. It is just that *The Domino Effect* is about markets, not policy or politics. That said, this book asserts that the shale revolution will continue to expand regardless of politics, global market competition, or even energy prices.

The Genesis of the Domino Effect

I do a lot of public speaking at industry conferences, for consulting client engagements and the like, explaining how energy markets work. At one such session, a Morgan Stanley midstream conference in New York on March 7, 2012, I introduced the domino effect as a single PowerPoint slide. It was the last slide in my presentation deck, intended to give the audience a neat summation of market developments. For much of 2012, I continued to use that slide to close my presentations. Toward the end of the year, a conference participant came up to me and said, "Boy, that last slide was really helpful. Your whole presentation would have made a lot more sense if you had started with it in the first place."

Hmm. I realized the domino effect was not just a summation device. It could be a framework for helping people understand how seemingly unrelated events in the shale revolution fit together, particularly if the underlying drivers for the domino effect could be isolated and explained. That became my goal: to lay out the market events that have shaped the shale revolution up until now and to provide a framework to make sense of the massive changes in this industry that are just over the horizon.

Please do not regard the domino effect as some unifying theory of the universe that will explain everything about the energy business. It isn't, and it won't. Instead, it is simply a way of grasping the new dynamics of the markets for natural gas, NGLs, and crude oil. I hope it will help explain the shale revolution so that it makes more sense to you.

Rusty Braziel
September 2015

PS. The ideas, concepts and analysis surrounding *The Domino Effect* are original work I have developed over four decades of involvement in energy markets. This book is not intended as an academic work; therefore, there are few footnotes or references except for those specifying data sources for graphs and charts. Most of the statistics are based on data from the U.S. Energy Information Administration (www.eia.gov). The sources for historical events include Internet articles, books, industry publications, and word of mouth, and are as verifiably factual as possible.

Acknowledgments

I AM ETERNALLY GRATEFUL TO JACK ROCHESTER, MY TEACHER, SPIRITUAL guide, taskmaster, editor, and good friend, who helped me every step of the way from a nebulous concept to a finished manuscript. Jack, it would have never happened without your persistence, discipline, and enthusiasm. Thanks also to Jack's team of Casie Vogel and John Woods for doing a great job in the book's production.

This book was made possible by the support and encouragement of the team at RBN Energy: David Braziel (my son), Ashley Braziel (my daughter-in-law), Housley Carr, Noel Copeland, Ron Gist, Christine Groenewold, Paige Hambric, Jeremy Meier, Callie Mitchell, Scott Potter, Omilla SinghAhamad, Rick Smead, Kelly Van Hull, Heather Wallace (my daughter) and Sheetal Nasta, who read the early drafts and helped get the logic straight. Special thanks to Brenda and Roger Ibanez for working long weekends, nights, and odd hours to pull the charts, diagrams, cover, and other graphics together. And to Sandy Fielden who cut me no slack in describing the conceptual underpinnings of the domino effect.

I would have never had the opportunity to tackle this project in the first place if not for my former colleagues at Bentek Energy who launched me on the adventure of energy market analytics—Porter Bennett, Jim Simpson and Rich Rinehart. At Bentek, we proved that information can change energy markets. And Bentek was just a start.

I've saved the most important acknowledgement for last—my wife, Teresa, who has endured endless non-weekends, writing "vacations," and perpetual declarations that "I'm finished." It is really done now. Thank you for your love and infinite patience.

Part I

The Times They Are A-Changin': The Domino Effect

Your old road is
Rapidly agin'
Please get out of the new one
If you can't lend your hand
For the times they are a-changin'.
—Bob Dylan

CHANGE. AS THE SONG LYRICS POINT OUT, THE TIMES ARE INDEED CHANG-
ing, particularly for oil and gas. Just a few years ago it was generally accepted that the oil and gas industry was one that had seen its better days.
However, about a decade ago, the world of hydrocarbon energy started
to change, and more changes are on the way.

The theme of this book—the domino effect—is based upon a simple
concept intended to help you understand the reasons behind these changes.
An event is represented by a domino. Something happens, causing a
domino to fall, striking another domino, which strikes another and so creates
a chain of cascading events that can lead to unexpected consequences.

Part I of this book explains the foundation of the domino effect as it occurs in the oil and gas industry, starting in the late 1990s. In order to help
you grasp the domino concept, Chapter 1 quickly reviews the first dominoes
to fall: dominoes one through sixteen. Chapters 2 and 3 then go back over
the dominoes in more depth to explain how and why they fell. Chapter 4
lays out the fundamental developments that changed the oil and gas business
and which led up to, and continues to drive, more falling dominoes.

Chapter 1

What Is the
Domino Effect?

THIS BOOK IS ABOUT UNDERSTANDING ENERGY MARKETS: PRICES, FLOWS, *infrastructure, value, and economics. It is a critical examination of the responses of those markets since the advent of the shale revolution, a framework for understanding what happens next, and an explanation of how shale will continue to drive the energy industry in the coming decades in the United States and throughout the world. It is most certainly not about geology or petroleum engineering, and for that reason, does not contain a scientific explanation of shale drilling or technologies. Instead,* The Domino Effect *is about markets: how those markets are being shaped by, and how they are in turn shaping, the shale revolution.*

Energy markets in the shale revolution do not behave the way they did pre-shale. Today's energy market realities have confounded many who have tried to make sense out of them, because they have attempted to extrapolate the way things worked in the pre-shale world. It simply does not work that way anymore. The shale revolution has demonstrated a unique capability to ricochet one market's effect onto others, tying energy commodity markets together in ways not seen before. One development triggers another that elicits another, and so on. Some of the causal relationships seem obvious, particularly in hindsight. Others, like the collapse of crude oil prices in late 2014 have been a surprise, if not a shock. Few of these relationships are understood outside a small cadre of industry insiders.

This cascading series of events is the domino effect and is the subject of this book. The domino effect helps explain how we got here, what is happening now, and where we are heading. Think of energy markets as a big puzzle. If you can figure out how the puzzle fits together, you win. By understanding the domino effect, you can do just that—win in energy markets—because you'll understand and anticipate developments in these markets. The domino effect is driving energy markets: their pricing, distribution, and investments. It will continue doing so for the foreseeable future.

The best way to explain the domino effect is by perusing a few of the dominoes, and the best place to start is at the beginning. This chapter is intended to get the domino-effect concept across by providing a brief overview of the first sixteen dominoes.

Running on Empty?

Beginning in the 1970s, there was a prevalent fear that the United States was running out of accessible crude oil and natural gas. It was becoming increasingly difficult to find conventional reservoirs that would yield commercial quantities of these hydrocarbons. Producers knew that shale— the source of the hydrocarbons from the conventional reservoirs—held vast quantities of oil and gas, but everyone knew that it was impractical and too expensive to get to it. Almost everyone. In the late 1990s, George Mitchell and his intrepid band of engineers at Mitchell Energy figured out how to extract natural gas on an economically viable basis from the Barnett Shale, just outside Fort Worth, Texas.

That was Domino 1: shale technologies came first to U.S. natural gas markets. Mr. Mitchell proved it could be done, and—just like what happened in aeronautics after the Wright brothers flew the first airplane— others jumped into the industry, intending to replicate Mitchell's success. Eventually many did.

But energy is not airplanes. Energy, particularly in the United States, trades in commodity markets. As anyone who has suffered through Econ 101 knows, free-market commodity prices are determined by the interplay of supply and demand, regardless of the industry or product. The energy business is no exception: energy products are commodities, and it is this interplay of supply, demand, and price that drives the domino effect. Here's a summary of what happened from the early Mitchell era through 2012:

- Shale technologies, *Domino 1*, significantly enhanced the returns producers were able to achieve by drilling for and producing natural gas. That led to much more drilling, which supercharged natural gas production. In turn, this led to an oversupply of natural gas, *Domino 2*.

- The laws of economics say oversupply results in lower prices, and that is exactly what happened with *Domino 3*: natural gas prices fell. It was good news for natural gas consumers.

- However, lower natural gas prices were not good news for everyone, especially producers of natural gas. Lower prices had a negative impact on their economics, resulting in poor financial returns from drilling for and producing natural gas. But there was a way for many producers to recapture those high rates of return—by shifting their shale-drilling activities to crude oil and to so-called wet gas that contained natural gas liquids (NGLs). Neither of these markets had yet to see their commodity prices crushed, as had natural gas prices. This shift of drilling activity was *Domino 4*.

- Once again, producers were too successful for their own good, which led to oversupply, first in the NGL markets. Increasing NGL production was *Domino 5* and resulted in supply surpluses, which in turn toppled *Domino 6*: NGL prices declined. This triggered *Domino 7*; those lower NGL prices launched a huge surge of profitability in the petrochemical industry (the largest market for NGLs) and resulted in an onslaught of new multibillion-dollar plant-investment announcements, intended to capitalize on the bounty of cheap NGLs.

- Just as low natural gas reprioritized drilling activity to NGLs, producers also shifted drilling activity to oil-rich areas. The impact on crude oil markets was similar to the impact on NGLs, though more regionally focused. In *Domino 8*, crude oil production increased, initially in the Williston Basin's Bakken play in North Dakota. Again a surplus developed, this time centered on the big crude oil trading hub at Cushing, Oklahoma. As a result of the excess oil supply in the region, *Domino 9* dropped and crude oil prices in the Midcontinent declined. This resulted in the fall of *Domino 10*, and refineries in the region realized huge profits. Not only was the crude cheaper, but the increase in production encouraged investment in new pipeline and crude-by-rail projects designed to get that crude to more refineries.

■ Ironically, as producers shifted away from developing natural gas production and looked to NGLs and crude oil to earn most of their profits, they also got a by-product of drilling for those commodities: even more natural gas, which comes along with the production of NGLs and most crude oil. So more dominoes dropped. In *Domino 11*, natural gas—driven by by-product gas production that came along with NGLs and crude oil—continued to increase gas volumes to all-time records, continuing oversupply conditions. In *Domino 12*, the price of natural gas remained low due to oversupply. That triggered *Domino 13*—lower fuel costs for power-generation companies, industrial plants, and residential markets.

■ At that point, those lower natural gas prices resulted in a shift by power generation companies from coal to cleaner natural gas, which was *Domino 14*. In *Domino 15*, the quantity of coal used for power generation declined, resulting in lower coal demand and hard times for coal companies. To wrap up this roll call of the first few dominoes, motivated by the abundance of natural gas supplies and low gas prices, scores of new industrial projects were announced. This was *Domino 16*.

Oh, oh, domino.

Each of these dominoes was a major market event or development in its own right, shifting billions of dollars out of the pockets of those on the wrong side of the energy markets—like coal companies—to those on the right side—like chemical companies. For those following individual markets hit by these dominoes, such as the markets for natural gas, NGLs, crude oil, coal, or petrochemicals, it may have seemed as though some of the events described here came out of the blue, each creating significant, unanticipated economic shifts. Not so. When looked at as a chain of mutually interdependent events, it becomes clear that these shifts were not only understandable, but also predictable.

And that is precisely the point. Because the domino effect does not stop with number sixteen. The domino effect has continued to tumble through energy markets, with implications for exports, flow reversals, prices, drilling activity, and ultimately global energy supply and demand. In the chapters to follow, we will examine a total of thirty dominoes that consider such developments. And we will assess the implications for many more dominoes that are just over the horizon.

As you've read about these first dominoes, you might have asked yourself, "What keeps the dominoes from being just a disparate listing of events?" They are much more than that. Nothing really occurred out of the blue. The connections and interdependencies across the natural gas, NGL, and crude oil markets can be understood, and the changes and disruptions can often be anticipated. Just as there are certain laws of mechanics that make real dominoes fall, there are certain laws or principles that govern what makes the domino effect occur in the markets for natural gas, NGLs and crude oil, collectively referred to in this book as the drill-bit hydrocarbons.

Described in the chapters to follow, there are six principles upon which the domino effect is based. They explain what has made the dominoes fall the way they have so far and why more will continue to fall in the future. It is these principles that are the essence of the domino-effect concept, but in order to fully grasp them, it is necessary to understand in more detail what happened with the first sixteen dominoes. That is where we will go in Chapters 2 and 3. Then, Chapter 4 will delve into the inner workings of the six principles to help you understand which dominoes will fall in the future. With this foundation, you will be able to make more sense of their economic impact on prices, production volumes, and the behavior of energy companies in these markets. *The Domino Effect* is intended to help you anticipate what's coming around the corner, because there is a lot more change just ahead.

Chapter 2

Drilling Down, Down, Down: A Closer Look at the Domino Effect

C HAPTER 1 WAS INTENDED AS AN OVERVIEW OF THE DOMINOES THAT FELL up to 2012, providing a general sense of the domino-effect concept. With that as a foundation, this chapter will drill down, metaphorically speaking, into the details: how and why the market events of those years happened.

As previously mentioned, the shale revolution had its genesis in the Barnett Shale formation near Fort Worth, Texas, where George Mitchell, the father of the shale revolution, and his team of engineers at Mitchell Energy, banged away—literally—at nearly impermeable rock for almost two decades. Their objective was simple: develop the technologies needed to extract what had been thought to be inaccessible natural gas from the massive shale deposits of the Barnett. They finally broke the code, so to speak, in the late 1990s and proved out the technologies in the early 2000s.

That code was a combination of drilling and well-stimulation technologies which made it possible to produce gas from relatively impermeable shale rock. The two most important techniques were (1) horizontal drilling—a vertical wellbore thousands of feet in the ground that turns to drill laterally through the shale for some distance away from the well site, and (2) hydraulic fracturing (what we now call fracking), which involves pumping fluid under high pressure into the well to break up the rock. These technologies had been around for decades—

There is no doubt that Mitchell's breakthrough was Domino 1. But it was a long wait for Domino 2. By the early 2000s, Barnett Shale production was a reality, but that single natural gas field in northern Texas wasn't nearly enough to offset the continuing production declines across the rest of North America. It would take a natural disaster to fully launch the shale revolution.

directional drilling since the 1920s and hydraulic fracturing since the 1940s—but it remained for Mitchell to figure out how to use these technologies together in shale rock to produce commercially successful natural gas wells.

Back in the early days of Mitchell's work in the Barnett, shale production had not hit the radar screens of most energy-market participants. The industry—and the world—was locked in a shortage mentality. Mitchell's shale production concepts were starting to filter out into the producer community at large, and some figured the combination of technologies had real potential. But they knew shale production was both a costly and risky proposition. Based on the economics understood at the time, natural gas price levels only marginally supported such high-cost, high-risk drilling. It would at the time take a massive catalyst to kick shale into high gear. That happened in 2005.

Although not directly responsible for the shale revolution, two back-to-back natural disasters provided the stimulus to launch it. Producers in Louisiana, Arkansas, and other areas of Texas beyond the Barnett were already experimenting with Mitchell's shale drilling techniques when two crippling natural gas disruptions occurred.

On Monday, August 29, 2005, Hurricane Katrina hit land in southeastern Louisiana, devastating the Gulf Coast and wreaking havoc on the offshore natural gas production infrastructure that much of the country relied upon.

A second storm, Hurricane Rita, blasted the Gulf Coast on September 18, less than a month later, just as the industry (and the region) had begun to recover from Katrina.

The two storms' combined impact devastated the Gulf Coast and took out almost 15% of U.S. natural gas production. With supplies cut so severely, prices skyrocketed to more than $15/MMBtu[1] from the $6–7/MMBtu range before the storms. With higher prices, those early shale producers saw dramatically improved cash flows and higher rates of return on new drilling activity. With more money to drill wells and substantially better well economics, due to the higher prices and increasingly efficient shale drilling, producers did exactly what you would expect: they drilled more shale wells. A lot more shale wells.

Knocking Down the Dominoes

As 2005 drew to a close, the domino effect had its catalyst: high natural gas prices induced by the two hurricanes. It is very unlikely the shale revolution would have occurred at anywhere near the rate of change seen in the late 2000s without such a price shock. With that as the preamble, we can now look more closely at how the domino effect unfolded. Figure 2.1 depicts the importance of 2005 as the launching point for the shale revolution. Production continued to fall that year, as it had since 2001, with the decline aggravated by the production lost from hurricane damage. When 2006 production statistics started to register increases, it was generally attributed to recovery of offshore production from hurricane damage.

Buried inside the U.S. natural gas production statistics was an important new development. Not only was offshore production coming back—

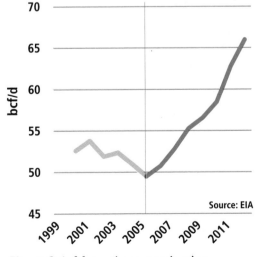

Figure 2.1. Natural gas production

onshore production was starting to surge. Some of the increase was coming from the Barnett. But by that time, production was also increasing from other newly discovered shale plays like the Haynesville in northern Louisiana and the Fayetteville in Arkansas. High natural gas prices whipped the producer community into a frenzy of shale-drilling activity.

The number of rigs actively drilling (a.k.a. the *rig count*) increased, and new, highly productive shale wells proliferated. By March 2006, less than a year after the two storms, total natural gas production was back where it had been before the hurricanes. Prices settled into a $5–$8/MMBtu range, no longer stratospheric but not in the cellar either. It looked briefly like the natural gas market had reached some kind of equilibrium. That turned out to be an illusion.

Natural gas production kept right on increasing, past where it had been before the two hurricanes, averaging between 2.5% and 7.0% growth annually for several more years. That was a surprise to many market observers. Such a shortge mentality had developed that some just could not believe that production was really increasing.

 Something had changed. At that point, few recognized it—much less understood it—as the start of an energy revolution. In fact, shale production had come into its own and was starting to shift the supply-and-demand equilibrium of the gas market. Shale technologies were driving a massive surge of natural gas production. For the natural gas market, Domino 2 had dropped, and there was no looking back.

Shale technologies were driving a massive surge of natural gas production. Domino 2 had dropped and there was no looking back. Unfortunately for a number of market participants, there *was* a lot of looking back going on at the time. Even though natural gas production was increasing into 2007, most participants in the natural gas marketplace remained mired in that shortage mentality of the previous years. More than a dozen companies were proceeding with plans to import huge quantities of natural gas in the form of *liquefied natural gas* (LNG) to make up for the perceived shortfall. Utilities geared up to increase electricity generation capacity, using just about any fuel other than natural gas. The extreme price volatility of the previous few years had given natural gas a black eye in that market sector. For the same reason, building a new industrial plant dependent on natural gas as a feedstock was unthinkable.

However, the shortage mentality did encourage a few positive developments. For example, a new high-capacity pipeline called *Rockies Express* (*REX*) was built to bring gas from the Rocky Mountains into the notoriously gas-starved market of the northeastern United States. It came fully online in 2009. At that time, it was difficult to imagine there would soon be a surplus of natural gas in the country, especially in the Northeast. More on that development later.

As 2007 and early 2008 rolled by, domestic gas production from shale ramped ever higher. Nearly every month an overheating economy edged natural gas prices upward as well, defying the conventional supply-and-demand expectation that more supply ought to push prices lower. It was a strange market. Financial institutions had seized on commodities as the next great thing for investors, and that meant crude oil and natural gas prices—some of the most actively traded commodities—got caught up in the turmoil.

Within the natural-gas-producing community, it was starting to become apparent that price increases were spurring even higher levels of drilling activity. Less obvious was that higher gas prices were driving an incredible wave of new technological innovation. Many other producers—essentially all independents—had gone to school on Mitchell's innovations and were throwing investment dollars at shale plays across Texas, Oklahoma, Arkansas, and Louisiana.

Then things got even crazier. In 2008, Wall Street went completely gaga over energy commodities. Natural gas took center stage in a wild commodity-price run-up. Just before the Fourth of July, 2008, natural gas prices skyrocketed to $13.58/MMBtu, almost as high as they had been right after Hurricanes Katrina and Rita. But this time the reason for the run-up was not a natural disaster. Rather, it looked like Wall Streeters were jumping into what appeared to be a speculative bubble. They were, and it was.

You know what happened next. In 2008, the worst financial crisis since the Great Depression blew up the economy. Commodity markets crashed and the ensuing chaos sucked the energy markets down with it. Crude oil prices plummeted from the bubble level of $120/bbl to less than $40/bbl. Natural gas prices collapsed, falling to $2.72/MMBtu, down 80%. Drilling slowed to a crawl and rigs were being idled—what is called *laid up*—all over the country. Oil and gas companies warned of dire consequences for energy supplies, not to mention the fragile state of their financial condition. Those were dark days for both the economy and for the oil and gas markets. As 2009 passed by, natural gas production did exactly what many industry pundits and a few oil and gas executives predicted: it started to decline, only slightly—but definitely on a downward trajectory.

The gas production decline continued throughout 2009. Natural gas prices remained low, but there was a seemingly obvious explanation for that: demand was down, due to the collapse of business activity caused by the financial crisis. Many industry analysts predicted it would be just a short time before demand picked up again, promising that prices would recover.

There was, in fact, a partial recovery. By the end of 2009, crude oil prices had doubled, back to the $80/bbl range. Having moved above $5.00/MMBtu, natural gas prices were also looking a lot better to producers. As the 2010 New Year rang in, the worst of the financial crisis for energy markets was in the rearview mirror. Oil and gas producers breathed a sigh of relief.

The prevailing wisdom in the producer community at the time was that natural gas prices would return to what had been considered "normal" before the meltdown. Sadly for these producers, however, that was not to be the case. By then, the economics of shale production were disrupting what producers understood to be the relationship between drilling activity, production, and prices. *Shale production, driven by new technologies, was creating an unanticipated abundance of natural gas and, in the process, had permanently disrupted the old supply-and-demand equation. Domino 2 had toppled and was leaning toward Domino 3.*

 Shale supercharged natural gas production and led to an oversupply of natural gas, subsequently disrupting the traditional pricing relationship between crude oil and natural gas.

Natural gas markets did indeed improve in 2010, but not nearly as much as the industry had anticipated. Prices started the year by increasing, but that respite was short-lived. Unexpectedly, the price of natural gas headed south early in the year. Producers scratched their heads, wondering what had happened after starting the year well above $5.00/MMBtu, then watching prices fall below $5.00 by the end of February and even lower, to $4.00, in March. These are peak demand months. Lower gas prices in the winter? That wasn't the way the gas market was supposed to behave.

Even more perplexing, crude oil prices were moving in the opposite direction, starting the year at $80/bbl and increasing to $90/bbl by year end. "Wait!" said the producers, Wall Street traders, and many others, "Gas and oil prices are supposed to move together, either up or down. Now natural gas prices are going down while crude oil prices are going up! What's going on?"

Domino 3, natural gas oversupply, had toppled, disrupting the pricing relationship between gas and crude. It was the first sign of *The Great Divide*, the point at which natural gas prices and crude oil prices began to diverge.

Increasing natural gas production surpluses from shale—landlocked in North America—were pushing gas prices lower. As gas production grew, there was nowhere for the gas to go, since no natural gas export facilities existed.[2] The oversupply drove gas prices down. But why was the crude oil price increasing? Well, it was actually perfectly logical. At that time, crude oil production had yet to see a big kick from shale production, and huge quantities were still being imported by the United States from international markets at global prices. Those global crude oil price levels were rising as the world economy moved back from the precipice. Few producers anticipated that prices for natural gas and crude oil would—or ever could—move in opposite directions so dramatically. But that was how it began playing out. The economy was starting to recover, oil and gas commodity prices were diverging, and the fourth domino was wobbling.

> Natural gas oversupply pushed gas prices down, while crude prices rose, and The Great Divide became a reality.

How big a deal was The Great Divide? Very. Figure 2.2 provides an indication of the significance of this divergence in prices. The light blue dashed line is natural gas futures at the Henry Hub, Louisiana. The dark blue solid line is West Texas Intermediate crude oil futures at Cushing, Oklahoma, on the right scale. Note that in 2006 and into early 2007, the prices bounced around within a trading range, then from mid-2007 through 2008, the prices of the two commodities moved in lockstep.

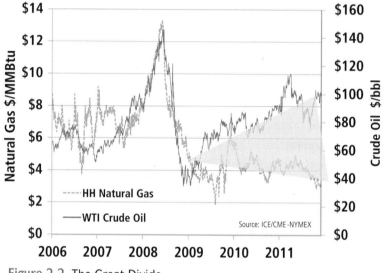

Figure 2.2. The Great Divide

That lasted until 2009, when crude oil prices started to recover. Crude jumped quickly back into the $70/bbl range while natural gas eventually fell below $2.00/MMBtu. A cold winter stimulated a short-lived gas price rally in early 2010, but after that, gas prices went into a long slide while crude oil ramped higher. The Great Divide yawned wider.

It was becoming apparent to producers that production of natural gas from shale was a double-edged sword. On one hand, production volumes were up (a good thing for producers). Shale gas was reversing the decline in domestic production. But on the other hand, without an increase in demand or outlet to international markets, oversupply meant lower natural gas prices.

In contrast, due to continued reliance on imports from overseas producers, crude oil was marching to an entirely different drummer: international supply and demand. Those prices were increasing, decoupling oil and gas prices and creating The Great Divide. *Domino 4 had toppled.*

It's an old story, relevant for us to resurrect here. The bank robber Willie Sutton was asked why he robbed banks. "Because that's where the money is," he replied. Like Willie, oil and gas producers want to drill where the money is. And in 2011, the money was not with natural gas.

With natural gas prices falling and crude prices rising, any producer with the ability to do so made the logical economic choice: shift drilling activity to crude oil and natural gas liquids where they had an opportunity to make a profit.

Savvy producers quickly realized it would not be profitable to continue producing large quantities of *dry natural gas,* although it was plentiful and many had profited up to that point. The term *dry* means natural gas that is mostly methane, the stuff that you think of as natural gas used for home heating, water heaters, and cooking. Dry natural gas prices had declined so precipitously that in some of the most prolific plays it made no economic sense to continue drilling more wells.

But some natural gas—called *wet gas*—contains significant quantities of NGLs, as discussed in Chapter 1. NGL prices had a tendency to be more aligned with crude oil than natural gas, and those NGLs could be extracted and sold for higher prices. The natural gas left over after the extraction of NGLs would be worth no more than dry natural gas. In fact, the leftover gas (called *residue gas*) is essentially identical in composition to dry natural gas and thus has the same market value. As a result, producers were getting a big profit boost from the extracted NGLs, but no less profit for the left-over gas. Consequently, any producer with access to wet gas shifted their drilling activity in that direction ... or to the one other drill-bit hydrocarbon commodity available to producers: crude oil. The shift to NGLs and crude was Domino 5.

With oil prices headed back toward $100/bbl, the economics of drilling for oil looked great compared to dry gas. There were only a

Shale-drilling activities shifted to natural gas liquids (NGLs) and crude oil, whose prices had not declined like those of natural gas.

couple of problems. First, producers had little experience applying shale

Rockin' with the NGLs

As the name suggests, NGLs—natural gas liquids—are liquids extracted from natural gas. To understand what this means, we need to go into a bit of explanation about the term **natural gas**. Natural gas from a wellhead must be treated and processed before it can be used to heat your home or cook your food. The natural gas delivered to homes is composed mostly of methane. Methane is a **hydrocarbon**, a compound containing hydrogen and carbon. It is the simplest of the hydrocarbons, with a molecular structure consisting of one carbon atom and four hydrogen atoms.

Natural gas from a wellhead contains methane, as well as many other compounds. Some of those compounds are impurities like water and sulfur that must be removed from the gas before it can be sold. Natural gas from a wellhead also contains some quantities of hydrocarbons other than methane. NGLs are by far the largest group of these other hydrocarbons, a family of five hydrogen/carbon compounds that can be economically extracted from natural gas provided it contains sufficient quantities of these products. It can make sense to extract NGLs from gas for two primary reasons. First, because they are frequently worth more than natural gas, and second, because there is a limit on the amount of NGLs that can remain in natural gas in order to transport the gas safely over long distances in pipelines.

If you are not familiar with NGLs, you might be surprised to learn what a pervasive role they play in industry and your everyday life. Products containing or derived from NGLs include plastic water bottles, antifreeze, some gasoline components, trash bags, and just about every other plastic you can think of. They are the propane in your BBQ grill and the butane in the lighter you use to start the grill. They are the propellant in hair spray and what makes your refrigerator stay cold.

There are five members of the NGL family.

1. **Ethane** is a feedstock used to make a number of petrochemicals, the most important of which is **ethylene**. Ethylene is used in the manufacture of **polyethylene** (plastic), **ethylene glycol** (antifreeze), and a host of other products you use every day.

2. **Propane** is primarily used for heating, BBQ grills, and petrochemical manufacturing yielding various chemical derivatives, including propylene, used in the manufacture of **polypropylene** (another plastic).

3. **Normal butane**, or **n-butane**, is primarily a component used in motor gasoline. When you see those vapors coming out of your gas tank at the filling station on a hot summer day, you are seeing mostly normal butane.
4. **Isobutane** is used in refrigeration, as a propellant in aerosol cans, and in the manufacture of a high-octane component in motor gasoline.
5. **Natural gasoline**, sometimes referred to as **pentane** or **pentanes-plus**, is used as a component of motor gasoline, in petrochemicals, and in something called **diluent**, which is stirred into heavy, viscous crude oil so that it will flow as a liquid in pipelines.

In NGL vernacular, ethane and propane are called the **light NGLs** while normal butane, isobutane and natural gasoline are called **heavy NGLs**. The dominant markets for light NGLs are petrochemicals and heating, while most heavy NGLs move to the transportation fuels markets, primarily motor gasoline.

While you ponder these products, consider the fact that rock and roll is and always has been highly dependent on NGLs. No kidding. All the old vinyl records were polyvinyl chloride, made from ethylene, which in the United States is mostly made from NGLs. Fast forward to today. CDs are made from polycarbonate, which in turn is made from bisphenol A (BPA), derived from propylene which is made mostly from—you guessed it—NGLs. Who knows, rock and roll may never have happened if not for NGLs. Think all of this is old fashioned? Well, whether you download your music from the cloud to your phone, tablet or computer, these devices are assembled and manufactured using polymers and plastics, most of which come from NGLs. So there you are.

gas technologies to crude oil. Many assumed that fracking shales containing crude could never be made to work like a natural gas frack job. And second, producers had few ideas about where producible crude shales might be hiding. At the time, the only plausible territory seemed to be the Williston Basin in North Dakota, in what is known as the Bakken play. Some producers with expertise in the Bakken started to adapt shale technologies for working that formation. (*Note:* Throughout this book we will be referring to a number of basins and producing regions. A basin map is provided for your reference on page ii.)

Other producers went on a hunt for more crude oil plays that were ideal for shale technologies. Due to the technological challenges, the shift to shale crude did not happen as quickly as the shift to wet gas and NGL production. But the motivation was the same: make use of shale technologies to produce economic quantities of something other than dry natural gas, which had seen its price crushed by overproduction. That sounded good. Unfortunately, changes in producer behavior do not happen in isolation, and more dominoes were waiting just around the corner.

Notes

1. Wholesale natural gas prices in the United States are quoted in $/MMBtu, which stands for dollars per one million British Thermal Units (Btus). Energy markets use MM as an abbreviation for million, M for thousand. To put that measure in perspective, the average energy consumption of a U.S. household in 2013 was about 75 MMBtu. As defined by the U.S. Energy Information Administration (EIA), this statistic includes electricity, natural gas, propane, and fuel oil.
2. Except for one liquefied natural gas export plant in Alaska, which had no impact on the supply and demand equation in the lower 48 states and Canada.

Chapter 3

More Dominoes Fall: NGLs, Crude Oil, and the Loop Back to Natural Gas

T*HE FIRST FIVE DOMINOES SET THE STAGE FOR WHAT WAS TO COME NEXT. The Great Divide—Domino 4—motivated producers to switch from dry gas drilling to wet gas in order to produce NGLs and shift into more crude oil production. This was Domino 5. But NGL and crude oil production growth did not start ramping up at the same time. NGLs came first. Production and completion techniques used for dry gas quickly transitioned into similar drilling techniques for wet gas. Every producer with drilling rights in the right places moved as quickly as possible from dry gas to wet gas. It was somewhat more difficult for oil. There were more technical issues to overcome in getting shale technologies working on a broad scale in the oil patch. Consequently wet gas production started to ramp up before crude oil. Within a few months, wet gas production was growing fast, yielding greater volumes of NGL production. This wet gas drilling activity happened in locations like the Eagle Ford in South Texas and the Granite Wash in the Texas Panhandle and Oklahoma. It didn't happen overnight, but once it began there was no stopping it, and it continued into and past 2012 as dominoes 6 through 16 illustrate.*

The Consequences of Increased NGL Production

By 2009, the shift to shale drilling for NGLs was in full swing and yielding big production volumes. Normally a significant amount of new infrastructure, like processing plants and NGL takeaway pipelines, would be needed to handle this growth in NGLs, but fortunately those early wet gas plays were in longstanding producing basins with legacy plants and pipelines. Their capacity was not enough to handle all of the wet gas that would eventually be produced, but it was enough to get the growth curve started without many delays for development of new infrastructure.

Thus the impact on NGL production should not have been much of a surprise. But it was. The sheer magnitude of the increase was a shocker. As producers drilled for more wet gas and more NGLs were extracted, NGL production continued to zoom upward.

As shown in Figure 3.1, NGL production rose from about 1.7 MMbbl/d in 2009 to more than 2.4 MMbbl/d by the end of 2012. That was more than 40% growth over the four-year period. And wouldn't you know, the law of supply and demand reared its ugly head one more time.

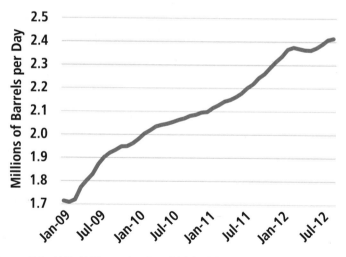

Figure 3.1. U.S. NGL production 2009–2012

The bounty from shale had changed the supply-and-demand balance in yet another energy commodity. Like natural gas, the oversupply of

NGLs resulted in declining prices. But from the domino-effect perspective, it is important to recognize that low gas prices drove producers to wet gas and NGLs in

Domino 6 fell. History repeated itself, once again. Just like natural gas a few years before, overproduction had come to the NGL markets.

the first place. Without the incentive of a gaping difference between low natural gas and higher NGL values, producers would not have chased NGLs the way they did when they did. So this time the oversupply in one market—NGLs—was the direct result of developments in another market—natural gas. One hydrocarbon domino had banged up against another. And this cross-commodity influence is fundamental to the workings of the domino effect. For three years, between 2009 and the end of 2011, NGL volumes increased while the value of NGLs—which tend to rise and fall with crude prices—also continued to rise relative to the price of natural gas. NGL prices followed crude prices higher as petrochemical plants and others steadily increased their demand for NGLs. Figure 3.2 depicts this increase. It shows the *frac spread*, one of the most important indicators of natural gas processing profitability. The measure compares the average value of NGLs on a Btu basis with the price of natural gas on a Btu basis. The frac spread has nothing to do with fracking (the well-completion technique), but instead is short for *fractionation spread*, the process by which mixed NGLs are separated into individual products like ethane and propane. By comparing the value of the input of a gas processing plant (natural gas) to the value of the NGL output of a natural gas processing plant, the frac spread is a rough approximation of the uplift in value for processing natural gas and extracting NGLs. With natural gas prices low and NGL prices high, these were very good years for natural gas processors.

In effect, the frac spread was mirroring The Great Divide. Gas prices stayed low while crude oil prices increased, dragging NGL prices up along with them. The frac spread hit a historically high level in 2011 when NGLs worth $15.00/MMBtu were being extracted from natural gas worth $3.00/MMBtu. The frac spread was $12.00/MMBtu ($15 minus $3). It was like turning lead into gold. For a while.

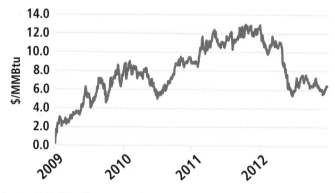

Figure 3.2. The frac spread

Finally, in early 2012 there was just too much NGL supply. NGL production overwhelmed demand, helped along by a warm 2011–12 winter which significantly reduced the need for propane as a heating fuel. As luck would have it, at about the same time, outages at some petrochemical plants cut the demand for ethane as a feedstock. The result was a supply surplus, leading to lower prices for NGLs in general, but especially for ethane and propane (known as the "light ends" of the NGL barrel).

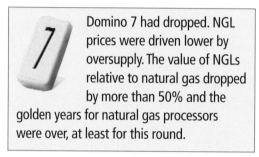

Domino 7 had dropped. NGL prices were driven lower by oversupply. The value of NGLs relative to natural gas dropped by more than 50% and the golden years for natural gas processors were over, at least for this round.

But note an important fact in Figure 3.2. The value of NGLs still did not get back to the level where they were in 2009. Not even close. The frac spread stayed at the $6/MMBtu level, which is not fantastic, but still not that bad. Thus drilling for wet natural gas continued to be considerably more economically attractive than drilling for dry gas. Just not as ridiculously attractive as it had been in 2011.

However, lower NGL prices did create ridiculously attractive economics for another sector of the market: petrochemicals. First, some background on the market for NGLs. There are three primary markets for the five NGL products: petrochemicals, residential and commercial heating, and the refining and blending market. As noted in the feature

"Rockin' with the NGLs" in Chapter 2, each of the NGL products—ethane, propane, normal butane, isobutane, and natural gasoline—has a unique market profile. Almost all recovered ethane (C2)[1] production is used in the petrochemical market as a feedstock to produce ethylene, propylene, and other building-block chemicals. Propane (C3) moves into both the petrochemical and heating market. Some propane is exported to Canada as well as offshore markets, mostly to Latin America, Europe, and Asia. Normal butane (nC4), isobutane (iC4), and natural gasoline (a.k.a. pentanes+ and C5+) move into petrochemicals, motor gasoline, diluent, export, and a few other markets.

The value of each of the NGLs is established within these markets in relation to the products produced and by the prices of other products that can be substituted for NGLs as raw materials, feedstock, or fuels in these markets. For example, just over 50% of all U.S. NGLs move into the petrochemical market to be processed by *olefin crackers* (sometimes called *steam crackers* or *ethylene crackers*). There are 37 of these olefin crackers in the United States, some of which have multiple units at the same location. All but four are located along the Texas and Louisiana Gulf Coast. The demand for NGLs from the petrochemical sector fluctuates with the downstream demand for petrochemicals (which is in turn influenced by economic activity, exchange rates, etc.), as well as the relative prices of NGLs to other petrochemical feedstocks, which can be used in place of NGLs, such as *naphthas* (low-grade gasoline) and *gas oils* (low-grade diesel).

When the price of NGLs dropped, particularly ethane and propane, the ethylene crackers designed to use this feedstock for the majority of their input received an economic bonanza. For the five years prior to Domino 7 falling, Gulf Coast ethylene crackers had subsisted on margins of $0.07–$0.15 per pound of ethylene produced, hardly enough to justify continued operation. Then the domino fell and Figure 3.3 shows what happened. As ethane and propane prices declined during 2011 and 2012 (shown in the graph on the left of Figure 3.3), margins for ethylene produced from these feedstocks increased (as shown in the graph on the right). There was a margin dip in late 2011, just before NGL prices fell hard. But during 2012, margins for petrochemical companies cracking ethane and propane were extremely attractive, ranging between $0.30 and $0.60 per pound. The petrochemical industry had entered its golden years.

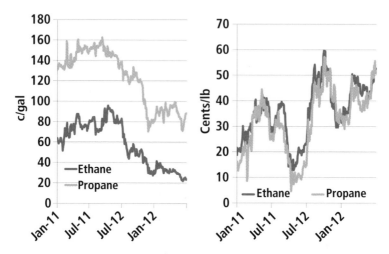

Figure 3.3. Light NGL prices (left), ethylene margins (right)

 This was Domino 8. By 2012, low NGL prices had completely changed the economic environment for the U.S. ethylene cracker industry.

At first, the petrochemical industry had a hard time accepting such a huge improvement in its economic prospects. But soon, press releases announcing new ethylene crackers designed to run on cheap ethane hit the streets. The U.S. petrochemical industry started to believe in a shale-driven industry resurgence. The domino effect, begun in the natural gas market, had ricocheted through the NGL market and blasted across industry lines into the petrochemical market. And there were more dominoes to come.

Dominoes and Crude Oil

In 2011, there was another hydrocarbon market also feeling the full brunt of the shale revolution: crude oil. In reality, the crude oil market had been in the midst of a transformation for a few years in the Bakken in North Dakota. But the success of producers in that state was obscured by a couple of developments that kept crude oil out of the spotlight until traditional price spreads went wacky in mid-2011.[2] The mainstream media began talking about the possibility of energy independence, usually defined as the elimination of crude oil imports. But we are getting way ahead of ourselves. To see how the crude oil side of the shale revolution got started, it is important to drop back a few years to put things in perspective.

As recently as the mid-2000s, U.S. crude oil was written off as dead. For the two decades between 1988 and 2008, crude oil production declined each year, falling from nearly 8.5 MMbbl/d to about 5.0 MMbbl/d, with occasional dips due to hurricane-related offshore production shutdowns (Figure 3.4). Even high crude prices before the economic meltdown of 2008 did not seem to stimulate production. Then the meltdown happened and prices fell to $40/bbl, killing off almost all remaining interest in crude within the United States. But *almost* is the key word here.

Figure 3.4. U.S. crude oil production

Despite these depressing numbers, a hardy band of crude producers would not take no for an answer. They drilled for crude in what seemed like the most unlikely of places: North Dakota, where a crude oil boom in the 1970s had revealed the presence of oil but not the technologies to produce it at consistent economic quantities. In the 1990s, a few companies like Continental Resources started to drill for oil in North Dakota. By 1995, Continental had discovered the Cedar Hills Field, which is now known to be one of the largest onshore crude oil fields in the United States. But back in those days, the only people interested in what Continental and other producers were doing in the Williston Basin—now better known as the Bakken—were the few locals up in North Dakota.

Little known to the rest of the industry, those Williston producers were starting to break the code on the Bakken shale formation. It was slow going at first, and times were particularly difficult during the crude oil price crash of 2008. But then in 2009, The Great Divide kicked in when natural gas prices stayed low while crude oil prices increased. Just as with wet gas, producers started to move resources into crude oil drilling. Up in the Bakken, the producers drilling the Williston before it was cool were joined by other producers eager to leave dry gas economics behind and deploy their development capital into a commodity with a higher price: crude oil.

The market started to shift, and all the new drilling activity started to yield results, as shown in Figure 3.5. Production increased, from about 200 Mbbl/d in 2008, up to 400 Mbbl/d in 2011, and then took off in 2012, increasing up to 800 Mbbl/d.

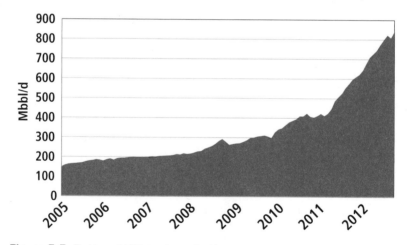

Figure 3.5. Bakken (Williston) production

It was not just the Bakken. Another little-known play in South Texas also started to attract capital targeting crude oil and *condensate*[3] production. Just like in the Bakken, it took producers some time to break the

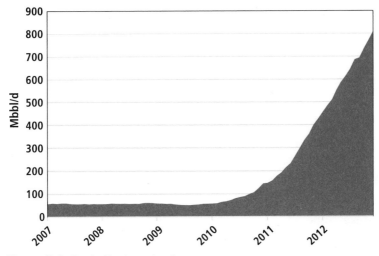

Figure 3.6. Eagle Ford production

code, but when they did, Eagle Ford production in South Texas came on the scene with a vengeance, increasing from little more than 50 Mbbl/d in 2010 up to nearly 800 Mbbl/d by the end of 2012 (Figure 3.6).

With all this crude oil production from the Bakken and Eagle Ford, you might wonder why the market did not seem to wake up to the significance of these developments back then. There were two complications that obscured the increases. First was the impact of the Macondo Prospect blowout (also known as the Deepwater Horizon) and subsequent oil spill in April 2010. Offshore production was halted for a time and a moratorium on new drilling was put in place that lasted six months, then extending several more months due to permitting delays. This resulted in a decline of Gulf offshore production from 1.6 MMbbl/d just before the accident to 1.1 MMbbl/d by August 2012. During the same period, Alaska production was falling another 0.2 MMbbl/d, continuing a pattern of decline from the late 1980s when Alaska production had peaked at about 2.0 MMbbl/d. This combination of Macondo and Alaska declines obscured what was happening in the shales.

In addition to domestic production, there was one more source of increasing crude oil supplies. For years, Canada had been working hard to increase production of a unique type of crude oil called *bitumen*, more commonly known as *oil sands crude*. Rather than drilling for this crude and producing it from a wellhead, over half of Canada's bitumen is mined in huge above-ground operations. These oil sands (essentially oily dirt) are then processed to extract a heavy, or viscous, oil. Other bitumen crude is produced by drilling wells that pump steam into the ground, which heats the oil to the point where it will flow out of other wells. Before the U.S. shale revolution started, the increasing production of Canadian heavy oil was expected to be the most important source of new crude oil supplies into the United States, and several pipeline expansion projects were planned to move more of this crude into the U.S. market. Of course, the most well-known pipeline project was Keystone XL. But before Keystone XL became so notorious, higher crude prices encouraged the production of more Canadian crude, and those barrels started moving to the U.S. on existing pipelines. Between early 2005 and late 2012, crude oil imports from Canada to the U.S. increased from 2.2 MMbbl/d to 3.2 MMbbl/d.

Domino 9 was falling. The combined impact of Bakken production, Eagle Ford production, Canadian imports, and increases from a few other U.S. basins finally overwhelmed production decreases still happening in other parts of the country. Crude oil supplies were increasing, and increasing fast.

As crude oil production from the Bakken grew, supplemented by growing imports of Canadian crude, supplies in the Midcontinent region of the United States started to exceed the capacity of its refineries. There were other refineries in other parts of the country that could use the barrels, mostly by backing out overseas imports, but at the time there was no way to get the crude to them. Either the pipelines did not exist—which was the case for East Coast and West Coast refineries—or the pipeline capacity available was inadequate, which was the case for the Gulf Coast. In fact, the Gulf Coast had an even bigger problem because two of the major crude oil pipelines from the Gulf Coast flowed north, designed to take crude oil imports into the Midcontinent region. In other words, the pipelines were flowing the wrong way to solve the problem of growing supplies in the Midcontinent. Northbound flows made sense before the Bakken and Canadian imports developed, but no longer. By 2010, the Midcontinent was developing a glut of crude oil and had no need for additional barrels from the Gulf.

The price impact of the Midcontinent crude glut hit in summer 2010. For years, prices for the international benchmark (Brent Crude) and the U.S. domestic benchmark (West Texas Intermediate (WTI)) had traded within $1–2/bbl of each other. Then in August 2010, WTI began to trade at a discount to Brent that widened out as far as $28/bbl in November 2011. This price disparity was the result of a buildup of crude oil inventories at the Cushing, Oklahoma trading hub. Growing crude production in North Dakota and Western Canada overwhelmed Midwest refinery needs and got caught in Cushing because of the inadequate pipeline transport capacity to Gulf Coast refineries mentioned above. The result was lower Midcontinent crude prices.

> That was Domino 10. Crude oil prices in the Midcontinent fell relative to the rest of the country, dropping significantly below prices in the rest of the world for that matter.

There was not enough pipeline capacity to move the oversupply of crude to other markets, and WTI crude oil prices responded by declining relative to Brent. While coastal refiners were stuck running mostly crudes pegged to Brent, Midcontinent refiners enjoyed those lower crude prices. It was particularly enjoyable since the prices for petroleum products—motor gasoline, diesel, jet fuel, and other products sold by those Midcontinent refiners—had a tendency to be about the same as those coastal refineries running more expensive imported barrels.

Similar to the jump in profitability seen by petrochemical plants due to low NGL prices, Midcontinent

> That triggered Domino 11. The margins of Midcontinent refineries ramped up to be much higher than refinery margins in the rest of the country.

refineries were making money at levels not seen in decades. It was another of those golden-year cycles. Again, the long arm of the domino effect had reached out with producers responding to low natural gas prices, shifting their focus to crude oil across commodity lines, and eventually creating a Midcontinent crude oil surplus that drove down prices in that region.

Dominoes and Natural Gas Revisited

The stories for NGLs and crude oil discussed previously were about producers shifting away from natural gas in order to take advantage of higher NGL and crude oil prices. So you might think the growth in NGL and crude oil production occurred at the expense of natural gas volumes. In fact, that is what many market observers expected would happen in the 2010–2012 period. As shown in Figure 3.7, it did not happen that way.

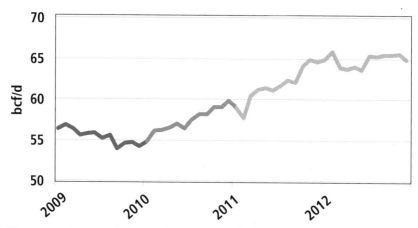

Figure 3.7. Lower 48 dry (residue) gas production

As discussed in Chapter 2, natural gas production did decline somewhat in 2009. At the time, prices were down in the aftermath of the economic meltdown, drilling activity had slowed considerably, and—as a consequence—production was falling. At least that is what appeared to be happening. But a more careful review of the statistics reveals there were two partially offsetting developments going on.

The first clue could be seen in the pattern of production in 2010. In that year, the natural gas price continued to be low but production kicked into a steep growth trajectory. *Prices were lower but production was increasing.* To many involved in the market, this looked counterintuitive. Lower prices should result in less drilling, which should translate to lower production. But production levels were not behaving that way. The market confusion was due to misunderstanding what happened the previous year, in 2009.

When prices dropped in 2009, there was, in fact, a decline in conventional natural gas production due to the fact that most gas drilling in conventional (non-shale) basins was uneconomic at then-current market prices. What was harder to see was that shale gas production capability was increasing substantially. Very large shale wells with two to ten times the initial production rates of typical conventional wells were being drilled and readied for production. Producers drilled these wells to keep up with a number of contractual and lease-related obligations and requirements like *held by production (HBP)* leases.[4] But many of these wells were not brought online when they were completed. In 2009, there simply was not enough pipeline or processing capacity in the areas where the new shale plays were located to accommodate all the new production. In other words, it was an infrastructure problem. All that changed in the first quarter of 2010, when midstream infrastructure caught up with production. At that point, total U.S. production took off.

Then three other factors took hold of natural gas production to drive it higher. First was wet gas production. Even though producers shifted their drilling from dry gas to wet gas in order to benefit from NGL production economics, they were still producing gas. Recall that NGLs are extracted from wet gas, leaving residue gas that is exactly the same as produced dry gas. Thus wet gas production was one factor that kept natural gas production increasing. The domino effect had crossed commodity lines again.

Second was associated gas production. When producers shifted drilling activity to crude oil, the focus of drilling was production of crude. However, crude frequently comes with significant quantities of natural gas out of the same wellhead. This natural gas production, called *associated gas,* increases when crude oil production increases and is especially prevalent in several shale plays. It was one more example of the domino effect crossing commodity lines.

And the third factor was the Marcellus, a huge shale play that was taking off in Pennsylvania and West Virginia. It turns out that in a certain part of the Marcellus (northeast Pennsylvania), the economics of dry gas production were still very attractive. In fact, they were extremely attractive, because the Marcellus wells in that region tended to be hugely productive,

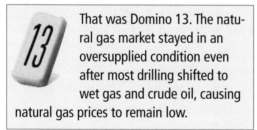

Put all three of those factors together and you had Domino 12. Even though overall natural gas drilling activity had slowed down, the combination of wet gas, associated gas, and Marcellus gas kept natural gas production increasing.

relative to their cost. That translated to high rates of return for Marcellus producers. For that reason, dry Marcellus gas production continued to grow, even as most other U.S. dry gas production was declining due to lower levels of drilling activity.

By now the market pattern should be pretty familiar. Natural gas production continued to increase. But there was little growth in demand. In fact, it got worse. The warm winter of 2011–12 was particularly bad for natural gas demand. Residential and commercial gas users burned a lot less gas that year, which resulted in significant inventories of natural gas remaining after the heating season was over. That translated directly into much lower prices, getting down below $2.00/MMBtu in spring 2012.

That was Domino 13. The natural gas market stayed in an oversupplied condition even after most drilling shifted to wet gas and crude oil, causing natural gas prices to remain low.

It was not good news for natural gas producers, especially for those left struggling in most of the dry gas plays. But even those more fortunate producers who were getting most of their economic uplift from NGLs or crude oil were stuck with low prices for their natural gas. In fact, many producers started to think of natural gas as simply a byproduct: a commodity to be disposed of so as to produce the moneymaking NGLs and crude oil.

The Winners and the Losers

However, those low gas prices were quite beneficial to other segments of the market. Local distribution companies (LDCs) delivering gas to homeowners and commercial companies were able to reduce their natural gas utility rates, benefiting some of those hit hardest by the economic meltdown. Large industrials also benefited from low natural gas prices, helping the recovery in that segment. And finally, low natural gas prices looked good to utilities and other power generation companies using natural gas to produce electricity.

Among all the demand segments benefiting from low natural gas prices, the rewards were particularly attractive to those electrical power generators who were under regulatory and public pressure for using coal as their primary fuel. With natural gas so cheap, replacing coal was ad-vantageous from both an economic and an environ-mental perspective.

In April 2012, for the first time since EIA began collecting the data, electricity generation from natural gas-fired generation equaled

In 2012, when natural gas prices dipped into the $2.00-$3.00/MMBtu range for much of the year, power generation companies made a massive shift to gas as their fuel of choice. That was Domino 14.

coal-fired generation, with each fuel providing approximately 32% of total generation. It was not long before coal recaptured the lead power gener-ation spot from natural gas, but the event was a wake-up call for coal pro-ducers. Low gas prices had made gas more competitive with coal, which, combined with environmental concerns, posed a downside risk to domes-tic coal demand.

Starting in 2011, the in-evitable occurred: favorable economics for burning gas over coal and tighter federal pollution limits for power plants led to a shuttering or idling of coal-fired generation plants. More than 100 coal-burning electricity generators have been shut down, both due to economic and envi-ronmental considerations. As

Domino 15 hit the coal indus-try. The use of coal for power generation declined by nearly 12% between 2011 and 2012 to about 825 million short tons, the lowest level since 1995. Most of the decline was due to displacement by natural gas. Coal demand made a partial recovery the next year, but the handwrit-ing was on the wall. Natural gas would be replacing a significant volume of coal for power generation.

coal plants continue to close, a number of coal mines have followed suit, unable to compete with lower natural gas prices. Once more, the domino effect crossed commodity lines.

Still another benefit of the shale revolution was developing in the industrial sector of the economy. Natural gas is used as a direct and indirect input in manufacturing. Direct input includes use as a process feedstock in certain petrochemical manufacturing processes (methanol, ammonia, etc.). Indirect use is fuel for boilers, heating, etc. The largest industrial natural gas sectors are chemical production (26%), refining (16%), and food manufacture (13%). These sectors and many others have been enjoying lower natural gas prices. Even more important, there is a rising level of confidence that natural gas prices will remain at attractive levels for years to come. Consequently, there has been a flurry of new industrial and manufacturing plant announcements.

 Low natural gas prices meant higher profits for industrial plants. That was Domino 16. A U.S. industrial resurgence was underway, driven primarily by attractive natural gas prices.

Literally thousands of new industrial facilities have been announced which, if all were built, would add about 5.0 billion cubic feet per day to U.S. natural gas demand. Although it is highly unlikely that all of these facilities will be completed, those that are built will validate the label *Industrial Renaissance* for U.S. manufacturing over the upcoming years. That is quite an impressive domino.

The Sweet Sixteen

These are the *Sweet Sixteen*, the first sixteen dominoes that dropped from the inception of the shale revolution to the end of 2012. Whether you work in the energy industry and lived through these events or are an energy market novice, hopefully the domino structure provides a good framework and the historical perspective for understanding how these seemingly disparate events fit together. Now that you have a general idea of what the domino effect is all about, let's drop back and take a closer look at each piece of the puzzle.

So far, all we have done is get the concept down and provide a historical perspective on how the domino effect has influenced energy markets. Next we will look at *why* the shale revolution has linked together the markets for natural gas, NGLs, and crude oil in new relationships, and we will examine the underlying principles that make the domino effect work. This deeper understanding will help provide a roadmap for anticipating future dominoes.

Notes

1. The designations C2, C3, etc. for NGL products are references to the number of carbon atoms in their molecules, and are frequently used as shorthand names in the NGL market. For example, there are two carbon atoms in a molecule of ethane, thus it is abbreviated C2.

2. In 2011, the price differential between the benchmark international crude oil, Brent, and the benchmark U.S. domestic grade, West Texas Intermediate (WTI), increased from its traditional level of only one or two dollars to more than $25/bbl as a surplus of WTI developed at the key crude trading hub in Cushing, Oklahoma.

3. Condensate is a very light crude oil produced mostly from wet natural gas wells but classified as crude oil in government and industry statistics. More on condensate in Chapter 7.

4. Under this type of lease, the producer is required to produce hydrocarbons from a well in order to continue holding the land lease, including the rights to drill and produce the well. Otherwise the production rights revert to the owner of the mineral rights. HBP drilling in areas such as the Haynesville in northwest Louisiana encouraged significant increases in production, even though the economics for the wells were marginal. Producers drilled enough wells to hold the leases, assuming they would come back some day and drill more wells on the secure leases once prices supported more drilling.

Chapter 4

The Six Domino Effect Principles

C HAPTERS 2 AND 3 TOOK US INTO THE DETAILS OF THE DOMINOES THAT *launched the shale revolution. Now that you are up to speed with the domino effect concept, we are almost ready to move into the energy commodity markets themselves. But first, it is important that we build a foundation to enable better understanding of those markets, including the role of gas, NGLs, and oil in the overall energy picture, the relationships between these three commodities (which we call the drill-bit hydrocarbons), and the six key principles that underpin the domino effect.*

Energy: The Big Picture

Energy markets are big. Energy is the largest market on the planet as measured by global exports, more than double either the food or automotive products markets. It is certainly the largest commodity market in the U.S. economy. Energy starts wars, shapes geopolitics, and shifts trillions of dollars in wealth from the energy have-nots, like Japan and India, to the energy haves, such as Saudi Arabia. The average U.S. resident spends almost a quarter of his or her after-tax income on energy—transportation fuels, home utilities, the cost of energy imbedded in manufactured products, etc. This all translates to energy having a very significant impact on our lives.

The three hydrocarbons we are focusing on—natural gas, NGLs, and crude oil—are, as they emerge from the wellhead, referred to as *commodities*. Once they have emerged from the ground and are transformed into different energy sources and subsequently transported and marketed, we call them *products*. Most people think about energy in the context of its *use*, for example, electric power for your lights and computers, gasoline for your car, or natural gas to heat your home. But when you think about our three hydrocarbons from a *market perspective*, it is important to differentiate them in the context of *energy products*—rather than as commodities—each one purchased from an energy vendor and delivered to your home or corner filling station by a complex network of pipes, trucks, and other transportation channels, for a price set either by the market or some regulatory agency.

To truly understand energy markets, it is even more important to broaden your perspective to consider the *sources of energy*. Just like any other product that is marketed, energy products are produced using raw materials from the natural environment: petroleum, natural gas, coal, hydropower, nuclear power, sunlight, or wind. Sometimes an energy product is produced from several sources. For example, electricity (an energy product, not a source) may be generated by burning coal, natural gas, or fuel oil. It can also be produced from solar energy, wind energy, hydropower, or a nuclear

Units of Energy Measurement

Comparing just how much each of the individual energy sources is used can be a challenge because each energy product or source can have its own unit of measurement. For example, coal is measured in tons, oil in barrels, and natural gas in cubic feet. Fortunately, all sources of energy share one thing in common: their **heat content**, which can be converted to a standard unit of measurement. The U.S. measures heat content with the **British thermal unit**, or **Btu**, which represents the amount of energy required to raise (or lower) the temperature of a pound of water by one degree Fahrenheit. The U.S. is about the only country still using the Btu measurement. Other countries use joules, calories, watts, and other measurements, but fortunately these measurements are readily convertible to Btu. Since this book is written primarily from a U.S. perspective, Btu will be used as the primary means to standardize measurement across energy sources.

power plant. What coal, hydropower, wind, crude oil, solar power, nuclear power, and natural gas all have in common is that they are sources of energy, the raw materials used to produce the energy products we consume.

And each energy product has a supply chain. Crude oil from wells is processed at a refinery into motor gasoline, as well as many other energy products. Those wells could be in North Dakota or Saudi Arabia. Similarly, the natural gas you use at your home was also extracted from a well and processed to make it usable as a home heating fuel. Each energy product has a supply chain that moves the energy from the point of production through processing, distribution, and eventually to market. Just like any other product.

Today's Energy Market

The pie chart below from the U.S. Energy Information Administration (EIA) shows the breakdown of the major sources of energy used in the U.S. market, compared using the common denominator of Btu (see Figure 4.1). That total U.S. energy consumption is 97 quadrillion Btu per year, which is about 18% of the energy consumed by the entire planet. The largest source of energy is crude oil (petroleum) with a 37.2% share of the U.S. market. Natural gas takes honors as the second largest market share with 26.9%, then coal with 19.4%.

It should not be a surprise to learn natural gas is a bigger energy source than coal. Natural gas has two large markets: a fuel for generating electricity and a fuel to heat homes, businesses, and factories. In contrast, coal has only one large major market—electricity generation—and a much smaller secondary market in the manufacture of steel. Nuclear energy, with about 8.2% market share, is used exclusively to generate electricity. The remaining balance in the pie chart is renewables, with a total share of 8.3%. About one-third of that small renewables share is hydropower (dams) and wood, with biomass, hydro, wind, and solar making up the other two-thirds of the renewables share.

Although the proportion of renewable energy sources is small, it is certainly a significant factor in energy markets today. From both political and policy perspectives, growth in the renewable energy slice of the pie

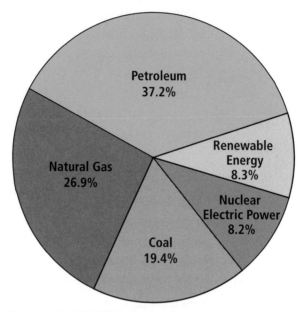

Figure 4.1. 2014 U.S. Energy Consumption by Source, 97 Quadrillion Btu. Source: EIA Annual Energy Outlook 2014

is important, and there is no doubt that investment dollars, government subsidies, and public attention will continue to focus on growing this sector. However, renewables are unlikely to become a major factor in energy markets for at least another decade. For example, generating electricity from wind currently makes up only about 1.3% of total energy production. Renewables have certainly experienced a huge increase over the past five years, and EIA predicts renewable-sourced electricity generation will grow 69% between 2014 and 2040. However, even in the distant future of 2040, EIA forecasts renewables to make up only about 12% of total U.S. energy consumption.

One more point about the big picture of energy. Note that in the EIA pie chart, NGLs are nowhere to be seen. NGLs are simply lumped into the petroleum sector, presumably because they are liquids, even though they are produced from natural gas. As a source of energy, they really belong in the natural gas energy sector, but that is not how EIA or most companies classify NGL products. Frequently NGLs are lumped in with crude oil or treated as a footnote to total liquids production. That can give the erroneous impression that NGLs are not that important.

NGL production is far from trivial. In 2014, the total production of petroleum liquids in the United States (crude oil plus NGLs) was about 11.6 MMbbl/d, according to EIA. Of that total, 8.6 MMbbl/d was classified as crude oil and 3.0 MMbbl/d was classified as NGL production. That means 26% of all the petroleum liquids produced in the United States were NGLs. As discussed in Chapter 3, NGL markets have been an unsung hero in the shale revolution. We will discuss the implications of NGLs' low-profile status later in this chapter.

Slicing and Dicing the Energy Markets

Most of our attention in this book is on the hydrocarbon slices of EIA's energy pie. We consider only nonrenewable energy sources, leaving out hydropower, nuclear power, and other renewables. And although coal is an important hydrocarbon fuel, unfortunately it has not benefited from the shale revolution, which is solely concerned with hydrocarbons produced from wells drilled into the earth, not digging subsurface or strip-mining. In fact, as discussed previously, some parts of the coal market have been casualties of that revolution.

That leaves us with just two sectors of the pie chart: petroleum (liquid hydrocarbons) and natural gas, which together make up 64.1%, or just over two-thirds, of total U.S. energy sources. All three of these energy commodities come from the same drilled hole in the ground and together define what is generically called the *oil and gas industry*, or sometimes collectively called the *petroleum industry*. The business of oil and gas production is generally split into three different segments:

1. **Upstream**, which is the business of finding oil and gas, drilling wells, and getting the raw product to the surface (in Texas vernacular, "The Awll Bidnesss");
2. **Midstream**, which is the business of processing and transporting the oil and gas to markets; and
3. **Downstream**, which is the business of packaging and distributing the finished energy products to consumers.

Although oil, natural gas, and NGLs share a common upstream sector, for the most part, each has its own unique midstream and downstream sector. Downstream markets for oil, natural gas, and NGLs are particularly distinct, meaning the products are used for different purposes. All oil is used in refineries, and those refineries use most of the oil to produce transportation fuels: motor gasoline, diesel fuel, jet fuel, bunker fuel for ships, etc. Most natural gas is burned to create heat, either for homes and factories, to produce steam used to generate electricity, or as a boiler fuel in a wide range of industries. Most NGLs are used in plastics manufacturing and the production of transportation fuels. One of the NGLs—propane—is used for heating homes and businesses, and of course as a fuel for BBQ grills.

Although the downstream uses for crude oil, natural gas, and NGLs are quite different, they are linked together by a common upstream sector: that hole drilled in the ground. This common production source—the well—has done much more for these three hydrocarbons than simply giving them common birth and sibling status. *It is the innovative application of both new and existing technologies to well drilling and completion that made the shale revolution possible* and caused a significant impact on each of the markets for crude oil, NGLs, and natural gas.

Drill-Bit Hydrocarbons

The shale revolution is about the impact of new applications of drilling and completion technologies on these three segments of the hydrocarbon energy market. Each segment has played and, as you will see throughout this book, will continue to play a distinctive role as the domino effect ricochets through the markets and topples one domino after another. Unfortunately, there is no generally recognized term for these market segments that gives equal weight to the three sectors. All we have is the "oil and gas industry." This old, catchall term fails to recognize NGLs that, in the shale revolution, make up the third leg of the hydrocarbon stool. Even though NGL production volumes are sometimes—but not always—included in oil and gas production statistics, NGLs generally don't make the A-list of big hydrocarbon markets. The EIA pie chart (Figure 4.1) is a good example of that. In fact, it seems when pundits, politicians, and laymen (i.e., non-energy business insiders) discuss energy topics, they rarely mention NGL production as a key driver in the shale revolution. In fact, NGLs are just as important a hydrocarbon energy resource as crude oil or natural gas. NGLs, in their own right, now drive huge investments in U.S. gas processing, pipeline transportation, liquids fractionation, and petrochemical markets.

In order to accurately represent all three of these sectors—crude oil, NGLs, and natural gas—that have driven and will continue to drive the shale revolution, it seems appropriate to introduce a new term for them: drill-bit hydrocarbons. If it's extracted by the business end of a drill bit boring a hole in the ground, it's a *drill-bit hydrocarbon* or *DBH*.

It is that drill bit, the way it is used to drill horizontally, and the hydraulic fracturing techniques applied down-hole once the well has been drilled, along with other technologies facilitating the process of drilling and completing wells, that distinguish the shale revolution from previous oil and gas drilling practices. From these shale wells emerge the drill-bit hydrocarbons, all three of which have seen the economics of their production radically changed by new technologies. The shale revolution is about the DBHs and the impact they are having on other energy sources, energy demand, and the need for billions of dollars in new energy infrastructure investment.

Howard Hughes Sr. and the Twin-Cone Rotary Drill Bit

Since our new term, DBH, is based on the three commodities' common heritage from the drill bit, it seems appropriate to provide a little (fascinating) history of the tool itself. The modern drill bit was born over 100 years ago at an oil well near what is today Baytown, Texas. Picture this: it is June 1st, 1909, at an oil well near Galveston Bay. Howard Hughes Sr., then a 40-year-old entrepreneur with multiple business interests—including oil exploration—is demonstrating for a rig crew a new invention: the twin-cone rotary drill bit. Although no one present is yet aware of it, this extraordinary drill bit will revolutionize oil and gas well drilling.

Up until then, wells were drilled with what is termed a **fishtail bit** (see Figure 4.2). Although of different designs, the fishtail bit looked like, well, a fishtail, similar to a woodworker's spade bit: wide, with sharpened edges or a sharp point.

It worked just fine for soft earth or sands, but it was not so good for drilling into rock. The thing just bounced off. Producers knew there was "oil

Figure 4.2. Photo credit: Fishtail Bits and Roughnecks ©Story Sloane, www.sloanegallery.com

in them thar rocks," and several engineers and inventors had been busy designing other types of drill bits to get through the dense stone.

Necessity is the mother of invention, but her offspring is rarely an only child. As many as six types of alternative drill bits were on the drawing boards. It is somewhat unclear just how Hughes ended up with the right design, but he was certain two bits, rotating together to break and grind through the rock, would work best. And it did work, ten times faster and more efficiently than the old fishtail design (see the rotary drill bit design below in Figure 4.3). Dubbed the **Sharp-Hughes Rock Bit** (to credit his partner Walter Sharp), it penetrated 14 feet of hard rock in 11 hours where no fishtail bit had ever been able to break through.

Sharp and Hughes did not invent the rock bit, but they did patent it and then formed the Sharp-Hughes Tool Company in Houston, in 1909. Sharp passed away in 1912 and Hughes became sole owner of the company, which licensed its Sharp-Hughes Rock Bit throughout the industry and began building the elder Hughes's fortune. Although Hughes Sr. died in 1924, his engineers ultimately developed the tri-cone rotary drill bit, introduced in 1933, which solidified the company's market dominance. Thanks to his father, who figured out a way to punch oil well holes into rock,

Figure 4.3. Photo credit: Sharp-Hughes Rock Bit (http://aoghs.org/this-week-in-petroleum-history/oil-history-august-5).

Howard Hughes, Jr. became a very wealthy man. That fortune provided the launching pad for his ventures into movies, aeronautics, airlines, electronics, and the Spruce Goose. Hughes was ultimately the subject of the Leonardo DiCaprio movie, "The Aviator."

A Marriage of Technologies and the Magic Dust of the Shale Revolution

The shale revolution was launched by drilling for dry natural gas in shale, migrated to wet natural gas containing NGLs, and eventually marched into crude oil. These commodities, all emerging from a hole in the ground created with a drill bit, are what the domino effect is all about. Of course, these three hydrocarbons have come from that hole in the ground since the earliest days of the industry, so you could say this is nothing new. Furthermore, the drilling and completion techniques we call shale technologies have been around since the early days of oil and gas exploration and production. So, the technologies are not really new either. But what is new—the magic dust, if you will—is the way producers have combined specific technologies together to produce hydrocarbons from tight formations—those with poor permeability—primarily shale. The true magic dust was combining the technologies so that a lot more of the wellbore has access to the hydrocarbon-bearing rock.

But how, exactly, did they do this? How does the combination of these shale technologies make such a big difference in the production economics for the drill-bit hydrocarbons? Although we address this question in great detail in Chapters 8 and 9, it is important to touch upon the high points of how shale economics work here. If you are a geologist or petroleum engineer, please forgive the layman's explanation; that said, please do not skip this section, if for no other reason than to make sure you agree with the logic. We will start with the basics, some of which will seem obvious. But read on. There is an important point to all this.

We will use the graphic in Figure 4.4 to help with this explanation. Numbers in parentheses before the paragraphs below refer to numbers in the figure. First, to provide a contrast to shale production, we will cover drilling and completion for conventional oil and gas: the way things were done before shale.

(1) Crude oil, NGLs, and natural gas (our three DBHs) are found in source rock, described back in the introduction as the birthplace of the three hydrocarbon fuels. Although there are several kinds of source rock, they are referenced in this book generically as shale. Shale is bedrock, a dense, sedimentary rock of low porosity that is found around the world, usually below the surface but sometimes appearing as rocky outcrops. These shales, deposited tens to hundreds of millions of years ago, contain hydrocarbons, which are the remains of plants and animals embedded in the bottom of some ancient bog.

(2) Hydrocarbons were trapped inside low-porosity shale, but over millions of years, some of the oil, NGLs, and natural gas seeped upward (*primary migration* in the graphic) into geological formations composed of much softer, more porous rock-like sandstones. Sometimes the hydrocarbons percolated to the surface and evaporated into the atmosphere. In other cases, the formations were capped by some geological feature, like a hard rock layer, that acted to contain the hydrocarbons. These caps holding the hydrocarbons inside are called traps, and they form what are called *conventional reservoirs.*

(3) These conventional reservoirs have been the source for almost all oil and gas production, from the first well drilled until the onset of the shale revolution. Most of these conventional reservoirs were ex-

ploited by drilling *vertical wells* from the surface straight down into the formation.

(4) After the vertical well is drilled, the drill bit is withdrawn and completion techniques are applied to prepare the well for production. *Casing*—a pipeliner that supports the hole—is set, typically cemented into place. Of course, there must be a way for the hydrocarbons in the formation to flow into the wellbore and up to the surface. There are a number of ways to accomplish this, but one of the most common is to set a length of casing into the formation, then *perforating* that casing—blowing small holes in it—so the hydrocarbons can seep through. Because the vertical well is drilled straight down through the formation, only a relatively short length of casing is actually in contact with the hydrocarbon-bearing formation, represented by the cylinder at the bottom of the wellbore (4).

These conventional wells tend to be relatively cheap, coming in at a cost in the $1 to $3 million range (in today's dollars). And in the past, conventional reservoirs were relatively easy to find. These two attributes were two of the key drivers of production economics for most oil and gas development over many decades. However, there was an important constraint to conventional well productivity. It was constrained by the relatively short length of pipe actually in contact with the hydrocarbon-bearing formation. In effect, the depth of the reservoir, which typically may be 100 to 200 feet, sets the limit on how much pipe into which the hydrocarbons can flow.

The other problem for conventional wells is that over the years, they became increasingly more difficult to find. Conventional reservoirs in the United States had been exploited for decades, and the number of new ones likely to be found was believed to be few and far between. This belief fueled the notion that the United States was rapidly running out of oil and gas. From a conventional drilling perspective, it was true. But then, shale technologies came together in ways that significantly reduced the per-unit cost of producing DBHs.

(5) A *horizontal well* takes advantage of the fact that most shale deposits are quite large. A horizontal well begins as a vertical well, drilled down to a prescribed depth, and then makes a long, gradual, ninety-degree turn over a distance of several hundred feet, thanks to a special

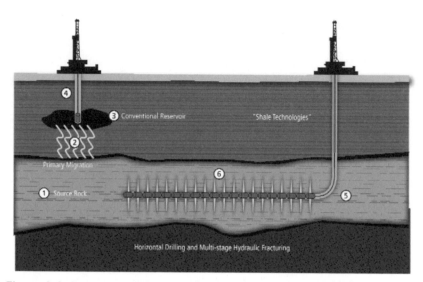

Figure 4.4. Horizontal drilling and multi-stage hydraulic fracturing

drilling motor that bends the wellbore. The wellbore then runs laterally, parallel to the surface. The well does not run out of reservoir, as happens with typical vertical wells, because the shale reservoir is large enough to handle the long lateral, which may be up to one or two miles in length. Once the horizontal well is completed, casing is set and perforated, similar to the vertical well, but it runs the entire horizontal length of the well.

Then the well is hydraulically fractured, or fracked. High-pressure fluid, mostly water and sand, is pumped into the well and flows through the holes in the casing out into the rock surrounding the wellbore to break up, or fracture, that rock. Later, the water is withdrawn and some of the sand, called proppant, stays behind, helping to hold the fractures open. The hydrocarbons in the shale are released through the fractures and flow around the sand, into the wellbore, and up to the surface.

(6) Here is where the magic dust comes in. The lateral is long, sometimes one or two miles in length as mentioned above. Hydrocarbons can enter the wellbore along the entire length of the lateral, which is many times longer than the short length of perforated casing connecting the formation in a conventional well. Think of a horizontal well as 20 or 30 vertical wells stacked end-to-end, represented by the multiple cylinders in the figure. There is a lot more surface area to collect hydrocarbons into

the wellbore. Using fracking to open fissures in the rock effectively funnels the hydrocarbons into that long length of the wellbore. The result is a lot of DBH production from each well. These are *big wells* that have ten to twenty times, if not more, the initial production of a conventional well. These wells might cost three to five times as much as a conventional well but can produce ten to twenty times the DBH volume, thus ten to twenty times the revenue. And that is the main driver of shale economics.

But this is not the whole story. There are four additional factors that make these wells even more economically attractive.

First, their production profile tends to be front-loaded, which means they produce much larger volumes in the first few months after completion, so the producer gets a much faster investment payback. The sooner the investment is recouped, the sooner the producer has enough cash to drill more wells.

Second, shale drilling results in far fewer dry holes than in the past. Conventional reservoirs were hard to find, with one consequence that sometimes wells were drilled that did not yield economically viable quantities of hydrocarbons—the notorious *dry holes*. Finding shale formations has been much less of a problem. The location of many shale deposits has been known for decades. The problem in the pre-shale era was the technologies did not exist to economically extract the hydrocarbons. Now these technologies are known and understood. Due to the information available on the location of shales and the large size of the formations, producers can achieve much better drilling results so the number of wells that do not earn a reasonable return are far fewer than with conventional drilling.

Third, producers are becoming much more productive in drilling these wells. In *pad drilling,* shown in Figure 4.5, several wells are drilled from one location, minimizing the time and cost of moving drilling equipment around, centralizing production at a single location, and minimizing the footprint needed to drill multiple wells.

These characteristics of shale production are powerful economic drivers, significantly reducing the *marginal per-unit cost of production* of the drill-bit hydrocarbons. That means if we divide the cost of drilling a well by the barrels (or cubic feet of gas) that the well produces, the per-unit

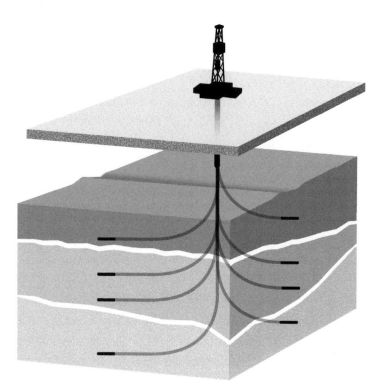

Figure 4.5. Pad drilling

of production cost of shale production is significantly less than the cost of conventional production. Yes, a shale well is more expensive than a conventional well. But the volume produced, and therefore the revenues generated, make up for it many times over. This concept is the hallmark of the shale revolution and the basis for understanding shale economics. It is the reason why shale economics are so much better than conventional economics and why shale has changed the markets for the drill-bit hydrocarbons.

Fourth, there is the matter of the starting production rates for wells, called the *initial production rate* or *IP*, and the steep falloff (*decline curve*) that occurs in shale well production. Since the early days of the shale revolution, various concerns have been expressed about the sharp decline experienced by most shale wells. While it is true that most shale wells exhibit these steep declines, their IPs are so much higher than conventional wells that the economics actually work better. That is because revenues generated from the high initial production volumes can recover the total cost of the well in a shorter period of time. After that point, most revenues are "gravy" from an economic perspective. Rapid recovery of investment capital is always good for investment returns. As the old saying goes, a dollar today is always better than a dollar tomorrow. Or potentially five years from now.

All of these factors translate directly into the huge increases in production of drill-bit hydrocarbons that the market has experienced over the past few years. Over the long run, energy markets will continue to benefit from these improvements in productivity and their consequent impact on producer economics. They represent the ultimate drivers of the domino effect.

The Six Core Domino Effect Principles: What Makes It Work?

The thesis of this book is that the domino effect creates the possibility for *a cascading series of cause-and-effect events, linking the hydrocarbon energy markets for crude oil, NGLs, and natural gas in ways never seen before in the pre-shale world.* What is it about the shale revolution that makes this true?

The underlying foundation of the domino effect can be understood in the context of six principles that explain why the Sweet Sixteen dominoes described in the previous two chapters dropped, which dominoes have dropped subsequently, and what dominoes can be expected to fall in the future.

Principle #1: All three DBHs are produced when drilling a well. In many cases, they are all produced at the same time from the same well. Thus each DBH benefits from the technologies that have reduced the marginal per-unit cost of production. Or, said another way, the cost to produce a barrel of crude, a gallon of NGL, or a cubic foot of natural gas has been reduced by shale technologies. At the same time, the industry's productivity has improved many times over. No such improvement has happened in the coal, nuclear, or renewable energy market sectors. The advances in the shale revolution have benefited the DBHs, and only the DBHs. Thus as a group, the cost of DBHs is falling relative to other energy sources, while at the same time supply is increasing. That puts DBHs in a very strong position when compared to competing sources of energy.

Principle #2: All three DBHs compete for the same investment dollar. Producers can decide to drill wells in *plays* (drilling areas) that produce predominately natural gas, predominately NGLs, or predominately crude oil. All three DBHs may be produced, but the proportions of each may vary significantly, depending on geography, geology, well depth, and other factors. That means producers can and do make investment decisions about where and how much to drill for each of the three DBHs, usually in direct proportion to how much money they will make (their rate of return) on each product. There are a lot of factors that go into the calculation of how much money a producer will make, but none more important than the price of that predominant DBH. This is one way that DBH markets can impact each other. For example, recall when the price of natural gas dropped in 2009 and stayed down while crude and NGL prices were increasing, producers shifted drilling budgets to crude and NGLs. That pulled investment dollars out of dry gas, significantly reducing drilling activity in many of those plays.

DBHs can compete with each other for all sorts of resources. Both public and private investors have had a big appetite for putting money into the shale revolution, but even those funds are limited. Dollars that go to NGLs might be diverted from crude oil investments. Or vice versa. And it goes beyond dollars. DBHs compete for labor. For example, almost all new construction projects need skilled welders. A welder working on building a gas processing plant means one less available to work on a crude oil pipeline.

Principle #3: The price drivers for each DBH are unique. The price of each of the three DBH is *formed*, or determined, in the market based on many factors, most of which are unique to that particular DBH. For example, the price for crude oil used to make motor gasoline and diesel fuel rises and falls mostly with global factors (conflicts and economics) and how much people are driving, while the price of natural gas generally rises or falls with the weather. The price of NGLs is influenced primarily by demand from the petrochemical industry. Crude oil trades in a global market, which makes it highly sensitive to global political developments, and the United States continues to import crude from those global markets. On the other hand, U.S. natural gas today is, by and large, landlocked into North America and thus relatively insensitive to global commodity price action. That is likely to change over the next few years as new LNG export terminal facilities come online. But today, North America is effectively a price island, insulated from global natural gas markets. Not only do NGLs trade in unique markets; each of the five NGLs has its own pricing dynamics. For example, ethane exports are quite small today, which makes the market relatively insensitive to global pricing pressure, while propane exports are increasing dramatically and are becoming much more connected to world prices.

Principle #4: All of the DBHs are subject to the same laws of energy markets regarding flow, capacity, and price differentials. The relationship between the capacity to move a DBH commodity, the volume of flow through that capacity, and the price for that DBH are intimately tied together. For example, consider what happens when the supply of a DBH in a particular region increases. If that volumetric increase exceeds the capacity of infrastructure to move that volume, then the result is a capacity shortfall. That capacity shortfall can have a dramatic impact on the difference in price between the supply source and downstream markets. The market mechanisms that cause and respond to these developments work exactly the same way for natural gas, NGLs, and crude oil and are explored in great detail in Chapters 12, 13, and 14.

Principle #5: The economics of one DBH influences the production of the others. As noted above, all three DBHs are frequently produced from the same well. So for example, a producer may move investment dollars to a play that produces predominately crude oil, but the wells drilled may produce a lot of associated natural gas along with the crude. In this case, the producer is going mainly after the crude, and the economics are based primarily on the revenue stream from crude oil sales. The associated natural gas becomes a *byproduct* produced and sold regardless of the price of natural gas (since the producer is making most of the money on the crude oil). The same holds true for natural gas as a byproduct of drilling for NGLs. Thus the decision to drill for one DBH can have unintended consequences for another DBH.

Principle #6: Supply and demand dynamics in the DBH markets are simultaneously distinct and interrelated. For example, incremental natural gas production has found a home primarily by growing its market share in power generation at the expense of U.S. coal. In contrast, increasing production of crude oil has found a home primarily by growing its market share in U.S. refineries at the expense of overseas imports. Furthermore, DBHs can compete with each other in some of the same markets. Homes can be heated with natural gas, propane (an NGL), or fuel oil (refined crude). If natural gas is cheaper than propane or fuel oil, homeowners may be willing to pay to switch fuel sources, and their suppliers may be willing to absorb the difference in distribution cost to get the fuel to them.

Here is the bottom line. DBHs are linked at their source—at the well—but differ from that point forward. They are used in diverse markets and have different values depending on how they are used. That common source is one way that a DBH's domino can knock over the domino of another DBH. The three DBHs can have quite varied responses to increases (and decreases) in supply in individual markets. What is good for one might not be so good for another, setting up one domino to topple another. Not only can these six principles be applied to help make sense of what has already happened in the shale revolution, they can be applied prospectively to anticipate what is likely to happen next. That is where this book is headed.

But first, to fully appreciate how these market linkages work, you need a deeper understanding of the overall marketplace. The next three chapters explore each individual market in detail, as well as their interrelationships.

Part II

The Three Amigos: Natural Gas, NGLs, and Crude Oil

AS YOU BEGIN THINKING MORE ABOUT THE THREE DRILL-BIT HYDROCAR-bons, consider three other amigos and their plethora of piñatas—in this instance, from the film "The Three Amigos":

Jefe: I have put many beautiful piñatas in the storeroom, each of them filled with little surprises.

El Guapo: Many piñatas?

Jefe: Oh yes, many!

El Guapo: Would you say I have a *plethora* of piñatas?

Jefe: A what?

El Guapo: A *plethora.*

Jefe: Oh yes, you have a plethora.

El Guapo: Jefe, what is a plethora?

Jefe: Why, El Guapo?

El Guapo: Well, you told me I have a plethora. And I just would like to know if you know what a plethora is. I would not like to think that a person would tell someone he has a plethora, and then find out that person has *no idea* what it means to have a plethora.

Jefe: Forgive me, El Guapo. I know that I, Jefe, do not have your superior intellect and education. But could it be that once again, you are angry at something else, and are looking to take it out on me?*

*"The Three Amigos" (1986), produced by L.A. Films and Home Box Office (HBO). directed by John Landis.

57

The three drill-bit hydrocarbons are *the three amigos* of energy markets. All three, in the words of El Guapo, are enjoying a plethora of production growth.

At one level, they have a lot in common. They are energy commodities that come from a well. They are actively traded in robust physical and financial markets. They move from production source to market primarily in pipelines which function as distribution networks. Each has its own central hub and corresponding regional hubs, where products are frequently stored for both operational and commercial purposes. They can be imported, transported to where they are needed most, and processed into other products.

But all that commonality is a 20,000-foot view. When you get down into the details of each DBH market, they are quite different. First, their physical characteristics are very distinct. Oil is a liquid that can be stored in containers at atmospheric temperatures and pressures, which means no special pressurized equipment is needed to store most crude oil. NGLs are also liquids, but to stay liquids most must be held in pressurized storage, like the thick-walled tank needed to hold propane for your BBQ grill. Natural gas is … well, a gas. It must be held under pressure unless it is super-cooled to the point it turns into a liquid—liquefied natural gas or LNG—primarily for overseas transport. That is a very expensive proposition.

There are other differences between the DBHs. Because of their dissimilar physical characteristics, the logistics infrastructure is individual to each. It takes different kinds of processing to prepare them for market. And of course, they are used for different purposes in distinctively different markets.

Beyond these physical differences, there are huge differences in the workings of each of the DBH markets. They have disparate commercial processes, different terminology, distinct trading networks, and unique regulatory structures. All of these characteristics grew up over many decades of history, in which each of the DBH markets effectively evolved independently from the others. For example, crude oil has been trading as a commodity for the better part of a hundred years, while natural gas commodity trading has only existed since the late 1980s.

To truly understand the shale revolution and the domino effect, it is necessary to have a solid grasp of both the commonalities and the differences between the three DBHs. The next three chapters provide an in-depth examination of how the three markets developed and how each transacts business. This foundation sets the stage for our understanding of the current and future dominoes and prepares you for learning to use the energy market tools in Part III.

One more matter before we begin. From time to time you will see mention of a *PADD*. It is an acronym for Petroleum Administration for Defense District, a geographic breakdown of the United States used by much of the energy industry for aggregating statistics for crude oil, petroleum products, and NGLs. The PADD system was established during World War II primarily to facilitate gasoline rationing for the war effort. Today, the PADD system is used by EIA to organize government energy data, and hence is used by most of the energy industry as a consistent way of organizing energy statistics. The five PADDs are defined as follows:

PADD I is the East Coast,

PADD II the Midwest,

PADD III the Gulf Coast,

PADD IV the Rocky Mountain Region, and

PADD V the West Coast (includes Alaska and Hawaii).

There are two additional PADDs: PADD VI, the U.S. Virgin Islands and Puerto Rico, and PADD VII, Guam, Northern Mariana Islands, and American Samoa. These two additional PADDs rarely show up in EIA energy statistics. The five primary PADDs also have further geographic breakdowns used for some EIA reports. (See Figure II.1 on the next page.)

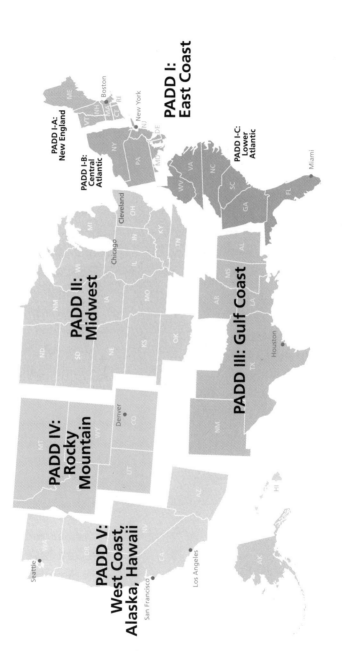

Figure II.1. Petroleum Administration for Defense Districts

Chapter 5

Natural Gas: The Hydrocarbon Energy Market That Started It All

I T IS ALWAYS SPOKEN OR WRITTEN "OIL AND GAS." NEVER THE OTHER WAY
*around. Gas is second, behind crude oil. It has always been that way. Natural
gas is a fuel burned for heat and, in the early days, for light. Certainly not used
as a highly valued transportation fuel, like oil. Natural gas is a quirky energy commodity: part deregulated, part highly regulated. Its road to becoming an energy
commodity was wild, rocky, and chaotic. In this chapter we examine the history of
natural gas, investigate how the natural gas commodity trades within its unique
infrastructure, consider what 50 years of regulatory hell did to the gas market, and
assess whether or not the market is geared up to handle the ongoing shale revolution.*

Beginnings

The U.S. natural gas industry grew out of what was once considered an
unwanted waste product. The first recorded commercial gas well in the
United States was 27 feet deep, drilled in 1821 by William Hart, a gun-
smith in Fredonia, New York, on Lake Erie. He piped the gas to a local
innkeeper. Eventually Hart's gas was piped to more shops, sparking more
demand in the area. By the late 1800s, natural gas was being used
throughout the Northeast. Streetlights were a big source of demand,
changing the way people regarded the night.

Nevertheless, the credit for drilling the first oil and gas well generally goes to "Colonel" Edwin Drake, whom history remembers for completing the first commercial oil well on an island in Oil Creek, near Titusville, Pennsylvania on August 27, 1859. Not only did this well launch oil production in the United States, it inaugurated a new phase of growth for natural gas because that first oil well came along with some natural gas. Drake ran a two-inch iron pipeline about five miles from the Oil Creek area to Titusville, and for most of the next 40 years, the Appalachia region was the center of the natural gas business in the United States.

Of course, following that Titusville well, natural gas soon took a back seat to oil. Producers went after higher-value crude oil for use in kerosene, the most widely used energy source for home and business applications. Not long thereafter the big growth market shifted to gasoline for automobiles, and the drive to produce oil vastly overshadowed natural gas. Eventually the demand for oil became so great that the producers that drilled for oil and found gas with the oil did not even take the time or trouble to bring much of the natural gas to market. It was often considered a nuisance and was *flared,* or burned off, rather than pipelined to market.

By the early 1900s, using gas for home cooking, heating, and lighting had started to take hold. Even so, it remained a relatively small, localized niche business. As the center of crude oil production shifted to Texas and Louisiana early in the twentieth century, significant volumes of gas, particularly in those states, continued to be flared. Most of that flaring did not end until state agencies prohibited the practice, driving producers to promote the construction of huge industrial and petrochemical complexes on the Gulf Coast, from Houston to the Mississippi River. The gas, not yet considered an economically viable, marketable commodity in its own right, was sold to the industrial and petrochemical companies at bargain-basement prices to incentivize the construction of those plants. In essence, it was treated as a by-product.

But things were changing. Even though the use of gas for home heating and cooking was a small market, it was starting to grow rapidly. As more and more communities and industries recognized the benefits of natural gas, the need for pipelines to move it from the production fields to the places where it could be used multiplied. That demand prompted a wave of pipeline construction projects.

Building out the U.S. natural gas pipeline infrastructure. In 1931, the first big natural gas pipeline was the 1,000-mile, 24-inch diameter transmission line built by what became today's Natural Gas Pipeline Company of America, now owned by Kinder Morgan. The pipeline runs through Louisiana up to Chicago. It was soon followed by many other long-line systems, constructed over the next 30 years to move gas from major producing states like Texas, Louisiana, and Oklahoma to major consuming states like Illinois, Indiana, Michigan, New York, and New Jersey.

The creation of this infrastructure enabled the widespread use and development of a fuel that had been thought to have little, if any, value. The result was a rapid growth in demand as consuming markets gained access to low-cost natural gas. Unfortunately, in the mid-1950s almost half a century of legal, regulatory, and commercial turmoil began as the natural gas industry groped its way to the market we know today. We will examine this regulatory chaos later in this chapter, but first we need to fast-forward to how the market works today.

Today's U.S. Natural Gas Market

The U.S. natural gas industry is highly fragmented. The companies involved in upstream are generally not involved in midstream (processing and transportation). Those involved in midstream are rarely involved in the downstream market, which is the domain of natural gas utilities (called *local distribution companies* or *LDCs*), commercial and industrial gas users, and power generators using gas to produce electricity. There are as many as 20,000 producers (although the top 40 produce over one-half of the reported volumes), hundreds of pipeline owners, approximately 1,500 local distribution companies, thousands of power generation facilities and industrial end users, and more than 71 million commercial and residential customers.

Almost all gas within the United States moves to market on pipelines. Many of those pipelines cross state lines and consequently are regulated by the federal government agency called the Federal Energy Regulatory Commission (FERC) as to their rates, terms, and conditions and are called *interstate* pipelines. Pipelines that do not cross state lines are regulated by the states in which they operate, so are not subject to FERC regulations. These state regulated systems are called *intrastate* pipelines.

Although the 305,000-mile U.S. natural gas pipeline network is comprised of hundreds of local distribution companies and thousands of producers offering a host of different logistical configurations, the fundamental flow and value chain is consistent throughout the market. Figure 5.1 lays out a simplified diagram of the physical gas market configuration.

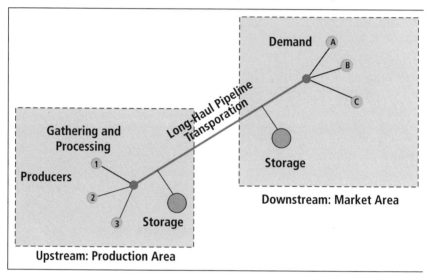

Figure 5.1. Natural gas pipeline network

In the upstream, or production area, gas is extracted from wellheads by producers, gathered through a network of usually small lines (called gathering systems) and carried to central treating and processing facilities. Gathering and processing plants are generally unregulated operations owned by midstream companies.

At the processing facilities, natural gas liquids and other impurities are removed and handled separately, the remaining residue gas delivered to long-haul transmission pipelines as pipeline-quality gas. It is moved into the downstream—much of it into distribution systems owned by LDCs—where the gas goes to homes, commercial companies, factories, and power generators. But not all gas goes through the LDCs. Some factories and electrical power generators take their gas supplies directly off the long-haul pipelines. Natural gas can be stored (and often is); storage may be located in the production area, the market area, or anywhere in between, as Figure 5.1 shows.

The extent and complexity of the transmission pipeline network, frequently called the *pipeline grid*, is apparent from Figure 5.2. This huge network spreads across the nation and truly defines the structure of the natural gas industry, where trading takes place, how reliability is managed, and how the commodity physically moves from the point of production to where it is ultimately used. This is by far the most extensive natural gas pipeline network in the world. As noted above, interstate pipelines are owned by FERC-regulated companies. Many of those regulated pipeline companies are subsidiaries of major energy companies that own both regulated and unregulated natural gas infrastructure.

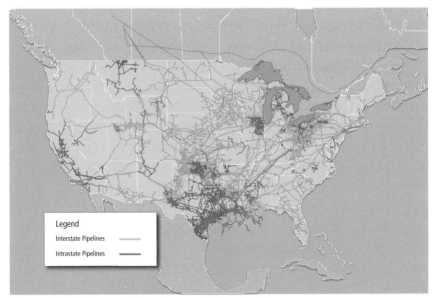

Legend
Interstate Pipelines
Intrastate Pipelines

Figure 5.2. U.S. natural gas transmission pipelines

Transporting Natural Gas

Even though the physical infrastructure of the natural gas market has remained relatively consistent over many decades, the commercial structure of the industry went through a massive, FERC-initiated *restructuring* in the mid-1980s. Until then, essentially all natural gas transported on interstate pipelines was owned by the pipeline companies. The pipeline companies bought gas from producers, moved the gas on their own pipelines, and then sold the gas to downstream buyers like LDCs, power generators, and industrials. At that point in time, natural gas did not trade at all, at least not as we know it as a commodity trading market today. Back in those days there was no spot market. No futures market. Nothing but gas engineers working mostly for major oil and gas companies selling their company's gas to pipeline companies mostly on very long-term contracts at prices set by the U.S. government. That all changed in the mid-1980s and early 1990s when the U.S. gas market was restructured, culminating in the government's FERC Order 636. We will get back to how all that happened toward the end of this chapter. But first, let us continue to examine how the market functions today.

Natural gas commodity transactions occur in what is now a very flexible, very complex, open, and transparent marketplace. In effect, any participant can conduct business with any other participant. That might not seem to be such a big deal, but it was not the case before restructuring. On the other hand, the transportation of natural gas is highly regulated, particularly for the largest portion of the market where interstate pipelines are involved. Interstate natural gas pipelines have rules. Lots of rules. Rules that are approved by FERC and apply to all shippers using the pipelines. Those stacks of rules—ensconced in the pipeline's *tariff*—define who can ship, how they ship, when they ship, and effectively everything about moving natural gas. So even though the natural gas commodity is freely tradable, the natural gas transportation system creates a highly regulated market structure within which the commodity must trade. That is why this market is characterized as partially deregulated, partially highly regulated.

Two types of gas transport contracts. To move gas on a pipeline the shipper must have a contract with the pipeline. There are two types of those contracts. The first type is the *firm* contract, meaning that the pipeline essentially guarantees that the capacity will be available to move the shipper's gas. These contracts are known by the acronym *FT*, standing for firm transportation. Under the basic market structure of interstate pipelines, *firm shippers* (producers, consumers, marketers, or any other entity engaged in gas transport) effectively charter capacity on the pipeline by paying a firm monthly reservation charge. The shipper pays the reservation charge whether gas is moved or not. Contracts for gas transportation may be for a few days or a few decades.

The second type is an interruptible contract, or IT, which stands for interruptible transportation. Under these contracts, the shipper makes no commitment to a fixed payment or fixed level of usage. The shipper only pays for actual volumes that flow for the shipper's account. However, this type of shipper has a lower priority than a firm shipper. This means that the pipeline does not guarantee that the gas will be transported as scheduled, only that the pipeline will move the gas if capacity is available. In practice, this means that the shipper's contract to move gas may be bumped or preempted by a firm shipper who has chartered capacity on the same pipeline. In effect, gas on interruptible capacity only moves if the pipeline's capacity is not fully subscribed or if the pipeline's firm capacity holders are not using all of their available capacity.

A key characteristic of natural gas is that it is, for the most part, fungible. When natural gas is received into a pipeline, it is required to meet certain quality specifications. Those specifications are relatively consistent across the nation. That fact has a variety of important implications.

First, gas from one pipeline can be used to meet demand on another pipeline, assuming, of course, the pipelines are connected.

Second, gas prices from one pipeline to the next are directly comparable from a quality perspective. They may be wildly different due to supply-and-demand conditions at a particular location at a point in time, but the commodity is generally the same stuff.

Third, natural gas pipelines work more like a bank than a UPS truck. Here's what that means. A shipper delivers gas to a pipeline at some receipt point (a metered connection with some gas production facility or gathering system) and can get that gas delivered hundreds or thousands of miles away the same day! Since all gas on a pipeline is of like quality, the pipeline can take a deposit (like a bank does with dollars) and make a payment, effective instantaneously, even though the physical gas only moves down the pipeline at about 20 miles per hour. It is not necessary to move the shippers' gas molecules to affect delivery. This single characteristic of gas transportation is a market feature with important implications for how gas is traded.

Physical Natural Gas Commercial Arrangements and Transactions

The sale and purchase of natural gas takes place both through one-on-one bilateral negotiated transactions (including long-term contracts) and through open and transparent trading on organized exchanges.

The market for physical natural gas, in which natural gas volumes are physically delivered from seller to buyer, includes several types of market structures:

Daily physical spot market. The most market-responsive sales and purchases are made in the spot market. In these deals, natural gas is bought and sold for delivery the next day: in other words, a transaction consummated today is delivered tomorrow. It may be traded by phone or instant (text) messaging between buyer and seller but is often conducted via the Intercontinental Exchange (ICE), an electronic, Internet-based trading system.

Once the trade has been consummated, schedulers take over. Since this is physical gas, schedulers for both the buyer and seller must coordinate with the pipeline to handle all of the details of receipt and delivery. For interstate pipelines, this is accomplished using a pipeline's web-based electronic bulletin board nomination system. All interstate pipelines are required to utilize such systems; rules for use are prescribed by FERC and the North American Energy Standards Board (NAESB).

Some daily spot prices are negotiated *outright*, at a fixed price (e.g. $3.50/MMBtu) agreed upon between buyer and seller. Others are based on a differential to the primary pricing location for natural gas in the U.S., known as the Henry Hub in Louisiana (e.g., $0.15 under the Henry Hub price). This price differential is called the *basis, basis spread*, or even more accurately, the *location basis* between some location and the price on the same day at the Henry Hub.

Monthly spot market. A significant volume of natural gas is bought and sold each month during a period called bid week, a time period 4–5 days prior to the first day of the month the gas is intended to flow. Again, pricing may be outright—i.e., negotiated at an absolute number, at a fixed basis differential relative to Henry Hub—or based on daily-traded index prices tracked and published by industry trade publications.

Long-term contracts. The market for longer-term physical gas supply is usually conducted under seasonal, annual, or longer-term deals with pricing based on the daily-traded published index prices as described above. LDCs frequently contract for seasonal (higher volumes for winter versus summer) deals to manage supply for both homeowners and commercial customers. Note that in the U.S. natural gas market, the heating season is usually defined as the five-month period between November 1 and March 31, and most LDC sales, transportation, and storage contracts are aligned in some way to this time period.

Many monthly and long-term contracts mentioned above are *firm transactions*, arrangements in which the parties are obligated to deliver and receive the volume specified in the contract unless an event of *force majeure* (explosion, hurricane, etc.) occurs. But in other cases, deals are *interruptible*, or *swing*, in which one party or the other can opt not to deliver or receive the volume committed. This is advantageous when either supply or demand is unpredictable or unreliable. Swing deals typically include a price premium to compensate the party providing the flexibility to the other.

Alternative index term market. Since most natural gas deals are either spot deals or are based on the index prices of spot deals, it is accurate to say that most natural gas in the United States is transacted at spot market-sensitive prices. However, various attempts have been made—and continue to be made—to structure deals based on a fixed price or pricing formula (e.g., prices adjusted for inflation and prices linked to another commodity). This is often referred to as an *alternative index term*. An example is the January 2013 ten-year contract between gas producer Chesapeake and chemical company Methanex, in which volume was indexed to the price of methanol. That said, such deals are very few in number and difficult to execute. For the producer to lock in a price or formula, some premium is usually required to compensate for the possibility of missing out on future natural gas price increases. That usually makes this kind of contract unattractive to the buyer. For these reasons, alternative index term deals are rarely consummated.

The transaction types described above are *physical markets*: gas is physically delivered from the seller to the buyer. But there is another kind of natural gas transaction that, for the most part, does not involve the physical natural gas product. Those are the nonphysical, or financial, transactions.

Financial (Nonphysical) Natural Gas Transactions

Various pricing mechanisms exist for purposes of *risk management*: the ability to assure a price for future deliveries as a hedge against what spot prices may be at the time. Risk management can also be used to protect against variations in the basis from Henry Hub pricing, with the objective of minimizing the risk and maximizing the return. Generally, the mechanics of these markets take place on the NYMEX futures market operated by the Chicago Mercantile Exchange (CME) or the Intercontinental Exchange (ICE). The CME/NYMEX contract for gas priced at the Henry Hub in Louisiana is the gold standard for natural gas pricing in the United States.

Like many futures contracts, although physical delivery is possible, CME/NYMEX deals rarely go to delivery. Instead, they are normally offset with trades in the opposite direction prior to delivery (e.g., a contract to sell at a price offsetting a contract to buy at that or another price). Transaction volume in the CME/NYMEX futures market is quite large. The trading value of the futures market is as much as ten times higher than that of the physical market.

In addition to the role of futures in managing risk, some industry participants use futures for speculation. Such activities are subject to ongoing regulatory scrutiny by both FERC and the Commodity Futures Trading Commission (CFTC).

Natural Gas Hubs and Basis

Theoretically, natural gas can be bought and sold anywhere on the pipeline grid. But in practice, buyers and sellers tend to do business at certain locations where, by convention and general market practice, it is easy to identify, consummate, and fulfill transactions. These locations are called *hubs*. Hubs are certainly not unique to the natural gas market. Both crude oil and NGLs also tend to trade at hubs. However, how the hubs work for each of the DBHs varies considerably.

For one thing, there are a lot of natural gas hubs. More than 130 around the United States are large enough to be tracked by industry trade publications. In some cases, hubs developed where multiple pipelines converged and there was a need for gas to change hands as it moved from one pipeline to another. In other instances, the structure of pipeline transportation contracts held by buyers and sellers simply made it convenient to do business at a particular location. Regardless, a hub is almost always characterized by high liquidity and high trading volumes, making it easy for sellers to find buyers and vice versa. Figure 5.3 identifies 24 prominent hubs, including the major pipeline corridors—routes between hubs containing one or more pipelines—with which they are associated.

Each hub can have a different price at which natural gas can be bought and sold at any point in time. The primary pricing location for natural gas in the United States—and the most important hub from a market price perspective—is the Henry Hub. The Henry location was elevated

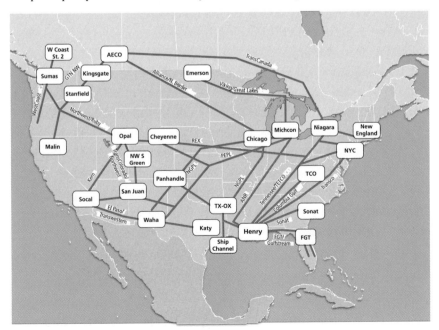

Figure 5.3. Natural gas hubs

to its lofty perch when, in April 1990, it was selected as the delivery point for the then-nascent NYMEX natural gas futures contract. It was not long before Henry pricing became the benchmark for all U.S. natural gas, with other hub locations trading in relation to the Henry price. The price differential between other hubs and the Henry Hub price is the basis spread discussed previously. In Chapters 13 and 14, we will cover the factors that drive changes in basis spreads.

Natural Gas Regulation

We started this chapter with the warning that natural gas is a quirky energy commodity: part deregulated, part highly regulated. In fact, the history of natural gas is tarnished by a fifty-year descent into regulatory hell. Your first inclination may be to skip this section, since who (besides regulatory attorneys) want to read about regulatory hell. But fight that urge. The regulatory history of natural gas still shapes what can and cannot be accomplished in the market today. After all, most of the pipeline regulations we live with each day have their roots back in the regulatory-hell period. To spare you too much pain, this is a much abbreviated version of natural gas regulatory hell. If, on the other hand, you are a glutton for punishment, go to the FERC website and read some old FERC natural gas orders from the era.

The regulatory hell period started in 1954 with something called the Phillips Decision. This was a Supreme Court case that interpreted a law from 1938 called the Natural Gas Act (which is still on the books). The court ruled that it was OK for the federal government to set the price of any natural gas crossing state lines. Yes, the government got in the business of pricing natural gas. Not surprisingly, that did not work out so well. Figure 5.4 depicts six major periods of regulatory and market evolution, starting with the Phillips Decision. The following paragraphs briefly outline what happened.

1954–1970. During this first period, the Phillips Decision by the U.S. Supreme Court kept prices artificially low, causing demand to grow while new supply remained undeveloped.

1970–79. By 1970, the result of the Phillips Decision was widespread shortages of natural gas. That led to the *Curtailment Era* which lasted until

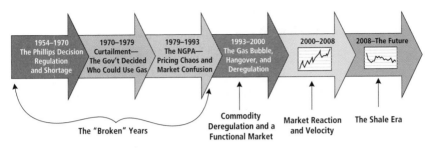

Figure 5.4. Six periods of regulatory and market evolution

1979. During this period the government allocated supplies. In effect, distribution companies, factories, and power generators could only use gas when and if the U.S. government declared it was legal for them to do so.

1979–93. Attempting to address those shortages, the U.S. Congress passed a very disruptive law: the Natural Gas Policy Act of 1978, creating no less than 27 different gas price categories ranging from $0.40 to $7.00/MMBtu. It was a huge, complex, artificial market structure and, even with all the categorical distinctions, *still* prohibited certain uses of natural gas. Years of pricing chaos and market confusion ensued, reaching into 1993. But in the mid-1980s, as described earlier, FERC started the restructuring process for the natural gas market. That process continued until 1993.

To understand the significance of restructuring, it is important to re-iterate that prior to the mid-1980s, the pipelines controlled much of the industry. As discussed previously, a pipeline company would buy natural gas from a producer on a "take or pay" contractual basis, meaning it would buy all the gas produced from a particular field for as long as it would last, typically 25 years. Pricing was set for the most part by the government; there were no negotiations, market trading, commodity futures, or any other characteristic of a commodity market. It was simply the producer selling for the price the government told the pipeline it had to pay. The pipeline company then sold the gas to local distribution companies (LDCs) or other end users for a gain, a regulated price based on the *cost of service*, a calculation approved by FERC. The situation was a mess. Fortunately an activist group of FERC commissioners took on the problem and started issuing a series of orders that transformed the business of buying and selling natural gas from a highly regulated activity to an open, flexible market. It took a few years, but by the late 1980s there were the beginnings of a robust commodity market in natural gas. However, there were still laws and regulations on the books which constrained the way commercial transactions were conducted. Those issues were finally resolved in the early 1990s.

1993-2000. In 1992, Congress finally deregulated wellhead natural gas prices. At about the same time, FERC completed the restructuring process in its landmark *Order 636*, formally and legally *separating the commodity, natural gas, from its transportation, the pipeline*. In a word, natural gas was *unbundled* from the pipeline companies and became an *unregulated commodity* which could be bought, sold, and traded on the trading floors and spot markets.

Commodity deregulation set the legal stage for a functional market, but what followed in the early 1990s was what became known as a *gas bubble*, a hangover of excess supply that held prices low for a decade, without significant expansion of the resource base. Surplus supplies pushed prices down, and low prices discouraged producer reinvestment.

2000–2008. The supply-and-demand balance finally tightened. Then in the mid-2000s, the back-to-back Gulf Coast hurricanes (see Chapter 2) and financial market disarray discussed earlier resulted in highly volatile prices. This persisted from early 2000 until 2008.

2008–The Future. By 2008, the shale revolution had come into its own, pushing the natural gas market into an oversupply situation. Prices fell and have been relatively low ever since, excluding the periodic impact of weather events like the polar vortex of 2013–14. It certainly appears that regulatory hell is in the rear-view mirror and that the legal and regulatory structures have settled into place for the long term.

Here's the bottom line for the end of natural gas regulatory hell and the beginnings of today's commodity gas market. FERC Order 636 mandated that purchases and sales of the gas commodity would be completely separate transactions from the transportation and storage services provided by pipeline companies. This separation allowed the gas itself to compete in an open, unregulated commodity market while most of the pipeline services and rates remain heavily regulated and rigidly structured. This is the way it still works today, and along with the rest of the natural gas market, it appears to be working pretty well. With these lessons of natural gas free markets and regulation under our belts, let us turn the page to NGLs.

Note

1. A pipeline's tariff is a published statement filed by an interstate pipeline with FERC that describes the rates (i.e., prices), terms, and conditions under which natural gas transportation services will be provided. Tariffs are extremely detailed, usually hundreds of pages in length, with every term and every cost-based rate being subject to FERC approval. Pipeline tariffs are public documents available on pipeline websites and in FERC databases.

Chapter 6

NGLs: The Unsung Heroes of Shale Development

N ATURAL GAS LIQUIDS. NGLS. IT IS A MARKET THAT MANY IN THE GENERAL *public have never heard of, even though NGLs have been out there for more than 80 years. Historically, NGLs were viewed as a byproduct of natural gas production, a nuisance that the producer had to remove from natural gas to make it safe to transport in pipelines. Within the energy community, NGLs were traditionally considered the backwater of the big crude oil and natural gas markets and did not receive much attention, even by the companies that produced the products. Being assigned to the NGL department was not a career-enhancing move at most energy companies.*

Over the past few years, shale has dramatically changed the status of NGLs, promoting NGLs from the tail being wagged by the natural gas dog to the other way around. The NGL market has mostly led the natural gas market since 2010, in some cases effectively making natural gas the byproduct of NGL production.

How did this happen? It was the domino effect. In the early 2010s, natural gas prices declined due to oversupply and crude oil prices remained strong; NGLs became more valuable relative to natural gas. Why? Because the prices of NGLs tend to be more closely related to the price of crude oil than the price of natural gas.

Here is the bottom line: NGLs are primarily extracted from gas. However, certain of the highest value NGLs are sold into markets priced in relation to crude oil. It is like modern-day alchemy. Not lead into gold. Instead, cheap natural gas into more valuable crude oil-related products. Don't take this analogy too far. Gas processors really do not make crude oil out of natural gas. They extract NGLs from gas. It is just that most of those NGLs are valued more like crude oil than they are natural gas. And for that reason, it is a bit like turning lead into gold, at least it was in the days when crude oil prices were worth far more than natural gas on a fuel equivalent basis.

Unlike natural gas, which mostly moves into fuel markets (i.e., it gets burned for heat), NGLs have a wide range of markets, from a petrochemical feedstock to motor gasoline and other fuels. Most NGLs can move into more than one of these markets, and do so based on their chemical composition and characteristics. The way different NGLs are handled varies greatly, depending on their physical characteristics. For these reasons, you cannot understand NGL markets without some understanding of the chemistry, manufacture, and handling of the various products. This chapter will provide that background and get into the inner workings of the NGL markets.

Beginnings

The story of NGLs goes back to the early days of the oil business in Pennsylvania, just before the turn of the last century. Much of the oil came along with associated gas, and that gas contained NGLs. If the gas was to be pipelined to a market, some of the more volatile NGLs needed to be removed to make the natural gas safe to transport.

At the time, the liquids that could be removed were extracted by compressing the gas, which produces a mixture of liquids. That mixture was mostly what we would call today either condensate, natural gasoline (one of the five NGLs), or a mixture of both, although other NGLs like butane and propane were mixed in with the condensate and natural gasoline. The liquid product was called *casinghead gasoline* (or *casinghead gas*) because it was a gasoline-like mixture that was produced at or near the wellhead (the *casinghead*).

The casinghead gasoline usually contained relatively high quantities of volatile hydrocarbons (like propane and butanes) and was typically left to weather, or sit for a while, in a tank for those volatiles to boil off into the atmosphere. That was a waste of potentially valuable hydrocarbons. Eventually, plant operators figured out ways to compress and store those volatile compounds instead of letting them boil off. Those compressed liquids were primarily mixtures of propane and butane. That was the genesis of what is now the *liquefied petroleum gas (LPG)* industry. LPG is generally synonymous with propane and butane. By the 1920s, LPGs were being used for heating, for cooking, and even as a fuel for blowtorches.

By the early 1920s, the big growth region for casinghead gas shifted from Pennsylvania to Oklahoma, where the crude and gas being produced had high concentrations of LPGs. Two of the early pioneers in the industry at that time were Frank Phillips (1873–1950), of Phillips Petroleum and Phillips 66 fame, and William Kelly Warren (1897–1990), founder of Tulsa-based Warren Petroleum Company that today can be traced as a predecessor company to Targa Resources. Phillips and Warren competed vigorously for rights to collect and process casinghead gas and LPGs in the early days of Oklahoma's energy boom.

Warren, often considered the father of natural gas processing in the United States, built his business by purchasing the production from the natural gas processing plants that had sprung up in Oklahoma in order to extract casinghead gas and LPGs. By 1925, Warren owned the output of 31 plants in five states; by 1929, the company had expanded to 50 plants. In 1953, Gulf Oil (now Chevron) purchased Warren Petroleum for more than $420 million, making it the largest exchange of money in the nation's energy industry up until that time. In 1955, Warren started development of underground NGL storage in Mont Belvieu, Texas, and went on to build the first fractionator there (see the feature titled "Thinkin' About Mont Belvieu"), cementing Mont Belvieu's role as the most important NGL hub in the United States and the world.

By the time the 1960s rolled around, LPGs had developed into an important industry segment in their own right, with several companies, including Phillips and Gulf-Warren, marketing propane to individual distributors around the country. However, most of that propane still moved by truck and rail. It took an ex-railroad man and entrepreneur named Robert "Luck" Thomas to develop the first liquid propane transmission pipeline. His company Mid-America Pipeline Company (MAPCO) developed a major pipeline system from New Mexico to Illinois and Wisconsin, putting LPGs on the road to becoming a fully integrated energy market. MAPCO is now owned by Enterprise Products Partners and is called MAPL.

No brief history of NGLs could possibly be complete without a few paragraphs on Enterprise, the largest player in the NGL industry today. In 1968, Joe Havens, a propane salesman for a company called Wanda Petroleum, launched a propane distribution company he called Enterprise with Rex White, an LPG dealer in Arkansas. Enterprise was successful out of the gate. Havens was soon expanding, purchasing tank cars that would allow him to access propane from distant supply points. Meanwhile, Wanda had been bought by Ashland Oil, on the strength of a deal put together by Wanda's accountant and EVP, Dan Duncan (1933–2010). Within a year, Duncan grew restless in his new position at Ashland. Havens offered Duncan, whom he had met when they worked at Wanda, a one-third partnership at Enterprise. Duncan accepted and became the driving force at the company. Throughout the 1970s, Enterprise expanded its midstream operations, laying pipe, building underground storage, and eventually building a fractionator at Mont Belvieu. By 1985, Enterprise owned a significant interest in Mont Belvieu fractionation facilities. Havens sold his interest in Enterprise to Duncan in 1990. Duncan took Enterprise public in 1998. He continued the buildout until his death in 2010, at which time the company's assets included nearly 50,000 miles of natural gas and NGL pipeline as well as 220 million barrels of storage. Since Duncan's death, Enterprise continued to expand to become what is today one of the largest integrated midstream energy companies and the largest player in NGL transportation and fractionation infrastructure.

The Five Siblings

As a drill-bit hydrocarbon, NGLs are unique: they are a family of products. We call them a family because NGLs are five different and distinct products when they are sold and used, although they are all mixed together when they are produced with natural gas and then extracted from that gas. To refresh your memory, the five members of the NGL family are ethane, propane, normal butane, isobutane, and natural gasoline.

Each member of the family has a quite different personality, and each is used in different markets for widely different purposes. However, they come from the same two sources. Most NGLs come from the processing of natural gas. But not all. Some NGLs are produced from crude oil refineries. When produced from refineries, NGLs are sometimes called liquefied petroleum gases, or LPGs, the same term used in the early days of Warren and Phillips. Whether the original source was a gas processing plant or a refinery usually makes no difference; when the products get to market, they are essentially the same stuff.

For example, both natural gas processing plants and refineries produce propane. About 70% of U.S. propane comes from natural gas processing, while 30% comes from refineries. This is the same propane you might use in your backyard BBQ grill or for heating and cooking in a rural home. Propane is also used as a petrochemical feedstock. Regardless of its source or its destination market, it is essentially the same product. Propane is also called C_3, reflecting that it is a hydrocarbon with three carbon atoms in its molecular structure. Due to this molecular structure, it must be held in pressurized containers. Propane boils at a temperature of 44 degrees *below* zero. This means if it is not held under pressure, it boils off quickly. This is one of the reasons propane works well as a portable fuel: as soon as it comes out of a pressurized vessel and mixes with air, it is ready to burn with a clean, hot flame. It is great for cooking steaks or frying up that Thanksgiving turkey. For more about hydrocarbon molecules and their properties, see the feature "Hydrocarbon Molecules."

The largest single domestic market for propane is residential and commercial, which consists of home heating, cooking, and BBQ grilling. That makes up about 45% of U.S. demand. Another 30% of propane goes into the petrochemical market, competing with ethane in the olefin crackers that we discussed back in Chapter 3. Some of those crackers run propane, ethane, or other feedstocks. They can pick and choose whichever feedstocks are the cheapest, relative to the products they produce. The balance of U.S. propane, a growing percentage of total demand, goes to export markets. Because a big use of propane is as a heating fuel, the price of propane tends to fluctuate with the weather. As a general rule, the colder the temperature in propane country (rural areas without access to natural gas pipelines), the higher the price for propane.

How about the other family members? Ethane is sometimes called C_2 and is the baby of the family. It has only two carbon atoms in its molecular structure and so is lighter than propane, meaning it is less dense. It has a boiling point of 127 degrees below zero, which means it must be held in vessels designed to handle much higher pressures than propane. In technical terms, the *vapor pressure*[1] of ethane is more than four times that of propane (for you engineers, ethane is 800 psia at 100° F). The implication is that tanks and pipelines for ethane must be made of strong, thick steel. A propane tank would burst if filled with ethane, due to the high vapor pressure of the latter product. Similarly, a tank designed for butane would burst if filled with propane. That characteristic is important for how ethane and propane are transported and stored, two topics that we will take up later in this chapter.

Ethane has but one use: to be a petrochemical feedstock, primarily to make ethylene in olefin crackers. These huge furnaces break (or crack) the feedstock molecules yielding ethylene and a variety of other petrochemicals like propylene and benzene. Ethylene is a basic building-block petrochemical used in the production of everything from plastic trash bags to PVC pipe to antifreeze for your car.

Hydrocarbon Molecules

If you like chemistry (or even if you hated chemistry in high school), there is a beautiful symmetry to molecules in the NGL family. This topic is not just interesting science. It is fundamental to understanding how and why NGL markets behave as they do.

Here's the basic physical fact of hydrocarbon chemistry. A carbon atom wants to have four bonds. By itself, carbon has four electrons. That means for a carbon atom to be stable (and all atoms want to be stable), it needs to find four other electrons to combine with. On the other hand, a hydrogen atom has only one electron. To be stable it needs to find one other electron to combine with.

Hydrocarbons are simply a combination of carbon and hydrogen molecules. However, different hydrocarbon molecules have different numbers of carbon molecules and thus different numbers of hydrogen molecules. The simplest hydrocarbon is methane, the primary component of the natural gas you use at your house. Methane has one carbon molecule, and since it needs to bond with four other hydrogen molecules, it takes four of them for our carbon molecule to be "happy" (i.e., stable). Methane is a very light molecule, which means it has a very high vapor pressure and a very low boiling point of only 260 degrees Fahrenheit below zero. You have to get methane really cold before it turns into a liquid. See the representation of a methane molecule in Figure 6.1. The chemical formula for methane is CH_4, meaning one carbon atom and four hydrogen atoms.

Figure 6.1. Ethane, Methane, and Propane

Ethane has two carbon molecules. That means that each of the carbon molecules has one electron that is satisfied by the carbons joining together. But to be stable, each of the two carbon atoms needs three more hydrogen atoms, so the molecule needs six hydrogen atoms in all. Ethane is heavier than methane, but still has a boiling point of 127° F below zero, so it is difficult to turn in to a liquid, but not nearly as difficult as methane. Ethane's molecular structure makes it a good feedstock for making petrochemicals, which is what essentially all liquid ethane is used for. The chemical formula for ethane is C_2H_6, often abbreviated in the NGL market as simply C_2.

Propane has three carbon molecules. Following the same logic as ethane, the three carbon molecules take up one bond each, leaving room for eight hydrogen atoms. Together ethane and propane are called the light NGLs because they contain the fewest number of carbon molecules in their structure. The boiling point for propane is 44° F, again below zero. The chemical formula for propane is C_3H_8, abbreviated in the NGL market as C_3.

It keeps on going like that. There are two types of butane as shown in Figure 6.2, both with a formula of C_4H_{10}. The boiling point of both butanes is about 32 degrees above zero. Pentane (the main component of natural gasoline) is C_5H_{12} with a boiling point of 97 degrees above zero. Together normal butane, isobutane, and natural gasoline are called the heavy NGLs.

That covers the five NGLs, but the carbon-hydrogen combinations do not stop there. After pentane, there are hexane, heptane, octane (the standard for gasoline quality), nonane, and several more compounds in what is known as the **alkane group** of saturated hydrocarbons.

So where is crude oil in all of this nice, neat molecular arrangement? It is not nice or neat. Crude oil is a mixture of various hydrocarbon molecules, from the lightest to the heaviest. The alkane group described above makes up about 30% of a typical crude oil barrel, but the other 70% is made up of entirely different families of hydrocarbons called **naphthenes, aromatics**, and **asphaltics**. The important point is that crude oil is a complex mixture of many different types of molecules, while natural gas and NGLs are relatively "pure" products.

The next two members of the NGL family are the twins: normal butane and isobutane. Both can be produced from gas processing plants and refineries, and both are heavier than propane, with four carbon atoms, and thus are called C_4. To tell them apart, normal butane is designated NC_4 and isobutane IC_4. The normal butane molecule has four carbon atoms linked in a row, or chain. Isobutane has one carbon molecule that acts like a central hub with the other three carbon molecules attached, giving it a 3D-ish shape. That little kink in the molecule makes a big difference in how the products are used and how much they are worth.

Normal butane, usually called just *normal* or *butane*, has two basic uses. The primary use is as a blending component in motor gasoline. When blended in gasoline, normal butane increases its vapor pressure and its volatility, making it easier to ignite. That is a good thing in cold weather. More normal butane is used in gasoline during the winter to make it easier for your car to start. However, in the summer, too much butane in gasoline tends to boil off and cause engine problems like vapor lock. As a result, the amount of normal butane used in gasoline during the summer season is much less. The amount of butane added to motor gasoline is federally regulated and varies from month to month and by geographic location. Colder regions have higher allowed vapor pressures for motor gasoline, while warmer regions have lower vapor pressures. Those wavy vapors coming out of your gas tank at the service station on a hot summer day (if your pump doesn't have a vapor recovery sleeve)

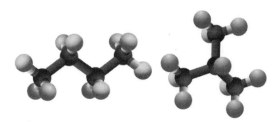

Figure 6.2. Normal Butane and Isobutane

are normal butane. In addition to gasoline blending, small volumes of butane are used as a petrochemical feedstock for olefin crackers. Since more normal butane is used in the winter, its price tends to go up in the winter and down in the summer but basically tracks the price of motor gasoline, since that is where most normal butane goes.

Isobutane, usually called *iso*, is a completely different animal. Most isobutane is used in a refinery process called *alkylation* to make a high-octane, low-vapor pressure motor gasoline blend component called *alkylate*. For example, premium gasoline will have more alkylate than regular gasoline to give it that additional octane boost. Isobutane is also used as a feedstock for petrochemicals, though not as a feedstock for olefin crackers.

Aside from gasoline blending and petrochemicals, about 20% of isobutane production is used for more specialized uses. For instance, isobutane is the clear liquid fuel in most Bic-type cigarette lighters. It is also the propellant used in most hair spray, cooking spray, and shaving cream cans. Since the early 1990s it has been used as a coolant in refrigerators, replacing a product called Freon.

In addition to the isobutane produced from gas processing plants, some isobutane is made purposely from the conversion of normal butane to iso in what is known as *isomerization units* (also called *butamer units*). Significant volumes of isobutane are produced in this way, so the price of isobutane in most of the large NGL markets tends to track normal butane closely, often with a premium reflecting the cost of isomerization.

The older brother of the NGL family is natural gasoline, which also goes by names like pentane plus and *plant condensate*. Unlike its sibling

NGLs, natural gasoline is a blend of several kinds of molecules, the most abundant of which is pentane, also known as C_5. The name natural gasoline is instructive. It is called *natural* because at one time it was naturally removed from natural gas, meaning little processing was required to separate natural gasoline from natural gas. It is called *gasoline* because it is similar in composition to a very low-grade, low-octane motor gasoline. Natural gasoline collected from traps at low points in natural gas gathering systems was used in the olden days as a fuel for tractors and other farm machinery. Today, most natural gasoline is like the other NGLs, produced at natural gas processing plants. However, some natural gasoline still comes from those pipeline traps. A product similar to natural gasoline called naphtha is produced from refineries.

Natural gasoline goes to a number of end-use markets. It is used in motor gasoline blending, as a petrochemical feedstock, as a denaturant in ethanol (denaturing makes ethanol undrinkable), and more recently as a diluent (thinner) to make it possible for very heavy Canadian crude to flow in pipelines. Today, more than half of natural gasoline is used for motor gasoline blending. As a result, natural gasoline values tend to track gasoline and, by extension, crude oil.

Natural Gas Processing and NGL Extraction

Approximately 80% of U.S. NGL production comes from natural gas processing plants. The other 20%, mostly propane, comes from refineries. Over the past few years, the big changes in NGL production have and will continue to come from the 80% of production from natural gas processing plants. These volumes are also what have benefited from Domino 5 (introduced in Chapter 2), with producers shifting drilling budgets to wet gas plays containing higher quantities of NGLs. For this reason, the primary emphasis of this chapter is on NGLs produced from natural gas processing plants.

When natural gas comes out of a wellhead, it contains a lot more than what we think of as natural gas, which is mostly methane. Mixed in with the methane are water vapor, carbon dioxide, hydrogen sulfide, nitrogen, oxygen, helium, various other impurities, and NGLs. Before the natural gas from the wellhead can be injected into high-pressure, long-distance natural gas pipelines for transporting the gas to markets, it must be treated, or cleaned up, to meet pipeline quality specifications. If natural gas is put into pipelines with too many of these impurities, it can result in serious problems including compressor malfunction, pipeline corrosion, or even rupture and explosion.

Removing impurities is called *treating* and is done in a treating plant or a treating unit. Extraction of NGLs is done in a natural gas processing plant, sometimes just called a *gas plant*. There are wide variations from one producing field to another—even sometimes between one well and another—in the type and amount of impurities and NGLs in the gas. Some gas is relatively clean and can go into pipelines with only a minimal amount of treating. Other gas contains significant quantities of impurities, some of which can be quite dangerous, such as hydrogen sulfide, a toxic gas. This gas requires substantial treating before it can be injected into a pipeline.

Dry gas. The amount of NGLs contained in natural gas can also vary greatly. Sometimes, the produced natural gas has such insignificant NGL content that it does not warrant extraction and is called dry gas, a term introduced back in Chapter 2. It is also called *lean gas*. The terms are synonymous and refer to gas containing only small quantities of NGLs. As it is used here, the term has nothing to do with the water vapor content in produced gas.

Wet gas. Wet gas, or *rich gas*, has a high NGL content. After it emerges from the wellhead it must be sent to a natural gas processing plant, where the NGLs are separated from the natural gas. There are about 800 of these processing plants across the United States, and most are located in the general vicinity of producing oil and gas fields. NGL supplies from gas processing plants are increasing rapidly, almost entirely due to the shale revolution. Furthermore, the market is experiencing a torrent of new natural gas plant construction.

What is driving all this activity? As a general rule, NGLs are valued higher than natural gas on a Btu basis. Due to the higher value of NGLs, most of the shales being drilled are in wet gas areas. Some of these shales are very rich, meaning they have a lot of NGLs. With more NGLs in rich gas and more producers drilling for rich gas, there has been a disproportionate increase in the quantity of gas containing NGLs, resulting in increasing NGL production. Recall that this is Domino 6.

Processing Plants: Baby, It's Cold in There

A natural gas processing plant is essentially a big super-cooling refrigerator. It lowers the temperature of an inlet stream of gas until the NGLs condense into a liquid, while the methane remains a gas. The outlet stream of natural gas (residue gas) moves to a natural gas pipeline for transportation to market. At this point, the extracted NGLs are all mixed together in a cocktail called *raw make, raw mix,* or most often *y-grade*. The mix moves via pipeline, rail, barge, or truck for further processing before it ultimately is moved to market.

That processing step between extraction of NGLs at a gas processing plant and delivery to market is called fractionation. A fractionator separates the y-grade NGL stream into ethane, propane, normal butane, isobutane, and natural gasoline, which the industry calls *purity products.* But do not be deceived by this name: none of the products produced from a fractionator are actually pure. Ethane may contain some propane. Propane most assuredly contains some ethane. The same is true for the other products; it is expected, and in most instances, not a problem. How much of the other products are mixed in is determined by the specifications of the products, the most prevalent of which are set by the Gas Processors Association, or GPA.

The vast majority of natural gas plants use one of three main processes that dominate the industry. As you might expect, the first processes used before World War II have steadily been replaced by the processes developed within the last couple of decades. However, some of the old plants are still out there and using those old processes. The three primary NGL extraction processes are *absorption, refrigeration,* and *cryogenics.* Most of U.S. processing capacity involves the most modern of the technologies, *cryogenic turboexpanders.* Less than 20% use older technologies such as refrigeration and absorption.

These processes are described in more detail below.

Absorption. As its name implies, absorption draws NGLs from the gas using *absorption oil.* When natural gas passes through an absorption tower,

Y-GRADE

This term is a mystery for many involved in the NGL markets, but its origin is actually quite simple. Y-grade is a throwback to an ancient quality specification on the MAPCO pipeline system. There was **p-grade** for propane, **g-grade** for natural gasoline, but what to use for the mix of different NGLs commonly transported? Someone decided y-grade and the name stuck, not only for MAPCO but for all other pipelines.

Y-grade is rarely traded as a product and there is no price quoted for it. All you can do with y-grade is fractionate it into purity products. Consequently, the value of y-grade is based on its content or yield of purity products. The mix is different from well to well, so of course the makeup of y-grade from each gas processing plant is different. One y-grade might have 42% ethane, 25% propane, and 33% other NGLs. Another might have 55% ethane, 23% propane, and 22% other NGLs. When you talk NGL markets, you are talking trading of the individual purity NGL products, not y-grade.

an absorption oil acts like a sponge to attract NGLs out of the gas. The leaner natural gas vapor exits the tower at the top, and the absorption oil, which is now rich with NGLs, exits at the bottom. The mixture then enters oil stills, where it is heated to boil off the NGLs. Though this process has a low ethane recovery rate at 0–30%, it can recover roughly 65–75% of the propane, 80% of butanes, and 90% of natural gasoline. It is the oldest, least used, and least efficient method for processing gas.

Refrigeration. Refrigeration is a slightly more efficient processing method that uses propane to cool the natural gas stream to around 30° F in order for the NGLs to drop out, or condense, into liquid. Refrigeration is sometimes combined with a Joule-Thomson (JT) expansion valve, which chills the gas stream with a quick pressure reduction. Ethane recovery rates increase using this technique. Refrigeration is capable of recovering as much as 40% of ethane, 70% of propane, and nearly all the butanes and natural gasoline.

Cryogenics. This process consists of sending the gas through a turbine, which causes the gas to expand at an extremely rapid speed, cooling it to roughly -120°F. These much lower temperatures make this form of extraction the most efficient: a cryogenic plant can recover 85%–95%

of the ethane, as well as nearly 100% of the other NGLs. Almost all newly constructed plants employ turboexpander technology.

Not only do turboexpander plants have the highest NGL recovery rates, they have the greatest operational flexibility for reacting to market conditions and thus maximizing revenues. For example, if ethane prices are sufficiently lower than natural gas prices, turboexpander plants are the eas-iest to configure to "reject" ethane as described in the following paragraph.

Ethane rejection. As NGL production from the big shale plays has con-tinued to increase, more than enough ethane is being produced than is necessary to meet demand from U.S. petrochemical crackers. Since the only use of liquid ethane is as a petrochemical cracker feedstock, some-thing must be done with the surplus ethane molecules. The solution to this ethane oversupply problem is *ethane rejection*. Rejected ethane is ethane that is not extracted as a liquid at a natural gas processing plant but is instead allowed to remain in the natural gas stream. It is sold as natural gas at natural gas values.

However, there are limits to how much ethane can be rejected, or left in the natural gas. Pipeline systems must adhere to certain quality specifications, and one of the most important of which is Btu content. Typically, natural gas (which is mostly methane) has a Btu content of 1,035 per cubic foot. To assure safe transportation, pipeline quality gas is often limited to no more than 1,100 Btus/cubic feet. Ethane has 1,758 Btus/cubic feet, so the more ethane rejected into the gas, the higher its Btu content. If the ethane rejection causes the gas to exceed a pipeline's quality specifications, it will not be accepted for shipment by the pipeline. The ethane rejection decision is an important aspect of natural gas pro-cessing operations. If natural gas prices are higher than ethane prices on a Btu basis, it makes economic sense to reject the ethane into the natural gas, up to the Btu limit of the natural gas pipeline's specifications.

The type of processing plant has a big impact on NGL recovery rates as described above. But the volume of liquids produced by a given plant mostly depends on the percentage of NGLs in the gas coming into the plant in the first place. As noted previously, the amount of NGLs in gas varies by region, by producing zone, even on a well-to-well basis. All other things being equal, the more NGLs in the gas, the more that can be extracted.

NGL Content in Natural Gas

The term frequently used to express the NGL content of gas is *gallons per Mcf*, abbreviated as *GPM*. Let's say that a given processing plant inlet natural gas stream has 3 GPM gas. That means that in 1,000 cubic feet of that inlet gas stream there are three gallons of NGLs that *could* be extracted. Figure 6.3 will help make sense of this statement.

Figure 6.3. Visualizing gallons per Mcf

This graphic represents a room 10 ft. by 10 ft. by 10 ft., or 1,000 cubic feet. The 6 ft. tall man is intended to give you a sense of perspective relative to the size of the room. In this room, there are three one-gallon buckets filled with liquid NGLs. (Don't try this at home. At room temperatures, those NGLs would vaporize and either asphyxiate the man or explode at the first spark.) The point here is 3 GPM of gas contains the equivalent of 3 gallons of NGLs in 1,000 cubic feet. of vapor. The NGLs emerge from the wellhead in a vapor state, mixed in with the natural gas. The NGLs are extracted and liquefied at a natural gas processing plant. How much of those NGLs can be extracted depends on the type of plant, its extraction efficiency, and the quantity of NGLs contained in the gas.

Not only can that quantity be measured in GPM, the amount of NGLs is also gauged using the heat content of the gas as measured in Btus. The more NGLs you have the higher the Btu content is, thus the higher the heat content in the total natural gas stream. Ethane, as noted above, has 1,758 Btus/cubic feet and the other NGLs have even more. For example, normal butane has 3,238 Btus/cubic feet, almost twice the heat content of ethane. In fact, the Btu content of a hydrocarbon fuel is directly related to how many carbons the molecule of that hydrocarbon has. So propane has a higher Btu content than ethane, normal butane more than propane, etc. That means as a general rule, the more heavy NGLs in a plant inlet natural gas stream (normal butane, isobutane and natural gasoline), the higher the Btu content of that stream.

Put that together with what we know about GPM and it becomes clear that usually the higher the GPM, the higher the Btu content. But it is not a 1:1 relationship, because the Btu content is also dependent on the percentage of each NGL in the mix. For example, since natural gasoline has a higher Btu content than ethane, a gas stream with a higher percentage of natural gasoline has a higher Btu content, even if the GPM of the gas streams is the same.

Given the above explanation of GPM, we can consider a crucial question for NGL markets: how much NGL content is in natural gas? As mentioned earlier, the answer is this: it varies all over the place. On average, across the entire United States, the number is about 2 GPM, which is relatively lean. However, the NGL content for any one region or play can be much higher, possibly more than 10 GPM. That liquids content makes a big difference to the economics of gas processing. The range of liquids content, the relationship between Btu and GPM, and the terms used to describe the different qualities of gas are shown in Table 6.1 below.

Dry gas processing. If an inlet gas stream has few NGLs—a Btu content of 1,050 or less, which corresponds to a GPM of 1 or 2—it is said to be lean or dry. Such a gas stream is typically pipeline quality, which means it can usually be delivered to a natural gas pipeline for transportation to market without processing to extract NGLs. This does not mean the gas goes straight from the wellhead to the pipeline. Most of the time, it still must be treated to remove impurities, but the NGL content is low enough to meet natural gas pipeline quality standards.

Wet gas processing. In contrast, a rich or wet gas stream with a Btu content ranging between 1,050 and 1,400 typically has a GPM of 3 to 4.

	Lean (Dry)	Rich (Wet)	Very Rich (Very Wet)
Btu	<1,050	1,050–1,400	>1,400
GPM	1–2	3–4	>4
Processing	Unlikely	Likely	Required

Table 6.1. Btu and GPM

This wet gas is nearly always processed to remove NGLs, both because the NGLs need to be extracted to meet pipeline specifications and because the extracted NGLs in liquid form can usually be sold at much higher prices. That higher value for NGLs is not always true. At various times in the past (bad days for gas processors), natural gas prices have been higher than most of the NGLs. More recently with the crude oil price crash of 2014, NGL prices are again very weak relative to the price of natural gas, resulting in marginal economics for gas processing in some areas.

Very wet gas processing. There is gas that is richer than rich: *very wet,* or *rich, gas.* Such streams have a GPM greater than 4 and a Btu value greater than 1,400. Processing this gas and extracting NGLs is absolutely necessary to move it through natural gas transmission lines. As producers shifted their drilling operations to shale in order to maximize wet gas production, the proportion of very wet gas produced has rapidly increased; the economics of producing gas with a high NGL content are almost always far better than lean or rich gas. For this reason, the average GPM of gas produced is on the rise.

And then, just like we have Warren Buffett and Bill Gates, there is *super rich gas.* This gas has a GPM content of 8, 10, 12, or higher. There are not many plays that can be classified as super rich, but some portions of the Eagle Ford in South Texas, Utica in Ohio, and Granite Wash in Oklahoma and North Texas fit this definition. The Btu content can be upwards of 1,600.

Fractionating NGLs into purity products. Natural gas processing as described above does not produce individual NGL products but instead yields the mixed stream of NGLs typically called y-grade. Y-grade is simply a mixture of the NGLs which is transported and stored as a mix. To produce the individual NGLs requires a *fractionator* that separates y-grade into the five purity products, each of which is sold into its own market. In one sense, an NGL fractionator is a massive, complex distillery. The mixed NGL stream is heated then fed into a sequence of towers where temperatures and pressures are controlled so that the boiling point will be reached by only one purity product in each tower. For example, y-grade enters a deethanizer tower, where only the ethane—the lightest of the five fuels—is allowed to boil and escape through the top of the tower. The remaining NGLs fall to the bottom of the first tower and are heated again as they make their way to the second tower, where propane, the next-lightest hydrocarbon, is processed and emerges as a gas. It is cooled until it condenses back into a liquid, then is sent to storage in preparation for transport to market. The process is repeated in subsequent towers for each of the remaining heavier NGLs.

Figure 6.4 shows natural gas being processed at a gas processing plant, with the y-grade then delivered to a fractionator and the processing units (de-ethanizer, depropanizer, debutanizer, and deisobutanizer) that separate the mixed NGLs into individual purity products.

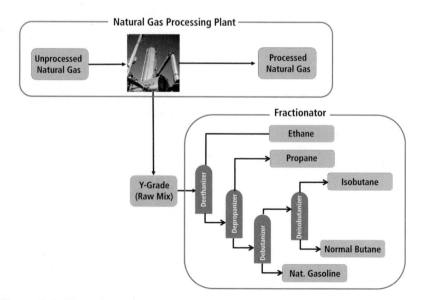

Figure 6.4. The processing of natural gas

There are currently about 100 fractionators in the United States with a total capacity of 4.5 MMbbl/d. Another 30 fractionation facilities are located in Canada. Several new fractionators are, as of this writing, under construction in the United States. More than half of all fractionation capacity is located in Mont Belvieu, Texas (see the feature "Thinkin' About Mont Belvieu"). As shown in Figure 6.5, most fractionators are located along the Gulf Coast. Other major centers of fractionation are Conway, Kansas, and the Marcellus and Utica shale regions in Appalachia.

Fractionation is only needed for NGLs extracted from natural gas processing. NGL products from crude oil refineries have usually already been separated into individual components.

At this point, it might be well to point out there is no relationship between fracking shale (breaking up rock underground with high-pressure fluids) and a fractionator (separating NGL products), except that fracking creates more raw mix for fractionation plants. More fracking means more NGLs, which means more fractionators, thus the surge in new construction.

NGL Transportation and Trading Network

NGLs are transported by truck, rail, barge, ship, and pipeline. Truck and rail are used mostly for smaller plants and in areas where NGL pipelines are not available. Rail also tends to be used extensively for refinery NGLs (called LPGs). Barges are primarily used to move product along the Gulf Coast and Mississippi River. Most large NGL ships are used for shipping propane and normal butane out of the Gulf Coast to international markets and have been used historically to bring propane into import terminals on the East Coast.

However, most NGLs move via pipeline. Several major systems move y-grade from gas processing plants to central fractionation facilities. Others move purity products from fractionation facilities to market. Figure 6.6 shows the major NGL pipeline systems in North America.

Y-Grade pipelines. Major transportation systems moving primarily y-grade (aka raw make) from gas processing plants to fractionators are:

1. The MAPL, or former MAPCO system owned by Enterprise, from the Rockies to Hobbs, New Mexico;

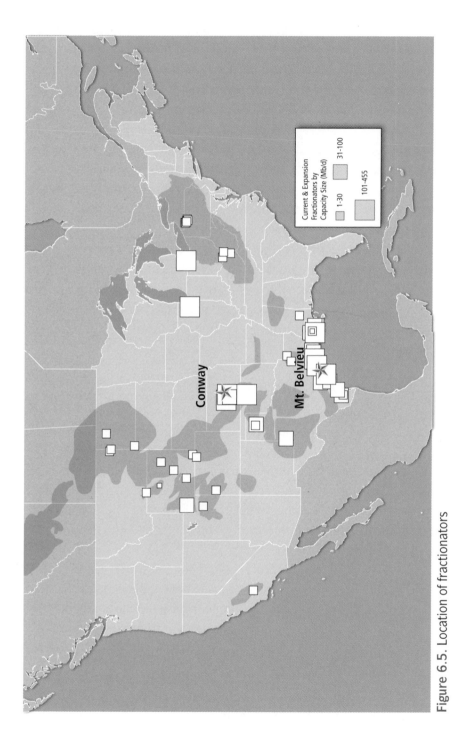

Figure 6.5. Location of fractionators

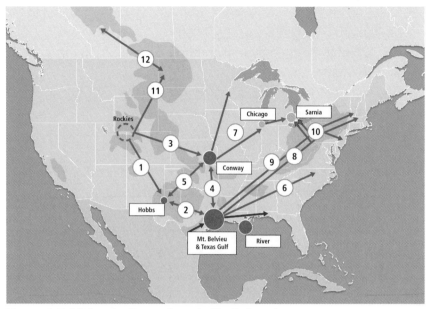

Figure 6.6. Major pipeline systems in North America

2. Enterprise's Seminole and Chaparral pipelines, from West Texas to Mont Belvieu;

3. The Williams/ONEOK (pronounced One-Oak) Overland Pass line from the Rockies down to Bushton and Conway, Kansas; and

4. Arbuckle and Sterling, two other ONEOK lines, from the Conway region to Mont Belvieu.

These are not the only y-grade systems, but do account for most of the y-grade volumes moved in the United States. In addition to these systems that move liquid NGLs, the Alliance pipeline (a 50/50 joint venture of Enbridge and Veresen) moves high-Btu gas containing significant volumes of NGLs from Alberta, Canada, to the Aux Sable gas processing plant and fractionator near Chicago, where the NGLs are extracted, fractionated, and moved to markets in the region.

Purity product pipelines. Key pipelines that move processed and separated NGLs—primarily propane—from fractionation centers to market include the following:

5. Enterprise MAPL system that moves mostly propane from Hobbs, New Mexico and Conway, Kansas into the Midwest market;

6. Dixie, an Enterprise propane line from the Mont Belvieu hub to the Southeast;

7. The ONEOK North System that moves propane from the Conway area to Midwest markets;

8. TE Products (often called by its former name TEPPCO), an Enterprise line from Mont Belvieu to the Northeast;

9. ATEX, an Enterprise ethane line between the Marcellus/Utica region and the Gulf Coast;

10. Mariner West and East, Energy Transfer Partners lines that move Marcellus/Utica NGLs west to Sarnia, Ontario and east to Marcus Hook, Pennsylvania;

11. Vantage pipeline, an ethane pipeline from North Dakota to Alberta, owned by Pembina.

Note that there are no NGL pipelines in the western part of the United States. NGL production in that region is relatively small and NGLs are moved in the region by rail or truck.

Hubs

NGL trading hubs are primary trading locations that work essentially the same as the natural gas hubs discussed in the previous chapter. There are just far fewer NGL hubs than gas hubs. NGL hubs tend to be located where there is a critical mass of infrastructure: fractionators, storage, pipelines, and access to markets.

Figure 6.6 also indicates several of the major trading hubs in North America:

■ Mont Belvieu, just east of Houston, Texas (See the feature, "Thinkin' About Mont Belvieu" on the next page);

■ Conway Hub, which includes four storage and fractionation facilities near the towns of Conway, Bushton, and McPherson in Kansas and Medford, Oklahoma;

■ Sarnia, Ontario and north of Detroit, Michigan, the location of underground storage, refineries, and chemical plants;

■ Chicago, the location of the largest gas processing plant in the United States operated by Aux Sable;

- Hobbs, New Mexico, a transit point for NGLs coming from the Rockies and moving on to Mont Belvieu, with an interconnect into the Conway market; and
- River, a generic hub along the Mississippi River that serves refineries and petrochemical plants in that region.

There are other small hubs around the country, but most large NGL transactions are consummated at one of the six hubs listed above.

Thinkin' About Mont Belvieu

Mont Belvieu, Texas (population 3,835), is located about 30 miles east of Houston, not far from the Gulf of Mexico. It is truly the center of the NGL universe. William Kelly Warren didn't decide to build the first major centralized fractionator here arbitrarily; no, he knew it made sense to build a fractionation plant at Mont Belvieu because it provided vast amounts of storage for NGLs in a huge, underground salt dome called Barbers Hill.

Mont Belvieu is the site of more purity NGL production than anywhere in the world. Below the numerous fractionators and labyrinthine pipelines is a vast cylindrical salt deposit, approximately 9,000–12,000 feet in diameter and about 2,000 feet below sea level. It extends approximately 33,000 feet beneath the earth's crust along the Texas coastline and is an ideal storage site for NGLs, petrochemicals, and pretty much any liquid product that must be held under pressure. The storage facilities themselves, called **caverns**, are created by drilling wells down into the salt, then using **solution mining**, a process of injecting fresh water that dissolves the salt and carves out the huge caverns. The resulting salt water, or brine, is then disposed of or used in the manufacture of chemicals. After a well has been completed, NGLs can be piped into the cavern, displacing any brine remaining in the cavern. When the NGLs are needed, more brine is pumped in. It is heavier than the NGLs, so it sinks to the bottom and gives lift to the product, effectively pushing it to the surface to be pumped out into a pipeline. Note that even though these big storage tanks are called caverns, it is not possible for a human to physically enter one. They are always full of brine, NGLs, or some combination of the two liquids.

Today, there are over 125 of these salt dome storage caverns in Mont Belvieu. Two major advantages for using a salt dome are its strength, which permits high-pressure storage, and its capacity to store vast quantities of hydrocarbons which can be quickly injected and withdrawn when needed.

Many of the caverns are tall, vertically oriented cylinders, while others look like upside-down mushrooms. They are large: really large. For example, according to 2007 construction records, Enterprise Products Partners built a cavern 2,175 feet tall and 300 feet in diameter, averaging 5,000 feet deep. Its capacity is 12.5 million barrels. To put that in perspective, consider that the Empire State Building has a roof height of 1,250 feet and, adding its antenna spire, stands a total of 1,454 feet tall. This single Enterprise storage well is more than 700 feet taller than the entire Empire State Building. And if you were wondering, the volume of the Empire State Building is 37 million cubic feet, or about 1.04 million cubic meters. It could hold about 6.5 million barrels of NGLs, or about half the capacity of that single Enterprise salt cavern.

Not all caverns are that big; some only have a capacity of one or two million barrels. But there are a lot of them: there is approximately 350 million barrels of NGL storage in the Gulf Coast region, most of which is located in Mont Belvieu.

Physical NGL Commercial Arrangements and Transactions

Like natural gas, NGLs can trade in both physical markets and financial markets. In the physical markets, NGL volumes are physically delivered from the seller to the buyer. The other alternative is financial markets (explained in more detail below), which only involve exchange of money based on changes in price. Physical NGL deals are consummated bilaterally, by phone or email, or on the Intercontinental Exchange (ICE) electronic trading system. Physical NGL deals done on ICE are transactions for physical barrels, not financial transactions (note that ICE also provides a trading platform for financial NGL transactions). This physical ICE trading system operates somewhat like an eBay for NGLs. After the deal is done, the parties are revealed to each other and then they handle the rest of the transaction process just as if they did the deal directly by phone.

Spot NGL trades for physical NGL barrels are valued differently, depending on when delivery is to be made. A deal for *prompt* barrels must be delivered within the next couple of days. An *any* barrel can be delivered any day before the end of the current month. An *out-month* deal is one which can be delivered any day the next month. Prices for the different vintages of spot deals are tracked daily by trade publications, which cover the major hubs and sometimes subdivisions within those hubs. Those reported prices, called price indices or *index prices*, are then used as price references in long-term, multi-month, and multi-year contracts.

After traders have consummated and documented a deal, it goes to schedulers who are responsible for physically moving the barrels. Schedulers deal with *noms*, or pipeline nominations. In the NGL world, a nom is the request from a shipper to a service provider (i.e., a pipeline or storage facility) to move barrels from the shipper's account in one location to the buyer, which can be either in the same location or somewhere else. If the nomination origin and destination are the same, it is simply a transfer from one company's account to another, which is called a Product Transfer Order, or PTO. The shipper must have an agreement in place with the service provider for the service. The transaction is done at rates and pursuant to the service provider's rules, contained in a tariff, similar to the gas pipeline tariff discussed in the previous chapter.

Historically, noms and PTOs were handled with faxes and a lot of clarifying phone calls. Today, many companies still use the 2012 version of the fax: email. The shipper emails the pipeline the nomination and the pipeline enters the information into whatever operational system they use to keep track of inventory balances, product movements, and other operational data. Fortunately for the industry, several of the larger NGL pipeline companies are investing in computer systems to handle these functions.

Financial NGL (Nonphysical) Transactions

Just as with natural gas, NGL transactions also occur in financial markets. Almost all financial transactions for NGLs are futures trades, transacted via either the ICE exchange or the CME/NYMEX exchange. These exchanges trade futures, which are standardized contracts for the purchase or sale of a standard quantity of an NGL product, agreed upon today but to be settled at some date in the future. Both exchanges settle these contracts financially, which means that no physical delivery is ever made. Instead, settlement is based on the difference between the price of the futures contract and a spot price index of the commodity being traded, with the index almost always being the one published by Oil Price Information Service, or OPIS, the gold standard for NGL price indices.

Like all exchange trades, the transactions are guaranteed by a clearing house, affiliated with either the ICE or CME/NYMEX exchange. In years past, some financial NGL transactions were consummated in *over-the-counter swap deals*, which means between two parties without an exchange or clearinghouse involved. However, due to complex new rules required by the Dodd–Frank Wall Street Reform and Consumer Protection Act (known usually by Dodd-Frank) signed into law by President Obama in 2010, over-the-counter swap deals are less frequent today.

Even though financial deals are done almost exclusively on exchanges, many are brokered. This means the third-party financial intermediaries (banks or other merchant companies) facilitate trades for their clients, many times in offline, verbal transactions. These transactions are posted on the exchanges after the fact and are cleared (guaranteed) by the clearinghouses.

Well, there you have it, the story of how the more-or-less youngest DBH came to play alongside the two old big guys. After reading this chapter, it should be quite clear NGLs have earned the right to be considered just as important as oil and gas. Even though "the oil and gas bidness" rolls nicely off the tongue in conversation, it is no longer an accurate description of the industry. That's why it is referred to in this book as "the drill-bit hydrocarbon business." But we get ahead of ourselves. We have one DBH left to discuss, and it's the big dog.

Note

1. Vapor pressure is the amount of pressure within a gas in an equilibrium state. As a general rule, a substance with a high vapor pressure must be held under pressurized conditions or at cold temperatures in order to stay in a liquid state. A substance with a low vapor pressure can be held at atmospheric pressures and temperatures and remain in a liquid state. Vapor pressure is related to the boiling point temperature of a substance. The lower the boiling point, the higher the vapor pressure. Vapor pressure is usually measured in psia, which stands for pounds per square inch absolute, defined as the force of a vapor applied to one square inch relative to a vacuum.

Chapter 7

Crude Oil: The Big Dog of Energy Markets

And we were casting [our young English soldiers] by thousands into the fire to the worst of deaths, not to win the war but that the corn and rice and oil of Mesopotamia might be ours."
—T. E. Lawrence, *Seven Pillars of Wisdom* (1921)

RUDE OIL IS THE BIG DOG OF THE DRILL-BIT HYDROCARBONS SUITE: THE *market is bigger, badder, and far more pervasive throughout society than its siblings, natural gas and NGLs. The global crude oil market is a $3-trillion-a-year business. Petrodollars are a huge wealth transfer from the energy haves to the have-nots. Have-not countries like Japan and India must buy theirs from the haves, such as Saudi Arabia and Russia. When gasoline prices go up, we all feel it at the pump. When they go down, it makes headline news. Wars haven't been fought over propane, and very few over natural gas. Crude is different. Disputes over oil have started wars, time and again, from the early twentieth century to World War II through the continuing conflicts in the Middle East.*

All three of the DBHs are important sources of energy and each has its own market dynamics. While supply and demand affects each differently, oil is unique in that its derivative products are primarily transportation fuels. In fact, motor gasoline, diesel fuel, jet fuel, and other liquid petroleum products derived from oil comprise about 97% of all U.S. transportation fuels. Oil is the only economical and practical fuel source for moving people and goods in the U.S. today.

A tiny percentage of the demand for natural gas and NGLs is also from the transportation sector. Natural gas accounts for about 2% of U.S. demand for transportation fuel. As of 2012, the United States had 250,000 vehicles (primarily buses) running on compressed natural gas (CNG) on the road, approximately 150,000 vehicles running on NGLs (propane), and 3,000 vehicles running on liquefied natural gas (LNG). That compares to the more than 265 million registered passenger vehicles and trucks in the United States powered by gasoline and diesel. Vehicles powered by gas or propane are trivial compared to these numbers, and the number of cars powered by electricity is even less. It will be a long time before there are tens of millions of cars on the road powered by anything other than crude oil-based fuels. Although there has been and will continue to be a robust dialogue around alternative transportation fuels, the reality is that hydrocarbon-based transportation is likely to be with us for many decades to come. It is not the intent of this book to debate the merits of hydrocarbon transportation fuels versus other alternatives, rather only to examine what this reality means for the crude oil market.

Beginnings

Crude oil is front and center in the energy independence debate and has been so since the oil shock of 1973. Until that fateful year, there was little discussion about crude oil dependence. Back in 1972, the United States was importing less than 20% of its needs. Crude oil prices were about $3.60/bbl, and gasoline prices at the pump were $0.36 per gallon.

But just a year later, in October 1973, the oil markets were roiled by the Yom Kippur War when OAPEC (the Arab members of OPEC, plus Tunisia, Egypt, and Syria) brandished the oil weapon and slammed the U.S. with an embargo. By 1974, the price of oil quadrupled—from $3.60/bbl to almost $12/bbl. Gasoline prices jumped to $0.55 per gallon in June 1974. The United States government instituted price controls on most petroleum products, motorists faced long lines at the gas pump, and oil moved into a central role in U.S. politics. Eventually the gas lines and price controls went away, but oil's political sway remains with us today.

Since those earliest days of the 1973 oil crisis, the U.S. domestic crude oil market has been overshadowed by the global oil market. In the 1972 pre-crisis year, U.S. crude oil production made up 21% of the world total. Twenty years later, in 1992, it was down to 13.5% and by

2002, it had fallen to 10%. In 2008, just before the shale revolution started to reverse the decline, U.S. production fell again to just 8.2% of the world total.

Not only did that shrinking production have a big impact on crude oil imports—which soared to 66% in 2008—it also had a depressing effect on the U.S. market generally. By the mid- to late-2000s, physical U.S. crude oil markets were roundly ignored by the global oil markets in general. Further production declines were anticipated. Infrastructure—pipelines, tanker trucks, rails, storage tanks, terminals, rigs, and equipment—was deteriorating. Refineries were unprofitable. Compared to previous decades when U.S. crude oil markets were vibrant, volatile, and actively traded, declining U.S. production volumes in the 2000s meant the market was in sad shape. Then the dominoes started to fall, and today we know what happened as the U.S. surplus pushed into global markets. But again, we are getting ahead of ourselves. Before launching into the crude oil market of today, it is important to turn back the clock and explain why today's crude oil infrastructure exists as it does, how the crude oil market functions, and what makes the trading markets value one crude oil over another.

U.S. crude oil markets have gone through several distinct phases of development since Edwin Drake drilled the first well back in the 1850s. Drake's is a story that most of us have heard many times, but it is a plain and simple fact that any review of the early U.S. crude oil market, which is essential to understanding the market of today, must start with Col. Edwin Drake in Titusville, Pennsylvania.

The Earliest Wells, Refineries, and Midstream

The first oil and gas spring in the United States might have been discovered by none other than George Washington near what is today Charleston, West Virginia, in 1770, but that is another story.[1] Although there are various claims as to who drilled the first well, it was Colonel Drake's 1859 Titusville, Pennsylvania, well mentioned in Chapter 6 that is generally recognized as the first commercial oil and gas well in the United States. Fortunately for Drake, his first well was drilled adjacent to Oil Creek, a tributary of the Allegheny River, thus he could put the barrels of crude on barges and move them down river to Pittsburgh. In Pittsburgh there just happened to be a refinery owned by Sam Kier, remembered today as grandfather of the American refining industry. Kier had developed the refinery in 1853 to refine *rock oil* from salt wells, first into a patent medicine and later into kerosene lamp fuel. Drake's transportation of oil down to Kier's refinery inaugurated crude oil logistics and distribution and, not coincidentally, the oil business. Horse-and-wagon teams delivering crude oil to railway heads followed but were hampered by equipment failures, terrible road conditions, and exorbitant rates charged by teamsters. There had to be a better way.

That better way was via pipe. The first pipe was wooden, little more than a trough. Soon after came cast-iron pipes, but they had a significant problem: leaks. In the early days, teamsters who wanted to keep crude moving on their wagons often damaged them. In 1865, Samuel Van Syckel, an oil buyer and shipper in the Oil Creek area, built the first wrought-iron pipeline from Pithole to Miller Farm, Pennsylvania. It didn't leak. Van Syckel charged a reasonable fee and established a firm business foundation for producers and distributors in the region. He became renowned as the father of the American crude oil pipeline system.

Before long, pipelines carried crude to rail depots for shipment in tank cars south to refineries in Pittsburgh, west to Cleveland, and to the East Coast. Throughout the 1870s, the railroads and pipeline companies fought with and against each other to monopolize crude transportation, driving the producers and other developers to lay their own large pipelines between the production fields and the refineries. By far the most significant of these pipelines was the Tidewater Pipeline. The Tidewater was the largest, longest pipeline across Pennsylvania in its era, crossing the steep grade eastward over the Allegheny Mountains to load crude into railroad tank cars bound for New York. Brought online in 1879, it had the least costly rates for moving product to market for East Coast independent refiners. John D. Rockefeller's Standard Oil of Ohio, a market force unwilling to settle for second place, countered with its National Transit Pipeline, which delivered crude to both Standard refineries and East Coast independents all the way to New York. Eventually, Tidewater came under Rockefeller's control. (For more about Rockefeller, see the feature "J. D. Rockefeller and The Standard Oil Saga.") The oil business continued to develop in the Northeast with more pipelines, refineries, and producers, but by the turn of the last century, momentum in the crude oil market had shifted south to Texas.

A Giant Arises in Texas

On January 10, 1901, a gusher—called the Lucas gusher—occurred atop Spindletop Hill, near Beaumont, Texas, heralding the Texas Oil Boom. While certainly a phenomenon unto itself, the Lucas gusher—named for its drilling engineer, Anthony Lucas (1855–1921)—was the first Spindletop well. It blew crude oil 130 ft. into the air for ten days at a rate of 70,000 to 100,000 barrels per day. Output was collected in a temporary reservoir hastily constructed by building up earthen levees around the growing pool of oil. The ensuing oil boom spawned nearly 300 wells drilled nearby, and the Beaumont area increased in size from 8,000 residents to more than 50,000 within a few months.

Oil exploration boomed all along the Texas and Louisiana Gulf Coast, as did the need to build out the infrastructure to support it. In the months after Spindletop, companies started developing the means to get all that crude to market. One of the most notable transporters was The Texas Company (which became Texaco in 1959), which initially moved Gulf Coast crude down to Port Arthur for delivery to sugar plantations, replacing coal as a burner fuel. In 1904, The Texas Company completed its refinery at Port Arthur, processing a total of 320,000 barrels in its first year. The Gulf Coast was on its way to becoming the largest center of refinery capacity in the world, not only because it was so near the production fields, but also because of its ready access to river- and ocean-going transportation for gasoline, diesel, and other refined products.

Unfortunately, the Spindletop oil fields succumbed to overproduction and declined rapidly. By 1903, most flow had ceased and before long, salt water invaded the wells. Output dropped from 62 Mbbl/d to 5 Mbbl/d a year later. Refineries operated by The Texas Company and others were able to stay in business only by acquiring crude from other plays, some near the Gulf Coast and others farther away. Increasingly, production came from just north of Texas, in Oklahoma.

Oklahoma Oil: How and Why Cushing Developed as the Main Crude Oil Hub

Today, the central hub for U.S. crude oil trading and pricing is at Cushing, a dusty Oklahoma town of about 8,000 residents. The events that created the hub at Cushing began just after Spindletop. Oklahoma's first major oil play was at Glenn Pool, west of Tulsa. On November 22, 1905, Robert Galbreath and Frank Chesley completed the first Glenn Pool well. By 1907 the field was producing 120 Mbbl/d, a huge volume at the time. Oklahoma became the leading oil producing state, a distinction the state held until 1928 and which was memorialized in the 1949 film *Tulsa* (keep a sharp lookout for the old photographs of Glenn Pool in the film). Glenn Pool was the first indication of an Oklahoma oil boom.

On March 12, 1912, Thomas B. Slick and C. B. Shaffer completed a well near Cushing, about fifty miles west of Tulsa, that produced 400 barrels per day at the outset. The Oklahoma oil boom kicked in with a vengeance, and the town of Cushing became its center. Over the next three years, new production in the area continued to be discovered. The Cushing-Drumright Field spanned 32 square miles and produced over 236 million barrels from the date the field was discovered until 1919. During this period, almost fifty small refineries and ten natural gasoline (then called casinghead gas) plants were built in the area of the field (see references to those gas plants in the previous chapter). Eventually pipelines were built to move Cushing crude oil to refinery centers along the Gulf Coast and other regions.

Unfortunately for Cushing, the oil boom did not last long. Annual production peaked in 1915 at 8.3 MMbbl/d; by 1916, production had declined by 50%. Eventually all the refineries in the area shut down, leaving only tanks and pipelines. Fortunately, Cushing was a central location between oil production in the Oklahoma area, the big refinery centers along the Gulf Coast, and the emerging refinery centers in the Midwest, particularly around Chicago. After the big rush of production growth along the Gulf Coast, volumes began to decline precipitously. Big refiners like Gulf and The Texas Company built 8-inch pipelines—large at the time—all the way from Oklahoma to their refineries in the Gulf Coast area. Several other pipelines from the Oklahoma fields were developing and were ultimately built down to the Gulf Coast.

The companies that owned these southern-moving pipelines mostly had interests in both the oil production and refining end of the value chain, so they were moving much of their own production to their own refineries. As pipelines were built from fields outside the state of Texas, these companies were able to assert that since it was their crude moving to their refineries, the pipelines should be considered private carriers and differentiated from common carriers, which were required by federal law to take on any producer requesting their oil be moved. By remaining private carriers, these pipeline companies were able to avoid common carrier rules and regulations.

That worked for a few years, but many independent producers protested. Led by the trust-busting fervor of the late 1800s and early 1900s, the Hepburn Act was passed by the U.S. Congress in 1906, decreeing that oil pipelines were, in fact, common carriers, subject to federal regulation (for example, nondiscrimination against independent shippers) and bound to apply "just and reasonable" tariff rates. With only a few modifications, this regulatory structure remains with us today for oil pipelines. It functions quite differently from the natural gas regulatory regime discussed in Chapter 6, although natural gas, NGL, and crude oil pipeline regulations are all administered by FERC.

J. D. Rockefeller and the Standard Oil Saga

In the 1860s, John D. Rockefeller was a young entrepreneur busily acquiring kerosene refineries and strong positions with the railroads. He was an astute businessman, competent in finance, transportation, and exceptionally good at identifying lucrative opportunities. When measuring wealth against the total economy, Rockefeller is considered the richest man in history.[2] This fact points to the importance of oil as the emerging primary energy resource of the twentieth century.

He entered into a refinery partnership with his brother, William, in 1866, selling and distributing kerosene. Through judicious business planning, borrowing, reinvesting, and managing of resources, the business grew to become the largest oil refiner in the world. The brothers Rockefeller expanded their interests by opening a marketing division, and in 1870, formed the Standard Oil Company.

Independent Pennsylvania oilmen, in a desperate effort to compete with Rockefeller's position in transportation, built the first crude oil trunk line: the Tidewater line described earlier in this chapter. The six-inch diameter pipeline, 109 miles in length, was built in the dead of winter between Coryville, Pennsylvania, through the Allegheny Mountains, to Williamsport, Pennsylvania. Construction began in February and the pipeline was completed in May 1879. But within a year, that competitive effort had crumbled. By that time, Rockefeller owned half of Tidewater and was busily laying more pipelines to Buffalo, Philadelphia, Cleveland, and New York.

Rockefeller looked to export his kerosene lamp oil production to Northern Europe and Russia, but about this time oil was discovered near the Russian sea town of Baku. Over twenty refineries sprang up in the region, and once again, logistics were key: a pipeline was constructed through the mountains east of Baku where Marcus Samuel, an enterprising merchant, developed the first organized kerosene shipping enterprise to compete with Rockefeller and send kerosene to Europe and the Far East.

Meanwhile, back in the United States, geologists were busy making new discoveries in Ohio, Oklahoma, and Kansas. Refineries sprang up near oil fields and new markets proliferated. Rockefeller's refinery on the southern shores of Lake Michigan in Whiting, Indiana, provided the impetus to expand his interests in distribution.

By this point in time, Edison's electric light bulb was starting to replace kerosene oil lamps (and gaslights). The oil business began shifting to motor gasoline in order to supply the proliferation of horseless carriages. When Henry Ford introduced the mass-produced Model T, the petroleum market changed permanently. Crude oil pipelines began crossing the country from the prolific fields in Texas, Oklahoma, and Kansas to feed the growing market for gasoline.

By the late 1800s, Standard Oil employed over 100,000 people and owned 20,000 domestic wells, 4,000 miles of pipeline, and 5,000 tank cars. John D. Rockefeller was said to be the most powerful man in the world. Not only did Standard have the production and supply market cornered, but transportation and distribution as well, which gave the company almost complete control over setting price. It was, plain and simple, a monopoly.

However, Rockefeller had his share of detractors. Competitors railed against Standard Oil, in some cases resorting to civil disobedience and property damage. In 1890, Congress passed the Sherman Anti-Trust Act.

Pipeline regulation followed in 1906: the Hepburn Act made interstate pipelines common carriers which were required to offer their services at equal rates to any shipper. In 1911, the Supreme Court ruled the anti-trust litigation was final: the Standard Oil Trust was busted. The company was dissolved into seven regional oil companies, as the table below shows.

Regional Company	Becomes	Which Is Now...
New Jersey	Humble, later Exxon	Exxon Mobil
New York	Mobil	Exxon Mobil
Atlantic	ARCO	BP
Ohio	Sohio	BP
Indiana	Amoco	BP
Continental	Conoco	ConocoPhillips
California	Chevron	Chevron

Table 7.1. Pieces of Standard Oil today

Rockefeller retired in 1906, the first American billionaire, and spent his remaining years in philanthropy. Early in his career, he was reputed to have said he wished to earn $100,000 in his lifetime and live to the age of 100. His first wish came true, many times over, but he died in 1937, just short of 98.

Oil Pipeline Development, From Sea to Shining Sea

Pipelines from the production fields to refineries grew to nearly 120,000 miles between 1919 and 1930, virtually tripling their reach. Pipeline integrity improved in the 1930s with the advent of electric welding and seamless pipes replacing bolting segments together. Many new pipeline companies were formed and another 100,000 miles of pipe were laid. Crude trunk lines radiated out from Louisiana, Texas, Oklahoma, and Midwest refineries like spokes on a wagon wheel.

The next two decades were a time of massive pipeline expansion for both oil and gas. In 1930, eight oil companies jointly built the Great Lakes Pipe Line, a spider web of pipes carrying crude oil stretching across a dozen Midwestern states. At 6,228 miles, it was the longest pipeline system in the country. By the end of the decade, with World War II looming, President Franklin D. Roosevelt authorized two government-subsidized pipeline companies, Southeastern and Plantation, to exercise eminent domain (the right to force the sale of land for the public good) for the first time in order to build two new petroleum product pipelines that would move gasoline, diesel, and other fuels, avoiding transportation by coastal tankers that would be at risk during wartime. That turned out to be a wise move, but it left much crude oil transportation still moving by ship to the East Coast. German U-boats began sinking oil tankers moving between the Gulf Coast and New Jersey in 1941. Within six months, over 55 tankers had been sunk, reducing oil deliveries by 80%. Then in the early 1940s, two huge joint government and private enterprise projects were set in motion to address this weakness. They would ultimately set new standards for capacity and time to completion.

These two pipelines were the War Emergency Pipelines, or WEP projects, which were built by a government-industry nonprofit consortium that included many of the largest oil companies. "Big Inch" was a 24-inch crude pipeline from Longview, Texas, to Phoenixville, Pennsylvania, where it split in two, going to New York and Philadelphia. "Little Big Inch," a 20-inch refined products pipe, ran from Beaumont, Texas, to Linden, New Jersey. Big Inch delivered its first oil in August 1943; Little Big Inch delivered in March 1944. They heralded a new generation of large-capacity pipelines, where before the largest was just 12 inches in diameter. After the war, the Big Inch pipeline was converted to move natural gas instead of crude oil and is today the Texas Eastern Transmission Corporation (TETCO) pipeline owned by Spectra Energy. The Little Big Inch is the TEPPCO (now called Products Pipeline System) pipeline owned by Enterprise Products Partners.

By war's end, U.S. pipeline mileage was growing fast. New pipelines, often 20 or 24 inches in diameter, were being built, along with the implementation of new technologies such as specialized pumps to adjust the flow and electronics for system monitoring.

There was a period of relative stability in world oil markets from the end of World War II through the 1960s. Prices were relatively constant with the market dominated by the majors, also known as the *Seven Sisters*: *Exxon*, *Mobil* (now combined into ExxonMobil), *British Petroleum* (BP, formerly Anglo-Persian Oil Company), *SoCal* (Standard Oil of California), now Chevron, *Gulf Oil*, and *Texaco* (both now Chevron), and *Royal Dutch Shell*. These major oil companies controlled much of the world's oil supply, either directly or indirectly through purchases from government-controlled oil companies. Fluctuations in the price of oil in international markets were measured in pennies. As late as 1972, the price of a barrel of crude oil from Saudi Arabia was under $3.50/bbl. Then the world changed.

The Run-Up to Hundred-Dollar Crude Oil

The events of the early 1970s bring us into the modern era, at which point in history we can fast-forward. You may have lived through all or part of this, so here is a brief summary:

Responding to the United States' support for Israel during the 1973 Arab-Israeli War, OPEC imposed an oil embargo on the United States. The result was a dramatic increase in the global price for oil, quadrupling to more than $12/bbl. The price shock resulted in hours-long waits at gas stations, government-controlled oil prices, and economic malaise.

A second oil shock hit in 1979 following the Iranian Revolution. The price of crude oil skyrocketed to almost $40/bbl and gas station lines appeared again. The Carter administration imposed a Windfall Profits Tax on oil companies and initiated all manner of programs to reduce oil consumption.

Responding to higher prices, U.S. crude oil production started to increase again. OPEC maintained its high level of production, but demand was down due to a weak economy and conservation measures. In five years, the market was awash in oil.

That precipitated the great crude oil crash of 1986. Prices dropped from the $30-40/bbl range down to $10/bbl. Drilling for oil in the U.S. screeched to a halt. Small wells, called *stripper wells*, were permanently shut down. The majors began exiting the domestic market and closing or selling refineries. Independent producers started to pick up the scraps. New companies were formed to cobble together pieces of the majors' fallen empires into new midstream entities.

Except for a brief run-up in 1990, it took fourteen years for crude oil prices to recover to pre-1986 levels. During this period, crude oil prices muddled mostly between $15/bbl and $30/bbl.

By 2004, growing global demand finally started to exceed the ability of producing countries. Crude oil prices moved to $40/bbl in 2004, $56/bbl in 2005, $62/bbl in 2006, and $72/bbl in 2007.

In 2008, as the economy was convulsing, Wall Street went completely gaga over energy commodities. On July 11, 2008, the price of crude oil in the United States ran up to $145/bbl. There was no war or other crisis, only Wall Street chasing a speculative bubble.

In October 2008, the bubble popped. By mid-December crude oil prices plummeted below $35/bbl.

But within six months, the world economy started to move back from the precipice and crude oil began a slow march back toward the $100/bbl level, where it remained until mid-2014.

Then in 2014, the U.S. shale revolution collided with stagnant demand in the global market. Crude oil prices again crashed, with significant implications for the petroleum industry and world economies.

Perhaps one of the most significant takeaways from this brief history lesson is this: Rarely does a single factor affect the crude oil market, but rather several conspire—some by accident, some by cause and effect—to create a rollercoaster ride for the world's most coveted energy source. It's true that energy markets are rarely efficient, but neither are they reliably predictable.

Today's Crude Oil Market

There are two vastly different crude oil markets: international and U.S. domestic. They are characterized by different procedures, pricing mechanisms, pricing benchmarks, and even a variety of participants. These two markets interact and usually track each other. However, other times they seem to march to completely different drummers, diverging and even contradicting each other.

The international crude oil market. The international crude oil market is huge, until the recent price decline transacting an annual dollar value of more than $3 trillion. Tankers carrying up to four million barrels each ply the world's oceans. When crude was $100/bbl, tankers were carrying $400 million worth *per tanker load*; therefore, the transaction size for international crude deals is very large even at lower crude prices. World production of crude is about 90 MMbbl/d, about 40% OPEC and 60% non-OPEC. National oil companies, i.e., governments, control about 75% of total world production. Major producers such as ExxonMobil, Shell, BP, and Chevron dominate the private side of the international markets.

International crude pricing is influenced by factors such as geopolitics, currency values, the world economy, and the global supply-and-demand balance for crude oil. Grades such as North Sea Brent and Dubai crude from the United Arab Emirates (UAE) are the most important price benchmarks for international crude oil trading.

U.S. domestic crude oil production. U.S. domestic crude oil production is about 10% of the global market. Most U.S. crude moves by pipeline in batches that may be only 100 Mbbl/d to 400 Mbbl/d at a time, or just 5% to 10% the size of those huge tankers. Thus the transaction size for domestic crude deals tends to be much smaller than international deals. U.S. independent producers like Devon, Anadarko, Apache, Chesapeake, Continental, EOG, Linn Energy, Occidental, Pioneer, Range Resources, and Southwestern Energy produce most of the crude, although majors like ExxonMobil, Chevron, and Shell also remain important domestic market participants. Much of that crude is sold not directly to refiners, but to midstream companies like Buckeye, Plains All American, Enterprise Products, Enbridge, and Energy Transfer. Those companies in turn sell mostly to independent refiners, such as Valero, Holly, Tesoro, Frontier, and Western Refining. These lists of producers, midstream companies, and refiners are not complete, but are intended to represent the fragmentation of the U.S. crude oil market. Unlike international crude oil, which is characterized by big, government-level entities, major oil companies, and huge transaction volumes, the small, independent entities and much smaller transaction volumes typify the U.S. crude oil market.

The factors that impact international crudes also influence U.S. domestic crude pricing but not always in the same manner or magnitude. In addition, U.S. crude is highly influenced by location, transportation costs, transportation constraints, and other factors unique to the U.S. crude oil market.

There is one more big difference between the international markets and U.S. markets: the rate of production growth. *Global production excluding the United States has been essentially flat, while U.S. production has increased by more than 50%.* That has thrust U.S. domestic crude into an era of radical change, while the international market is muddling along with about the same production dynamics it has had for the past several years. Except, of course, for the fact that the United States needs much less crude from those international markets, which has had important implications in recent crude oil market developments. Due to the size and importance of international crude oil markets, there are many books and other resources that provide information on their history and workings. The focus of this book is primarily U.S. domestic energy markets—the drill-bit hydrocarbons—therefore, domestic crude oil is the focal point for the remainder of this chapter along with its sibling, Canadian crude.

Transporting U.S. Domestic—and Canadian—Crude Oil

The U.S. crude oil market is highly integrated with the Canadian crude market. Canada produces about 4 MMbbl/d of crude, exporting about 2.8 MMbbl/d to the United States. That is about 70% of total Canadian production. The United States takes essentially all of Canada's crude oil the country does not use itself. Canada is the largest supplier of imported barrels into the United States responsible for more than 40% of all imported crude oil in early 2015. Most of this crude comes across the northern border by pipeline, although rail is growing in importance as a transportation alternative. Due to the importance of Canadian crude to U.S. supplies, and because of the pipelines connecting the two countries, the crude oil market is best viewed from the perspective of an integrated North American marketplace.

Like natural gas and NGLs, a significant amount of crude oil changes hands at hubs, which generally exhibit the common hub characteristics of pipelines coming together: storage capacity and processes which facilitate price liquidity. There are eight primary crude oil hubs in North America, six in the United States, and two in Canada, as shown in Figure 7.1.

The hub in Cushing, Oklahoma, has historically been the largest and most active hub in the United States. As mentioned earlier, Cushing was once an important oil field, perhaps second only to Spindletop in the early days of U.S. oil production. However, once its reserves declined, it became a storage depot and transshipment hub for moving crude back and forth from the Gulf Coast to the Midwest. Eight major pipelines and several smaller pipes connect into and out of Cushing. As a storage and distribution facility, Cushing has a storied history reviewed earlier in this chapter, equaled only by its reputation as the benchmark location for all U.S. crude pricing and the prime oil futures trading hub. In 1983, NYMEX selected Cushing as its official delivery point for West Texas Intermediate (WTI) light-sweet crude futures contracts, which cemented its role as the U.S. crude oil benchmark.

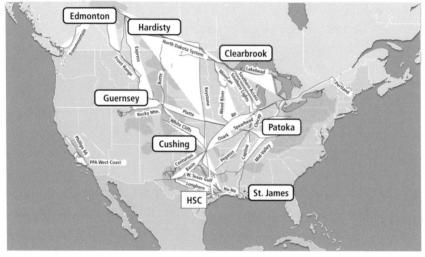

Figure 7.1. Crude oil shipping hubs

St. James, Louisiana, located on the Mississippi River about 40 miles south of Baton Rouge, Louisiana, and 50 miles northwest of New Orleans, is arguably the second most important crude trading hub and the key pricing location for another important benchmark crude grade, Light Louisiana Sweet, or LLS. St. James has been an active point for transit of Gulf Coast crude imports and is growing as a destination terminal for crude by rail as well.

Other important crude trading hubs are listed below:

- The Houston Ship Channel, or HSC, is the region between Houston and Port Arthur, Texas. Boasting the world's greatest concentration of refineries, it is also served by numerous pipelines, storage terminals, and dock facilities.

- Patoka, Illinois is a hub serving Chicago and other Midwest refineries, connecting to Canadian crude, Cushing, and St. James.
- Guernsey, Wyoming is the key crude hub for Rockies crude and also a transit point for Bakken crude coming south from North Dakota.
- Clearbrook, Minnesota is a transit point for Canadian imports and Bakken crude.
- Edmonton and Hardisty are two hubs located 112 miles apart in Alberta, Canada, about halfway between Calgary and the major oil sands production areas farther north. The importance of these hubs to the crude oil industry is related to the major pipelines either originating or passing through them. These pipelines serve two purposes. First, they are the main gathering points for onward distribution to market of crude oil production from the oil sands region, as well as conventional heavy and light oil production in Alberta. Second, they are distribution hubs for incoming supplies of natural gasoline and condensate used as diluent or thinner for heavy Canadian bitumen oil so it will flow through pipelines.

All crude oil production eventually moves to a refinery. Unlike natural gas delivered to thousands of factories and power generation plants, as well as millions of homeowners and businesses, almost all crude oil produced in North America is consumed by a refinery. There are 139 operating refineries in the United States. The U.S. crude oil pipeline system is designed to get crude from the point of production to U.S. or Canadian refineries.

There are about 25 major crude oil pipeline systems serving North America shown in Figure 7.1, along with a number of smaller pipelines. The two largest systems bringing Canadian crude to the United States are Enbridge Mainline and TransCanada Keystone (the one that already exists, not Keystone XL). The representative list that follows covers many of the major systems:

- The Spectra Platte and SemGroup White Cliffs pipelines bring Rockies crude oil to Patoka, Illinois, and Cushing, Oklahoma, respectively.
- Magellan Longhorn, Energy Transfer/Sunoco Permian Express, and Occidental/Magellan BridgeTex move West Texas Permian crude to the Gulf Coast.

- The Enbridge Spearhead and Flanagan pipelines move crude between Patoka and Cushing.
- The Enterprise/Enbridge Seaway pipeline and the TransCanada Marketlink system move Cushing crude to the Gulf Coast.
- The Capline system moves crude from the St. James area up to Patoka.
- The Shell Ho-Ho system (now known as Zydeco) moves crude from the Houston Ship Channel area to refineries in the Beaumont/Port Arthur area as well as refineries along the Louisiana Gulf Coast.

Note in Figure 7.1 that all of these pipelines are essentially in the middle of the United States. Today there are no pipelines that move crude to either the East Coast or West Coast. Prior to the shale revolution, refineries in coastal regions were supplied crude via tankers, either imported crude or, in the case of the West Coast, partially Alaska North Slope crude. Much of the supply to those coastal refineries is shifting to rail, a topic addressed in much greater detail in Chapter 15.

Crude Oil Quality and Value

Not all crude oils are made the same. Suffice to say that there are hundreds of varieties of crude oil and each one is slightly different. Or *very* different. How they differ and their key qualities are a primary determinant of the prices they will bring on the open market: a low-quality crude fetches a lower price than a higher-quality crude.

There are many ways crude oils can vary in quality, but the most important criteria are *gravity* and *sulfur content*. Gravity is a measure of the viscosity of crude oil or, more accurately, its *density*. The measure used is API gravity, from standards published by The American Petroleum Institute. The lower the API, the greater the crude's density. A crude with an API gravity greater than 10 will float on top of water. If it is less than 10, the crude will sink. Low-gravity crudes such as Canadian Oil Sands are 10 API or lower and are so thick they will only pour when heated or mixed with diluent (the thinner mentioned above). Super-light crudes called condensates have an API of 50, 60, or even higher, are transparent or translucent, and are more like low-quality gasoline than crude. The benchmark West Texas Intermediate crude oil has a gravity of 39.6 API.

The other important quality criterion is sulfur content. A crude with low sulfur content is said to be *sweet*, while a high sulfur content is said to be *sour*. Crude is generally considered sweet if it contains less than 0.5% sulfur. The more sulfur in the crude, the more it must be processed to remove that sulfur to make gasoline, diesel, jet fuel, and most other petroleum products, thus increasing the cost of processing.

Frequently, though not always, heavy crude is also sour, while light crude is more likely to be sweet. For example, the heavy Canadian Oil Sands crude is quite sour, while most of the new U.S. shale production is light-sweet. Heavy-sour crude must go to refineries with equipment designed to accommodate these crudes. Light-sweet crudes can go to almost any refinery, but some refineries, particularly older and smaller refineries, can only take light-sweet crudes.

Generally speaking, the lighter the crude, the greater its value to a refiner because of the lower processing cost. But there is a limit to the lighter-is-better rule. Super-light crudes tend to yield a lot of lower-value NGLs and are light (so to speak) in their yield of distillate products (diesel, jet fuel, kerosene) that generally command higher prices. So the refiner wants a crude oil that is just right: not too heavy, not too light.

Refineries value any particular crude according to its *yield* for that refinery. Each type of crude oil yields a different mix of products, depending on the quality of the crude oil and if the refinery has the equipment to process a particular crude oil. Refineries determine the price they can pay for a crude based on the yield of products (gasoline, kerosene, diesel, jet fuel, etc.) from that crude and the price it expects to get for those products. Of course, just because a refinery calculates the price does not mean it will be able to acquire the crude for that price. What it does mean is the refinery has set its target price, which is the basis for negotiating with crude sellers.

Crude Oil Commercial Arrangements and Transactions

Three primary market mechanisms are used to sell and purchase physical crude oil in the U.S. domestic market: postings, futures-related contracts, and outright price deals. All three structures evolved to meet specific market needs for crude transactions along the way from the point of production to a refinery.

Posted price. The earliest pricing mechanism was the posted price. Back at the turn of the nineteenth to the twentieth century, domestic refiners *posted the price*, literally nailing a sign to a post with the price they were willing to pay producers for their crude oil. Eventually other mechanisms were used to communicate the postings, but the name stuck. By definition, a crude oil posting is the price a buyer is willing to pay. The posted price mechanism is still used today, although mostly midstream crude oil aggregators like Plains All American or Enterprise post prices. However, some refiners also post prices for crudes that move directly into their refineries. Postings are used mainly for crude purchased from smaller producers *at the lease*. Usually, the midstream company or refiner provides transportation to get the crude from a tank near the well itself to some central location—storage facilities or a refinery—referenced by the posted price. The purchaser pays the producer the posted price, less the cost of transporting the crude to that central location. Crude oil posters usually list crude types by location (frequently the state) and a common description. Postings are generally available on the websites of companies that buy crudes based on posted prices.

There is an important potential "gotcha" in the pricing calculation that is ultimately paid to the producer: the quality adjustment. The posted price is adjusted based on the quality of the crude purchased. That quality is measured in a tank or in a pipeline, and the price is reduced (the adjustments are almost always deductions, called *deducts*) generally based on API gravity and sulfur content. Without going into the details here, suffice to say that the value of those deducts can have a significant impact on the price that the producer ultimately receives.

Spot and contract price. Most physical U.S. crude trades are linked to CME/NYMEX WTI crude futures. In other words, physical crude prices are calculated in part based on futures prices. The differences between futures and physical trading arrangements make physical pricing complex. Two formula mechanisms are commonly used in physical transactions that link directly to the NYMEX settlement prices: the *calendar month average*, or *CMA*, and WTI P-Plus.

In the domestic crude oil market, spot transactions (whether priced according to CMA or WTI P-Plus) are almost always for crude to be delivered in the next month. That is because crude oil scheduling is done on a monthly basis at the end of the current month for next-month delivery. In the decades before the futures contract came into its own, crude prices were simply negotiated outright prices, for example $70/bbl. But as the CME/NYMEX contract grew, it ultimately came to dominate all domestic crude pricing. Crude oil traders linked their physical deals to the heavily traded NYMEX futures market, which is hard to manipulate and easy to hedge. Understanding spot crude pricing for WTI and other U.S. domestic grades therefore requires an understanding of futures pricing and the differences between futures and physical crude markets.

Pricing elements. In theory, the terms and conditions for physical crude oil trades are entirely specific to each transaction. Traders can literally agree on anything to decide the price. In practice, however, the majority of trades follow fairly standard terms with which any two counterparties can feel comfortable. Many crude transactions take place under long-term contracts that last for years. The contract defines the general conditions of the trade, including the volumes to be transacted every month, delivery location, product specification, credit terms and conditions, payment terms, and pricing mechanism. Once the contract is set up, subsequent transactions simply reference the established contract terms. Most use the CMA and WTI P-Plus pricing mechanisms mentioned above and normally include the following terms:

- **NYMEX pricing element:** a price that is related to prompt NYMEX crude oil at the time of delivery (more about this below).
- **Grade differential to the NYMEX price element:** a premium or discount to NYMEX depending on the crude grade (similar to the posted price quality adjustment discussed above).
- **Transport element:** reflecting any transport costs to the pricing location, normally a pipeline and/or trucking fee.
- **Custom price differential:** a discount or premium to the sum of the three aforementioned elements, negotiated by the participants in the transaction (a.k.a. the fudge factor).

The first three of these pricing elements reference daily prices during the delivery month (usually a calendar month) but are averaged to create a monthly price. The transaction cannot be finalized until after the delivery period when all the pricing elements are available. The details behind CMA and WTI P-Plus pricing are described below in the section titled "CMA and P-Plus calculations."

Futures and physicals pricing. NYMEX WTI futures are linked to pricing for physical crude deliveries. Before we delve into this subject, here are a few basic concepts.

For each futures commodity, NYMEX lists a variable number of futures contracts that are available to trade, each for one month further into the future.

Every NYMEX WTI futures contract in the list is for delivery during a particular calendar month in the future. The name of the futures contract, for example "December 2017," represents the calendar month when the crude will be delivered: the delivery period.

Each futures contract has a lifespan that starts when it is first traded and ends when the contract expires. The contract expires at a predetermined time before the delivery period starts.

Most futures contracts are sold and bought back into the futures market before the contract expires; they are just financial transactions. A small percentage of contracts are held by participants to expiry and therefore go to delivery.

A NYMEX WTI futures contract contains detailed instructions about delivery, stating that it must occur at Cushing, Oklahoma, into a pipeline or storage facility during the delivery period.

Any pipeline deliveries made in the U.S. domestic crude oil market for a particular month must be scheduled by the 25th day of the month prior to actual delivery (or the closest business day before the 25th).

To give the holders of those NYMEX crude futures contracts—designated for prompt delivery—a chance to schedule their deliveries with a pipeline (if they decide to take delivery instead of closing out their futures position), the NYMEX prompt contracts expire three business days before scheduling ends.

Physical barrels of U.S. domestic crude are traded based on the *trading month*, or monthly pipeline schedule. That schedule runs from one pipeline schedule deadline to the next. Physical barrels for that "December 2017" delivery are traded in the physical market up until the scheduling deadline in late November.

Each NYMEX futures contract is for 1,000 bbl of crude. In practice, many pipelines specify a minimum 10,000 bbl parcel and most spot market transactions involve moving a specified number of barrels within a calendar month.

CMA and P-Plus calculations. As mentioned above, in the U.S. domestic crude oil markets, the prices for physical barrels are usually linked to the prices of NYMEX futures. The most common of these linking mechanisms is the NYMEX CMA (calendar month average).

There are two pricing aspects to the CMA: a basic figure and a more complicated *NYMEX roll* calculation. Some contracts use both, while others forego the NYMEX roll. The basic CMA is simply the average of NYMEX closing prices during the month when the physical crude is delivered. The roll adjusts the basic CMA up or down based on whether the prices for the current month were higher or lower than the CMA prices in the next month. So for example, the roll adjustment would represent the cost of rolling, or moving, a September futures position into October. More information on the calculation of the CMA roll can be found on *The Domino Effect* website at **www.dominoeffect.com/cma**.

The second common pricing mechanism for domestic spot crude is called *P-Plus*, or WTI P-Plus, which is similar to the CMA. Again there are two calculations, a base price and a premium. The base price is an average of company crude postings during the delivery month. The premium is a differential to the crude oil posting average (P-Plus) that represents the value of WTI delivered into Cushing from the production field during the current calendar month. Although this price mechanism is based on company postings, the postings themselves are actually derived from the same NYMEX settlement prices used in the CMA. In other words, the crude postings—those same postings discussed above—tend to be determined by formulae based on NYMEX settlement prices. In effect, the P-Plus mechanism has evolved to become a NYMEX-derived price as well. More information on computing P-Plus prices can be found on *The Domino Effect* website at **www.dominoeffect.com/pplus**.

The P-Plus price mechanism is used almost exclusively for WTI or West Texas Sour (WTS) crude purchases delivered to Cushing. The CMA price mechanism is used more widely because it can be adjusted by quality and location differentials for any U.S. domestic crude grade. Because the WTI crude postings are based on NYMEX, the two base price mechanisms end up being very similar. However, the roll adjustment mechanism for the CMA is more reflective of the futures market structure than the WTI P-Plus adjustment, which only reflects localized physical crude transport costs in the Cushing market.

The two Cushing WTI-based crude price mechanisms are quite similar in concept but suited to different purposes. WTI P-Plus is a local market price for physical WTI barrels, while the CMA NYMEX price is the benchmark underneath the price of most U.S. domestic crude transactions. There are numerous variations in the formulas used to calculate these prices. The fundamental linkage between these base prices and the NYMEX WTI futures market provides the assurance of a liquid market and transparent prices to both buyer and seller. That said, the crude oil world is changing. More of the new shale crudes, such as Eagle Ford and Bakken, are moving to the Gulf Coast, as is crude from Cushing. There has been a great deal of market discussion regarding new crude oil pricing mechanisms along the Gulf Coast, including the possibility of a Gulf Coast futures contract.

So there you have it, a primer on the history and structure of the three drill-bit hydrocarbon markets. Although there are many differences in how the commodities evolved, how they are transported, and how transactions are handled, it should be apparent that they have a lot in common. And by far the most important thing they have in common is that hole in the ground. That common source of production is what is driving the shale revolution and is the linchpin of the domino effect.

Notes

1. Historians from the great state of Virginia like to tell the story that George Washington was the first to discover oil. The Virginia area was covered with hundreds, if not thousands, of seeps (places where oil and gas bubble up from the earth's innards and form puddles). Mostly they were things you wanted to avoid stepping into. General Washington had distinguished him-

self in the French and Indian Wars of the mid-1700s and was awarded a tract of land as his compensation. It was on his land that one of the first seeps was publicly acknowledged, although American Indians had for generations skimmed oil from seeps. Of course, neither General Washington nor the Indians made any commercial use of the oil.

2. www.nytimes.com/ref/business/20070715_GILDED _GRAPHIC.html

Part III

Takin' Care of Business: How Things Work in the Energy Markets

PART II PROVIDED THE FUNDAMENTALS OF THE ENERGY BUSINESS IN ORDER to prepare you for Part III. This is the heart of the matter, where the three DBHs coming out of the ground as raw energy resources are transformed into businesses and markets, both physical and financial. The following chapters are devoted to exploring just exactly how energy markets work. Chapters 8 and 9 provide a foundation in production economics, detailing why drilling for shale oil and gas has become so much more productive. Chapters 10 and 11 go on to show how these production economics impact markets and why shale has changed everything about the interrelationships between energy commodities. Chapters 12, 13, and 14 reveal the secrets of energy market behavior: how supply, demand, and infrastructure interact to drive prices and how prices drive infrastructure investment. Let's roll up our sleeves and get to work.

Chapter 8

Production Economics: The Basics

<hr>

WE'VE SPENT THE LAST THREE CHAPTERS LEARNING HOW AND WHY *drill-bit hydrocarbon markets behave as they do. Hopefully it is becoming apparent that these three energy markets—natural gas, NGLs, and crude oil—have a lot in common when they emerge from a wellhead. They may have dissimilar physical characteristics and different uses, but each trades as a commodity. Each requires huge investments in infrastructure for processing and transportation to market and fluctuates according to supply and demand, responding to changes in market price.*

With the advent of the shale revolution, they have another thing in common based upon their shared wellhead source: the economics of extracting drill-bit hydrocarbons has changed radically. As a general rule, producers drilling in shale plays are making far more money on each well than are their counterparts drilling conventional wells. Shale gas producers can turn a profit even when prices are much lower than they were a decade ago or even a few months ago.

To reiterate, it is shale technologies—horizontal drilling, hydraulic fracturing, and other productivity-enhancing techniques—that are responsible for producing these improved returns. Why shale production is so much more lucrative is one of the most misunderstood aspects of the entire shale revolution. As we discussed back in Chapter 4, shale wells are certainly more expensive to drill. A typical conventional well can cost upwards of $2–3 million, while a representative shale well *might cost $7–12 million. Can a cubic foot of shale gas or a barrel of shale oil be sold at a higher price than production from a conventional well? No, not a penny more. It is all the same stuff. The quality differences between shale production and conventional production range from minimal to nonexistent. In some cases, the realized price for shale wells can actually be less than conventional production, due to cost differences in transporting the production to market.*

And what about those decline curves? It was mentioned earlier that production from shale wells tends to fall off rapidly, declining in the second year by 50–80% below first-year production. That is a fact. Doesn't that mean cash flow falls at an equally steep rate, cutting deeply into the economic return on the producer's invested capital? If that is the case, how are shale producers making more money than conventional producers?

It all seems so counterintuitive. There must be something very different going on in the way these wells produce. There is. The purpose of this chapter and the following two chapters is to provide a detailed understanding of how shale technologies have turned traditional oil and gas production economics on its head.

Size Matters

There are many reasons why today's shale wells are so much more profitable than conventional wells of the past. One of the key factors contributing to well profitability is *well size*, which is defined in terms of the initial production rate (*IP rate*) of the wells. It turns out that most shale wells being drilled and completed today (the big wells we covered in Chapter 4 when discussing the real impact of shale technologies) exhibit much higher IP rates than conventional wells.

When you get to the bottom line, it is those IP rates that really drive the economics of shale wells. The initial production rates for shale wells can come in between 3 to 10 times that of conventional wells, and sometimes much larger. The IP rates can be so large that the producer may generate enough cash flow in the first year or two to earn back the entire well investment cost. Of course, everything after that is gravy. Yes, shale wells tend to exhibit rather steep decline curves over the first few months of a shale well's life. But the starting point of production is so high that producers in some of the most productive plays can recoup most of their drilling and completion costs in just a few months if prices are high enough. That makes their rate-of-return calculations look great and provides enough cash to go drill more wells.

So, exactly how do these economics work? How much does it cost to drill a well, then to operate it? Once the well is drilled, what is necessary to get the hydrocarbon commodities out of the ground and to market? How does a producer determine whether a well is profitable or not? The answers to these questions are the basis for an understanding of how and why the shale revolution is driving energy markets.

Oil and Gas Production Economics: Why Should We Care?

Before getting to these answers, we need to step back and consider an even more fundamental question: why should we care about production economics? The simple answer is that production economics drive the entire supply side of the supply-and-demand equation for our drill-bit hydrocarbons. Oil and gas production economics define how producers make money drilling, extracting, and selling the three hydrocarbon commodities. Not only do producers need to know how these numbers work, but anyone trying to understand energy markets needs to have a solid understanding of the dynamics of drilling and completion costs, operating costs, transportation costs, and of course the revenues generated from the marketed commodities. Why? Because there is a direct cause-and-effect link between production economics, drilling activity, and production. If the economics support drilling more wells, then more wells will be drilled and overall production can be expected to increase. Of course, this works vice versa: If the production economics do not justify drilling new wells, they simply won't be drilled. Due to the natural decline rate of all wells, whether shale or conventional, not drilling new wells means overall production can eventually be expected to fall.

Note that the relationship between drilling activity and the level of production is far from perfect. Increased productivity from the shale revolution has translated into the need for fewer drilling rigs to maintain and grow production. However, the fundamental relationships between production economics, drilling activity, and the level of production remain the leading indicators of energy market behavior and, consequently, the domino effect.

The Link to Price

Price is one of the most important triggers to toppling dominoes. More accurately, it is the impact of *changes* in price. This gets us back to the significance of production economics. These calculations are the link between the supply side of the supply-and-demand equation and the pricing of the commodity, clearly the most significant single variable in any commodity market. To make this point, let's consider the different economics of two different wells that are exactly alike except for their initial production rate. Each costs $7.5 million to drill. Each exhibits the same decline rate in production. Each has the same operating costs, royalty arrangements, and taxes. But Well 1 has an IP rate of 150 barrels per day and Well 2 as an IP rate of 350 barrels per day. Using the production economics model described in the next two chapters, the calculations indicate that the producer needs a price of $100 per barrel just to break even for Well 1. But Well 2, with a much larger IP rate, would need a price of only $50 per barrel to break even. Consequently, if Well 2 production can be sold at more than $50 per barrel, the producer stands to make additional profits and will be encouraged to drill more wells and thus increase production.

There is also the follow-on impact from increased production which we examined in earlier chapters. As production increases, unless there is a corresponding increase in demand there is a tendency for prices to fall as oversupply puts downward pressure on markets. That is exactly what happened to natural gas prices in Domino 3, then to NGL prices in Domino 7, to Midcontinent crude oil prices in Domino 10, and eventually to global crude prices in dominoes that will be covered in later chapters. Consequently, the higher IP rate for shale wells has been, more or less, the direct driver of lower prices for all three DBHs. This fact is the essence of understanding production economics and how and why this linkage exists. In the next chapter, we'll get into the variables of our production economics model and the calculations that make it work.

All Shales Are Not Created Equal

In the introduction of *The Domino Effect*, we discussed the wide disparity between the prices for the DBHs, particularly in the period from 2009

Unconventional Is the New Conventional

In this book the terms shale gas and shale oil are used loosely. What we are really referring to is more accurately described as unconventional production: obtaining natural gas, NGLs, and crude oil from shale rock. But that's not all. There are other unconventional production sources we lump into our definition of shale gas and shale oil which are *not* produced from shale rock. One example is tight sands. You may hear others use the terms **tight oil** or **tight gas** to describe what we are calling shale gas and shale oil.

Our definition of shale liquids and gas includes gas, oil, and NGLs produced from wells requiring artificial stimulation (fracking) to yield economically viable quantities of hydrocarbon production. Almost all of these wells are also horizontal. Essentially, if the producer has to frack the rock and drill horizontally to achieve an economically viable well, then we call it shale regardless of whether the rock is really shale or not.

This gets us back to the terms conventional and unconventional, also used loosely when describing the shale revolution. This can be confusing; not all unconventional production is shale oil and shale gas. There are other forms of unconventional production that do not fit into our shale definition. So what do we mean when we use the terms conventional and unconventional?

Conventional production is usually applied to more traditional, vertical wells in legacy production basins, while the label **unconventional production** is slapped on shale plays being exploited with horizontal drilling, hydraulic fracturing, and other shale technologies. The more accurate use of these terms refers to the specific kind of hydrocarbon resource being produced. As a general rule, conventional resources are easier to produce but harder to find. Unconventional resources are easier to find but harder to produce.

For example, natural gas production from tight sands, coal bed methane, shale, and gas hydrates are all classified as unconventional, meaning the producer must do something special (fracking or another drilling or well completion process) to get the resource to give up its hydrocarbons. On the other hand, if all it takes to get the resource to give up its hydrocarbons is to drill a well and sit back and wait for the hydrocarbons to emerge, then it counts as conventional.

The real problem with the term unconventional is that unconventional production is becoming conventional. Years ago, when the terms came into vogue, unconventional was only a tiny percentage of total production. Today, unconventional natural gas (gas produced from shale, tight sands, and coal bed methane) has risen to about 60% of total U.S. gas production. Thus, unconventional production now exceeds conventional production. For this reason, it seems the terms have become misnomers. Consequently, it makes sense for us to stick with our equally inaccurate but more descriptive terms: shale gas and shale oil.

through late 2014. Those price differences translated directly into differences in profitability for different shale plays for the simple reason that different plays tend to yield different proportions of each of the DBHs. Some plays are dry gas only and that's it. Others are wet gas or gas that can be processed to yield both natural gas and NGLs. Then there are the pure crude plays which produce only oil. But most shale oil plays also produce some associated gas (which is usually wet gas) and also yield NGLs, or what are sometimes called *triple plays*. Even with lower oil prices, the triple play continues to have a big economic advantage in the market due to its multiple sources of revenue: sales of gas, NGLs, and oil.

To calculate the economics of an individual well, you need to consider the total cost of drilling and completing the well, the cost of moving all of the hydrocarbons produced from the well to market, and the revenues generated from selling all those hydrocarbons at market prices. It is in calculating those revenues that the differences between the prices of the DBHs demonstrate their impact on well economics. As you have probably already figured out, just what those prices are makes a big difference in the rates of return from one play to the next.

The map in Figure 8.1 shows the rates of return for several shale plays as of Fall 2014 (just before the crash in crude oil prices), as calculated by the production economics model to be introduced in the following chapters. At that point, WTI crude oil was priced at about $90/bbl while natural gas at the Henry Hub was $3.75/MMBtu. The map shows typical producer rates of return for dry gas (light blue squares), wet gas (grey-blue squares), and crude oil (dark blue squares). Note that these are representative returns only; there is a wide range of returns for individual producers and even a wider range of returns for individual wells.

However, these numbers were indicative of the range of returns for the different commodities in different geographies in pre-crash 2014.

These returns are calculated using what is termed *half-cycle economics*. That means the calculations only consider the cost of drilling and completing the well, not the cost of exploration activities or acquiring the lease. The values are discounted cash flow rates of return, sometimes called Internal Rate of Return (IRR). IRR calculations will be discussed in more detail in the next chapter.

As shown in Figure 8.1, based on pricing in the fall of 2014, the dry gas plays were at the low end of the spectrum: 5% in the Haynesville of northern Louisiana, 6% in the Fayetteville in Arkansas, a negative value -2% in the Piceance in the Rockies, but a robust 16% in the Marcellus Dry in northeastern Pennsylvania. You might wonder why the rates of return for these dry gas plays are so different. It is because the costs to drill and operate each well are different, the volumes produced from each well (the IP rates) are different, and the production decline rates are different. To state the obvious, cheaper wells that produce higher volumes have higher rates of return than expensive wells producing less volume. There is a broad range of well costs and production yields from the different shale plays.

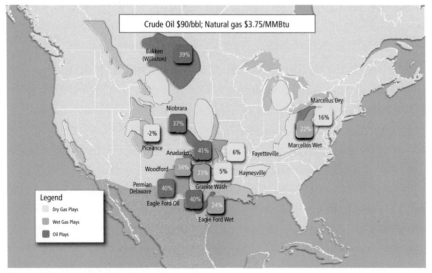

Figure 8.1. Rates of return for shale oil plays

Then there are the NGL plays. Not only can drilling costs and natural gas production volumes vary from well to well, but the amount of NGLs in the gas (the GPM of the gas) can vary greatly. That NGL content can have a big impact on returns, particularly when NGL prices are high relative to natural gas. When that is the case, the returns from wet gas wells—those with greater concentrations of NGLs in the gas—are higher. Wet gas returns, shown in the grey-blue squares, are considerably more attractive than dry gas plays, with a 23% IRR in the Granite Wash in Oklahoma, 24% in the NGL-producing area of the Eagle Ford in South Texas, and 22% at the Marcellus Wet (southwestern Pennsylvania and West Virginia).

Finally, there are the dark blue squares: the crude oil plays. Crude oil prices at the time these numbers were calculated were still relatively high which translated into attractive rates of return, with the Permian in West Texas and New Mexico averaging 40% IRR, 39% in the Bakken, and 37% in the Niobrara in the Rockies. Just like the gas plays, the differences in returns for the crude plays relate directly to economic factors for those plays. As you might expect, producers tend to drill more wells where the IRR is the highest. DBH economics drive supply growth in the profitable plays. And conversely, production usually tends to decline in the less profitable plays.

The Numbers They Are A-Changing

The numbers we've just reviewed demonstrate typical producer returns based on costs, reported volumes, and prices at a specific point in time. But of course, these numbers change frequently. Prices can swing dramatically as supply-and-demand balances shift, and they certainly did so when crude oil prices dropped dramatically in late 2014. But other factors are also at work in production economics calculations. Over time, producers continue to become more efficient, driving drilling and completion costs down. It seems like there is a story in the news every few weeks showing big increases in well production from some of the more prolific plays like the Marcellus or the Permian. And with lower crude prices have come lower drilling services costs, which improve producer economics.

Because these numbers are so volatile, it is important that we look beyond simple rates of return to the underlying calculations themselves. These are important in considering how the individual cost and revenue elements of drilling and producing a well come together in an economic analysis to determine if they yield a viable return.

In order to analyze the calculations, you need to understand the calculation process. In Chapter 9, we will examine the inputs, formulas, and economic outputs from our production economics model as applied to a representative well in the Permian Basin. To put a finer point on the process, if the well doesn't work in a spreadsheet, it isn't going to get drilled. With that determination, we will next consider the details of how such a well production economics spreadsheet actually works.

Chapter 9

Production Economics: The Math

N ow that we've covered the basic concepts of shale economics, we turn our attention to the numbers: production rates, declines, and costs. Only by examining the mechanics of the economic calculations can you really understand how shale production is changing oil and gas markets. Since every shale play is different, it is far beyond the scope of this book to look at all of them, or even a few of the most important plays. Instead, we will focus on a single example of an important shale play, one with multi-commodity economics: the Wolfcamp play in the Permian Basin of West Texas. Over the past few years, Wolfcamp producers saw high returns on their typical, average wells. This was due to a combination of factors but was primarily a function of the triple-play nature of most Permian wells, which enjoy revenue streams produced not just from crude oil but also natural gas and natural gas liquids.

To demonstrate how these returns are calculated, in this chapter we walk through the inputs required to apply The Domino Effect Production Economics Model for our representative Wolfcamp well. Note that these factors are intended only as examples or rough approximations. The values shown were derived from studying various publicly available resources including investor publications, industry reports, and statistical data. The numbers represented in this fictitious well were not derived from any one producer or county but instead have been aggregated to create a composite well representing what might be expected from the Wolfcamp play. Its sole purpose is as an instructional model.

Before getting into the numbers, there are a few more caveats and expla-nations to consider:

- *The methodologies for calculating the economics of oil- and gas-producing wells by producing companies are quite complex, requiring sophisticated models, considerable technical expertise, and much more data than is usu-ally available to independent analysts. However, it is possible to approximate the results from these sophisticated models using a simple spreadsheet and a few critical input variables. This is the approach used here.*

- *No matter what model you use, it is just a view at a particular point in time, no better than the data used in its calculations. There are a lot of assumptions that go into the data. Different analysts making these calculations at different points in time can produce quite different estimates of production economics from any given basin or producer. For example, the costs used in the calcu-lations below are as of late 2014. In 2015, drilling costs declined substan-tially following the collapse in crude oil prices.*

- *We will not get into the mechanics of using the model. If you are interested in more details on the spreadsheet itself, you can read more about it and download a copy from* The Domino Effect *website at* **www.dominoeffect.com/prodecon.**

Production Economics Modeling: The Variables

The Domino Effect Production Economics Model uses these seven input factors:

- **Drilling and completion costs:** what it costs to drill the well and ready it for production.
- **Operating expenses:** the ongoing cost of operating and maintaining the well.
- **Production taxes:** what is due the government entities based on oil and gas production.
- **Royalty rates:** the amount owed to the owner of the mineral rights where the well is located.
- **Initial production rate:** the rate of flow for the well when it first goes into production.
- **Decline curves:** the rate at which production drops over the life of the well.

- **Commodity prices and pricing:** the price at which the oil, NGLs, and gas will be sold.

Note that the cost of acquiring the minerals lease for the property to be drilled and any exploration costs are not included in our list of variables for the analysis that will be reviewed here. This analysis is confined to half-cycle economics, a term introduced in the previous chapter, which refers to the rate of return computed based on the incremental cost of drilling the well and offset by the revenues from products sold from that well. Since any exploration costs and the cost of acquiring the lease are for the most part already *sunk costs*, they are not included in the analysis. In other words, a producer will most likely elect to drill and produce a well if revenues over incremental costs provide positive returns, even if the economics do not fully recover costs that have already been paid out. We will examine this issue of sunk costs more in later chapters. Note that The Domino Effect Production Economics Model spreadsheet does have a provision for including these costs in the analysis.

Drilling Costs

The cost of drilling a single unconventional horizontal well is chiefly a function of the vertical depth of the formation and the lateral length drilled through it. Our representative well in the Wolfcamp play of the Midland Basin (a sub-basin of the Permian Basin), has a vertical depth of 9,250 feet with a lateral, or horizontal, length of approximately 5,000 feet. This is a relatively short lateral; they can get up to 12,000 feet or longer and are considerably more expensive than this representative well. Drilling and completion costs for our representative well are $7.5 million, in line with other wells in the area with similar specifications in mid-2014 and roughly five times the $1.5-million cost of a vertical well in the same region.

Developing a well is a two-part process. The first is drilling: prepping the site through actually drilling the well. The second part is completion: hydraulic fracturing to stimulate flow from the well and putting the infrastructure in place to get the well's production to market. The split for our representative well between drilling and completion cost works out to roughly 45–55% as shown in Figure 9.1.

It is a bit difficult to characterize an average well in the Wolfcamp play; it is quite a heterogeneous acreage, and the choices of how to drill

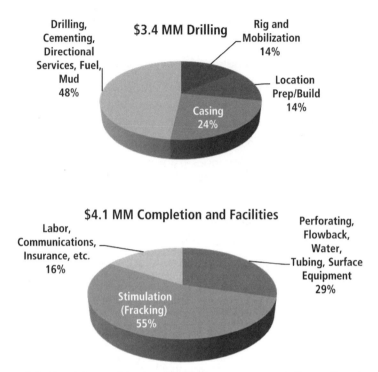

Figure 9.1. Breakdown of horizontal Wolfcamp representative well costs

and complete a well are so varied. That said, this representative well model is reasonably indicative of this area.

The following is a breakdown of the component costs and representative percentages of the $3.4-million estimate for horizontal drilling:

- **Location preparation** ($465,000, 14% of drilling costs). Regardless of whether a drilling site is located in the middle of the desert in New Mexico or just outside Midland, Texas, drill sites often require a great deal of site preparation to enable efficient drilling operations. These costs generally include putting in roads to the well site, leveling dirt for the drilling pad and platform, mobilizing the rig, drilling the well, cementing the casing, and constructing retention areas for drilling fluids.

- **Rig mobilization and demobilization** ($490,000, 14% of drilling costs). One of the larger costs incurred in the drilling of a well is simply getting the rig (usually rented or leased) out to the site for drilling and then moving the rig off the drill site when finished.

- **Directional drilling, cementing, and fuel** ($1.65 million, 48% of drilling costs). The largest cost associated with drilling a well is, of course, drilling the well to the desired depth and lateral length (*making hole*) and then cementing in the casing. Upon completion of cementing, the well should be fully prepared for perforation and hydraulic fracturing, discussed below. These costs are quite variable, depending on the depth and length of the well, and are subject to additional fluctuations due to the rise and fall of fuel and other costs.
- **Casing** ($815,000, 24% of drilling costs). Since casing is such a significant cost, it makes sense to break it out separately. Depending on local water resources and geology, varying lengths of overlapping steel well casing are installed to provide structural integrity for the well, isolate it from the surrounding geology, and protect fresh-water aquifers.

Completion and Facilities Costs

By far the largest part of completion costs is generically called fracking or, more accurately, well stimulation. Well stimulation dates back to the 1860s, when dynamite and nitroglycerin were used; modern fracking using fluid proppants began in the late 1940s. Other costs include perforation of the well casing, handling of flowback water, tubing and surface equipment, and facilities costs.

The number of fracturing stages is a primary determinant of completion costs. Recall the magic dust from Chapter 4: The well casing is perforated and water, followed by chemicals and proppant, are injected under high pressures into the shale to cause fractures in the rock. When the water recedes, the proppant (usually silica sand) holds open the fractures so that the hydrocarbons can flow into the wellbore. This is done in stages across the lateral; only one stage is fracked at a time. The well in our example has 22 fracturing stages. Total completion costs are $2.2 million for stimulation, $1.2 million for perforating, handling the flowback water, piping, etc., and $0.7 million for facilities, for a total of $4.1 million.

The following is a representative percentage breakdown of completion costs:

- **Stimulation** ($2.2 million, 55% of completion costs). Hydraulic fracturing requires an impressive number of trucks and rented equipment, tons of proppant, sophisticated engineering, labor and supervision, and, like drilling, mobilization and demobilization costs. Fine-grade sand, often a silica, is critical for use in proppant. As the shale revolution ramped up, demand soared for fine-grain sand from northern states like Wisconsin, as well as other spots including Brady, Texas, northwest of Austin.

- **Perforating, flowback water, piping, and surface equipment** ($1.2 million, 29% of completion costs). In addition to perforation, well completion requires a huge amount of water—typically between two and five million gallons—to accomplish the desired number of frack stages. Furthermore, environmental regulations have strict and costly requirements for the treatment and disposal of *flowback water*, or water returning to the surface from the well. Lastly, well completion includes piping and surface equipment to get the hydrocarbons to market.

- **Labor, communications, insurance, and other costs** ($0.7 million, 16% of completion costs). This includes the support costs essential to drilling the well.

Operating Expenses

Well drilling and completion costs can be considered the *fixed* costs of production. Once the well is producing hydrocarbons, there are a number of *variable* operating costs. These variable costs may be broadly grouped into two buckets: (1) operating expenses and (2) royalties and taxes.

In our representative Wolfcamp well, typical operating costs are estimated at $10/bbl for each barrel of oil produced, $1/Mcf for natural gas, and $0.30/Mcf for NGLs. In some cases, costs for natural gas and NGLs can be incorporated by the well operator into processing agreements known as *percent of proceeds*. In such deals, a gas processor typically takes responsibility for marketing the residue gas and NGLs and kicks back a percentage of the net sales to the producer. Instead of using such a structure, which varies from one instance to the next, the cost structure used in our representative model assumes that the operator is directly marketing the gas and NGL production.

The operating expenses estimated above are actually made up of a number of direct costs associated with operating each individual well, along with the gathering system connecting the wells to a processing plant or pipeline interconnect. These operating expenses can be split into the following two components.

Lease operating expenses. These are simply the day-to-day costs of operating the well on the land leased from the owner of the mineral rights. These expenses include:

- **Labor cost.** A typical well crew worker can earn in excess of $100,000 a year with duties covering the operation and the maintenance of field equipment.
- **Water disposal costs.** Vast quantities of water can be produced from the well along with hydrocarbons. Like the flowback that occurs during hydraulic fracturing, produced water is regulated by the Environmental Protection Act (EPA) and Clean Water Act (CWA). In accordance with these regulations, an operator must properly dispose of produced water.
- **Fuel costs to operate wellhead equipment and pumps.** Variation in fuel costs can have a significant impact on operating expenses.
- **Property taxes.** Depending on where the lease is located, the operator may have to pay an *ad valorem* tax on the value of the property, which may also include a tax on the value of the equipment used to operate the well.
- **Other expenses.** This includes materials and supplies used to operate the well and insurance.

Gathering and transportation costs. These are the costs of moving the hydrocarbon commodity out of the hole in the ground from which it emerged and routing it through various upstream gathering systems to midstream storage and pipelines, including:

- **Gathering expenses.** The costs to move the hydrocarbons, usually in small diameter short pipelines from the wellhead to field treatment facilities.
- **Treatment costs.** Hydrocarbon treatment includes any combination of dehydration (removing water), removing carbon dioxide (CO_2), and removing hydrogen sulfide (H_2S), called sweetening, each at a corresponding cost.

- **Compression.** The costs of compression in order to move gas from gathering system and treatment facilities onto market transportation pipelines operating at a much higher pressure than gathering systems.
- **Extraction of NGLs.** NGLs are removed from the natural gas when required to meet gas quality specifications and when it makes economic sense to do so. These processing costs are included in the cost of operating and marketing production from the well.

Production Taxes

In most U.S. oil and gas fields, producers are required to pay a production or severance tax based on the gross production revenue generated at the wellhead. *Gross production revenue* is the sale price of the oil and gas, less the transportation cost to get it to market. Our representative well economics uses a 4.5% rate for crude oil production taxes.

Royalty Rates

The *royalty* is an agreed-upon percentage of the gross production revenue, before production costs, paid to the mineral rights owner. Usually, producers do not directly own either the land or the mineral rights for drilling locations and must lease those mineral rights from the owner. Bear in mind the owner of the mineral rights may or may not be the surface landowner. The minerals lease will typically include a bonus, paid up front (and ignored in this analysis since these figures assume half-cycle economics, as described previously), and a royalty rate.

This analysis uses a typical royalty rate for the area of 25%. So, for oil, if production starts at 475 barrels per day at $100/bbl, gross revenue from oil would be about $47,500 per day. If gas production is 1,100 Mcf/d and the gas price is $4.50/Mcf, gross revenue before production costs would be about $4,950 per day. In total, the owner of the mineral rights would receive approximately $13,000 per day [($47,000 + $4,950) * 25%].

Estimating Well Production

Two of the most important factors to get right with any analysis of well economics are the initial production rate per day (IP rate) and the rate at which production from the well declines. Ideally, producers want a high initial rate of production and a slow rate of decline so that they can

Modeling Multiple-Commodity Streams

Modeling triple-play, multiple-commodity (crude oil, natural gas, and NGLs) production economics, such as the representative Wolfcamp well in this example, might be a little more complex than for a single-commodity well. However, it is a good problem to have in today's volatile price environment. If gas prices are below $3.50, some dry gas wells may be under water, meaning their economics do not justify drilling new wells. Even natural gas wells currently in the black might not recover their $7.5-million drilling and completion costs for many years. However, the picture for wells that produce predominantly crude oil can be different, dependent on the price of crude oil. In the days of $100/bbl crude, IRRs for crude oil wells in shale plays of 40% to 70% were common and over 100% was not unheard of. As this book goes to press, the price of crude oil is below $50/bbl, but that does not mean that some wells are not profitable. In fact, the well in our representative model has a crude oil breakeven price (at 0% IRR) of $34.83/bbl. This means the producer is neither making nor losing money at this price and is making an attractive return if the crude oil price is above that level.

Essentially, the **three-commodity model** is just that: one single set of assumptions for the cost of the well and three revenue streams, based on IP rates, decline curves, and prices for the three hydrocarbons produced. The model used in this example makes a number of simplifying assumptions to make the inputs easier to manage. The most important assumptions are these:

Assumption #1: The decline rate of all three commodities is assumed to be the same. In actuality, most of the time the mix of hydrocarbon production from an individual well changes as the decline rate of the different commodities varies over time. But to keep things simple for this model, we assume our representative well maintains the same mix of hydrocarbons, and thus the same decline rate can be used for all three commodities.

Assumption #2: NGL volumes can be calculated based on the Btu content (the gallons per thousand cubic feet of gas or GPM) of the inlet gas stream at a processing plant. Thus the NGL output volume is a function of the natural gas volume. Likewise, the gas volume is reduced by the naturally occurring **shrinkage** which occurs when NGLs are extracted from the natural gas.

Assumption #3: It is assumed that the price for NGLs is fixed in relation to the price of crude oil. Economics in this model are calculated on the total costs of the well and the sum of the sales from the three revenue streams.

get as much of the well's cash flow as possible in the early years, which greatly improves the well's economic value. However, if the well is produced too fast, it can impair the well's long-term productivity. Producers must balance economics with production engineering to arrive at just the right flow rates. Making the calculations to determine these flow numbers is part science and part art. Developing the production plan in a producer organization typically falls to reservoir engineers, whose job it is to estimate well production, production decline, and well life. Reservoir engineers use complex geophysical models to arrive at these estimates. Such models and the data required to use them for particular wells and plays are rarely available outside production companies.

There are various methods of approximating the results from these complex models that the rest of us—analysts and investors with access only to publicly available data—must be content to use. Public production data is usually derived from producer presentations to investors or from data published by state oil and gas resource departments. This state data is collected by a number of data vendors who provide access, along with useful software designed to help analysts forecast production.

The minimum data elements required to estimate production are the following:

1. The IP rate,
2. the decline rate over time (usually either monthly or annually), and
3. the life of the well.

Given these three variables, the question is then how to smooth out the decline curve so that it most accurately represents the actual decline rate experienced at most wells. There are a number of methodologies used to make this calculation. If you are interested in the details, see *The Domino Effect* website at **www.dominoeffect.com/declinecurves**.

The technique used in The Domino Effect Production Economics Model is the *Arps Curve*. This method was developed by a mining engineer named J. J. Arps and detailed in his 1944 paper, "Analysis of Decline Curves."[1] Effectively, the Arps method fits a hyperbolic curve to a series of decline rates. For our purposes here, suffice to say it is a way to mathematically smooth out a production curve so it looks like the downward sloping line in Figure 9.2 (downward sloping line, left axis).

Estimated Ultimate Recovery (EUR) and BOE

The bottom line for a production estimate is the Estimated Ultimate Recovery, or *EUR*, which is the total volume of recoverable hydrocarbons from a well. EUR is simply the cumulative production forecast for the well over its life. In the Permian/Midland Basin, typical EURs have risen healthily as producers have moved closer to the sweet spots in the play, shifted from vertical to horizontal wells, and have continuously improved their drilling techniques.

For a multiple-commodity well, EUR is frequently measured in *barrels of oil equivalent*, or *BOE*. It puts volumes of crude oil, natural gas, and NGLs on an equal footing by converting all output into a volume equivalent to crude oil. The official Internal Revenue Service definition of BOE is the energy (on a Btu basis) obtained from burning one barrel of oil. Practically speaking, BOE is the volume of crude oil production in barrels plus the volume of natural gas production (measured in thousands of cubic feet, or Mcf) converted to equivalent barrels of crude oil. The conversion is based on the assumption that a barrel of crude oil has approximately 5.8 million Btus, and that a Mcf of gas has approximately 1,000 Btus. Since an Mcf has 1,000 cubic feet and a cubic foot has 1,000 Btus, a Mcf has 1.0 million Btus. That means that a barrel of crude oil has 5.8 times more Btus than a Mcf of gas (5.8 million divided by 1.0 million). So BOE is calculated by adding the volume of crude production in barrels to the volume of gas production in equivalent barrels, which is gas in Mcf divided by 5.8.

For example, the representative well examined in this chapter has a crude oil IP rate of 475 bbl/d and a gas IP rate of 838 Mcf/d (after shrinkage). Ignoring NGLs for now, the daily BOE would be 620 BOE/d as shown in the calculation below.

$$475 \text{ bbl/d oil} + (838 \text{ Mcf/d gas} / 5.8) = 620 \text{ BOE/d}$$

The presence of NGLs in richer natural gas makes the calculation somewhat more complex. There are a number of approaches available to account for NGLs. In this model, we simply add the volume of NGL barrels to the crude oil barrel total and calculate the natural gas BOE based on gas production after shrinkage. The representative well has a NGL IP rate of 170 bbl/d, thus the total BOE is $620 + 170 = 790$ BOE/d.

The example above demonstrates the BOE calculation; however, the number most often expressed in BOE is the EUR. When measuring EUR on a BOE basis, it is typically necessary to quote the numbers in thousands of barrels, or MBOE. For example, the calculated EUR on an MBOE basis for our representative well is 1,158 MBOE.

The Relationship between IP, Decline Rate, and EUR

The relationship between IP rate, the decline rate, and EUR is extremely important to well economics. Figure 9.2 plots the relationship between the daily crude oil production curve (downward sloping line, left axis) and the cumulative crude oil production curve (upward sloping line, right axis) for the 25-year assumed lifetime of our representative Wolfcamp well.

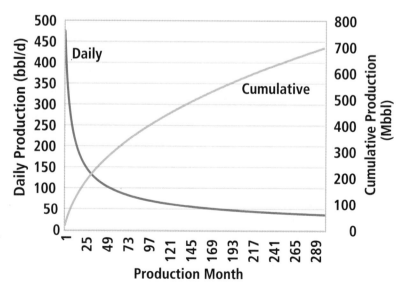

Figure 9.2. Daily oil production curve and cumulative production curve

The well has a relatively high crude oil IP rate of 475 bbl/d (downward sloping line, first month of production). The rate of production falls off steeply: 55% in the first year, 30% the second year, and a declining percentage each year thereafter until the decline curve comes close to flattening out (numbers detailed in the following table). By the end of the fifth year (60 months), the well is still producing about 93 bbl/d. Even after 300 months (25 years), the well is still expected to be producing 36 bbl/d.

Month	0	12	24	36	48	60
Annual Decline	55%	30%	20%	15%	10%	9%
Annual Production bbl/d	475	212	152	123	105	93
Cumulative Production MMbbl	14	120	183	232	273	309

Table 9.1. Declining Production

The upward sloping line in Figure 9.2 is cumulative production over the life of the well. Because of the high IP rate, the cumulative production builds quickly in the early years and then continues to grow at a slower rate over the entire life of the well, eventually reaching an EUR of about 700 Mbbl (cumulative production in year 25). Almost half of the well's EUR is produced in the first five years. From an economic perspective, this front-loaded cash flow is good news. In effect, the producer's well costs are recovered sooner, which improves the discounted cash flow rate of return for the well.

Commodity Prices

The final variables needed for our model are prices for each of the three commodities. These prices should reflect expected market prices, adjusted for regional price differences, and costs for delivering the energy commodities to the trading hubs. Such prices are generally available from price reporting services or from futures exchanges.

The price assumptions used for our model are $70 bbl for crude oil and $3.50/MMBtu for natural gas. Although the model provides the functionality to escalate these prices (presumably in accordance with future price expectations). To keep the example simple here, they are held constant for the life of the well.

Model Results

The model itself and more detailed instructions on its use can be downloaded from *The Domino Effect* website at **www.dominoeffect.com/prodecon**. The summary results are as follows: this representative Wolfcamp well produced a discounted cash flow (DCF) of $10.2 million, also known as the *net present value*, or *NPV*. The discounted cash flows are the cumulative pre-tax cash flows per year, summed for all three commodities discounted at 10% with the $7.5-million well cost subtracted out. That discount factor could be the interest rate the producer pays to finance drilling and completing the well, or an internal company interest rate used to compare alternative investments. When comparing well economics across companies, or in order to assess the generic return for an entire basin, the 10% before-tax figure is frequently used as an industry standard. For more information on understanding discounted cash flows and returns, visit **www.dominoeffect.com/dcf**.

The *discounted IRR* is the rate which discounts the series of before-tax net cash flows to zero. The calculated value for the representative Wolfcamp well is 31%, a very attractive return. To put that number in perspective, we can use the model to run a sensitivity case. If the crude oil price is reduced to only $34/bbl, and the natural gas price is held at $3.50/MMBtu, the rate of return comes out zero. This means the well is *breakeven* on a discounted cash flow rate-of-return basis at a crude price of $34/bbl.

What the Production Economics Model Reveals about the Wolfcamp

In walking you through all of this operational and financial detail, the intent is not to illustrate the definitive economics Permian producers are realizing. After all, each part of the play is different, each well is different, the expertise each producer brings to drilling and completion technologies is different, and prices change on a daily basis. There is a wide gap between successful wells and those that are not so successful across the Permian, and so there is really no such thing as the average well.

Instead, the goal here is to illustrate how Permian producers are achieving such attractive economics. This representative well cost $7.5 million to drill but generated *$5.5 million in cash flow in the first year!* After only five years, the well will have produced almost $12 million in discounted cash flows. These projections are possible not only because crude oil price projections in this analysis remain relatively attractive but also because crude oil proceeds are supplemented by substantial revenues from natural gas and NGLs—a Permian triple-commodity play.

Permian horizontal plays are quickly evolving into some of the best in the country. Here, as elsewhere, the technology that started the dramatic expansion of shale production over the past decade is constantly evolving and becoming more efficient. Costs are decreasing while rates of production are increasing. That is doubly good news for rates of return. Of course, for individual producers it depends on where they are located, the specific plays they target, their ability to have takeaway capacity available when they need it, the know-how they bring to the drilling and completion process, and the all-important variable: price. These well results clearly indicate that rates of return for shale wells can be extremely attractive if the right combination of factors are brought together. The next two chapters explore this combination of factors and how, in different mixes, they can coalesce to produce big winners for shale producers.

Note
1. The original paper may be read at the following link, courtesy of Texas A&M University. http://bit.ly/1JKRptR

Chapter 10

All Shales Are
Not Created Equal

THE HORIZONTAL PERMIAN WOLFCAMP INVESTMENT USED AS THE REPRE-
sentative well in the last chapter realized an attractive IRR of 31%, based
on a crude oil price assumption of $70/bbl. One of the most significant
factors that made its economics so attractive is the fact that the well is a triple
play. The combined sales of all three commodities from the same well make the
well economics very attractive.

But not all wells with attractive economics have to be triple plays. Some of
the best economic results in the United States can be achieved in the dry gas-only
part of the Marcellus in northeastern Pennsylvania–if producers in that region
have access to pipeline transportation capacity that gets their gas to good markets.
Liquid-rich gas production from Eagle Ford wells in South Texas can generate superior returns when commodity prices are right. Some vertical wells in the Permian
which don't even meet our arbitrary definition of a shale well can yield reasonably
good returns if crude oil prices are in the $70s per barrel range or above. However,
if we turn to one of the first big shale gas producers in the United States, the Haynesville in northwest Louisiana and East Texas, we see that returns are no better
than average, with most drilling investments rated poor. Just a few years ago, the
Haynesville was hot and returns were attractive. What changed for the Haynesville? Why can shale economics work for the Marcellus, Eagle Ford, and Permian, but not for the Haynesville and some of the other first-generation shale plays
like the Fayetteville and Barnett? This chapter addresses these questions.

The Big Three Variables

It goes without saying that producers want to make as much money as they can. This is why they are in business; they want to drill wells where the rate of return is highest. That said, not all drilling locations are alike. As we've seen, a number of variables go into a producer's rate-of-return calculation. While all are important, there are three primary determinants upon which wells win—or lose—economically. We touched upon these in Chapter 9, but a recap will help you better understand some of the differences, distinctions, and anomalies just mentioned.

The first key variable is the cost of drilling and completing the well. Shale wells are expensive. Horizontal wells have long laterals that take a lot of time and sophisticated equipment to drill. Shale wells in a number of plays are relatively deep; the deeper the well, the more time and money it takes to drill it. The whole process of fracking—hauling in sand, water, and other frac fluids, setting up multiple frac stages, pumping the fluids into the formation under exceedingly high pressure, and disposing of the waste products—costs a lot of money. Much more than a conventional vertical well. Since it is so expensive, the producer must have a way to recoup all these costs, or there is no way an acceptable rate of return can be achieved.

The second key variable is the IP rate, which establishes the magnitude of the well's revenue stream. As pointed out in previous chapters, the IP rates for shale wells can be many times those of conventional vertical wells. Most shale wells enjoy high IP rates due to the more recent advances in technologies used to drill and complete the wells, in particular horizontal drilling and hydraulic fracturing. You might think that the decline rate would be considered one of our key variables, and it is important in figuring well economics. However, we have not included decline rate in our list of key shale-well economic variables because it is almost always a given that shale wells will have steep decline curves. As long as the IP rate is at a high enough starting point, the steep rate of decline is simply the *modus operandi* of shale development and can be expected to be somewhere in the 50–90% range in the first year. For that reason, the decline rate is not on our short list of the most important economic variables.

The third key variable is the price of the commodity. There is no variable more important than price in well economics calculations. But as we use the term here, price is not just a single number. Instead, price is the *revenue per unit of production* generated by selling production from a well. There are three aspects of price we must consider whenever discussing well economics. They are commodity value, netback, and the commodity mix.

The Components of Price

The first component of price is the *commodity value*, which generally is the price realized at a liquid hub or location where energy commodities are bought and sold. You are already familiar with these major hubs from Chapters 5, 6, and 7: Henry Hub, Louisiana for natural gas, Mont Belvieu, Texas for NGLs, and Cushing, Oklahoma for crude oil. Commodity value is the number that gets all the attention from the media when prices rise or fall.

The second aspect to price is *netback*, the price a producer receives, commonly referred to as *netback at the wellhead*. It is the price received once all the treating, processing, gathering, and transportation costs have been paid. Thus it is the commodity value less the costs to get the hydrocarbons from the well to the hub, which yields the price received *at the well*. There can be big netback differences from one play to another, due to a number of factors. The most important one in the shale era is usually access to transportation capacity to get the commodity to a liquid market hub. Consider these examples:

In early 2012, transportation capacity for crude oil out of the Bakken was constrained. The result was a crude price of $75/bbl, which was 25% below the $100/bbl crude price at the Cushing hub at the time. If the Bakken producer had access to transportation capacity to move the crude to the Cushing (about $10/bbl by pipeline), the netback would be the Cushing price less the transportation cost to get there, or $90/bbl ($100 less the $10 transport cost). Otherwise, the producer would be stuck taking a price $15/bbl lower.

A similar situation has existed since 2013 for natural gas in the northeastern Pennsylvania Marcellus region, which sometimes was discounted several dollars below the price at Henry Hub. If the producer has the pipeline transportation capacity to get to higher-priced markets like Boston, the netbacks can be well above Henry. If not, the producer is stuck with netbacks well below Henry Hub.

The third aspect of price is *commodity mix*, or the combination of hydrocarbon commodities the well yields. Each hydrocarbon has a different value, sometimes radically different. Consider an example scenario for a triple-play (oil, gas, and NGL) well in the period before crude oil prices crashed. The price of crude oil at our wellhead is $100/bbl, the price of natural gas is $4.50/MMBtu, and the price of NGLs is 40% of crude oil, or $40/bbl. Recall the estimate of 5.8 MMBtus in a barrel of crude. Thus on a Btu basis, the price of crude oil is $17.24/MMBtu. That is nearly *four times* the price of natural gas at the time. Or consider a post-crash, first-quarter 2015 value. Crude oil at $50/bbl would be the equivalent of $8.62/MMBtu gas, while the price of gas was about $3.00/MMBtu, again a factor of almost three. NGLs are not as attractive as crude oil but are usually more attractively priced than gas. So it should come as no surprise that in an era of high crude prices, any producer with the option will switch as much of their drilling budget as possible to crude oil, followed by gas yielding significant quantities of NGLs, and will only fall back to dry natural gas if it is the only DBH available. Of course there are exceptions to that rule, such as dry gas wells in the Marcellus and the Utica in Ohio that have huge IP rates and thus high rates of return. But as a general rule over the past few years throughout most of the United States, the more liquids, the better.

The Good, The Bad, The Ugly

It is the relationship between these big three variables—well cost, IP rate, and price—that determines which wells make money and therefore where producers drill, where production growth happens, and ultimately how the drill-bit hydrocarbon markets behave. The big three variables can be combined in a number of ways to achieve winning rates of return. Conversely, just because a particular well enjoys one advantageous variable does not mean it will achieve an attractive rate of return. To clarify these relationships, here are a few examples.

■ Given that we have just examined the Permian Wolfcamp well in detail, it is a good place to start. At a cost of $7.5 million, it is a middle-of-the-road well, certainly expensive relative to vertical wells, but at the low end of horizontal well investment in the Permian based on 2014 cost levels. The lower cost is largely because it is a short lateral (5,000 feet) well. Its IP rate is also middle of the road, with a crude oil IP at 475, NGLs at 170, and natural gas at 145 BOE (838 Mcf X 5.8). Thus the total IP rate is 790 BOE/d, which ranks as a high-medium range well on a BOE basis. The price at the wellhead is based on $70/bbl crude oil, $28/bbl for NGLs, and $3.50/MMBtu for natural gas. Its DBH mix is 60% crude, 18% gas, and 22% NGLs. Consequently, the weighted average price on a BOE basis is about $52 per barrel, again in the high-medium range. As you've seen, put that in the model and the economic results are in an *attractive rate-of-return* range.

■ Near the other end of the spectrum is the Haynesville, former darling of the shale revolution but relegated to the backwater of basins for the past few years, suffering from a very low rate of drilling and declining production. Haynesville wells are deep, and therefore the cost was upwards of $10 million per well again, based on 2014 cost levels. Let's say a 100% gas Haynesville well has an IP rate at the high end of about 10 MMcf/d, which equates to around 1,700 BOE/d. Unfortunately with a gas-only well, if we assume a price of $3.50/MMBtu, the BOE price works out to be only $20/bbl. At $2.50/MMBtu, the BOE price drops to $14.50/bbl. Obviously both of these numbers are at the very low end of the range. That is enough to take the rate of return below zero. With an expensive well cost and a low product price, the result is a *not-so attractive rate of return* that does not support an investment in drilling.

■ Does the Haynesville example mean rates of return for gas-only wells will always be low? The answer is a resounding no. As noted earlier, some of the most attractive wells in the country are gas-only. If producers improve drilling performance to boost IP rates, or if natural gas prices increase, rates of return in the Haynesville could improve significantly.

As you can see, there is more than one way to win at the shale game. Whether a given well will earn awesome returns, passable returns, or be economically under water depends primarily on the relationship between the big three variables.

There are no standards or rules for what makes a high well cost or a low IP rate, but toward our goal of helping you understand how these numbers fit together, we have created an arbitrary grading scale in Table 10.1. Certainly some industry experts will find all sorts of fault with our subjective definition of these variables, but this table is not for experts. It is a simple template that describes the workings of production economics for those who want to understand why some shale plays work and others do not. As you will see, we can learn a lot by using the same three variables we have been discussing.

	Well Cost in the Millions	IP Rate in BOE per day	Price in BOE
High	>$8	>900	>$70
Medium	$3–8	200–900	$50–$70
Low	<$3	<200	<$50

Table 10.1. Arbitrary grading scale

The first column is well cost. Three million dollars to drill a well is cheap. A well below $3 million is probably a vertical well, but not necessarily. Wells above $8 million are getting expensive. A very expensive well is one that costs more than $12 million to drill.

The second column is the initial production (IP) rate measured in barrels of oil equivalent, or BOE per day. We use BOE because it is an industry-accepted convention for putting oil and NGL wells on the same footing as natural gas wells. A well over 900 bbl/d is a big well, while a well that produces less than 300 bbl/d BOE is small. Monster wells get up into the thousands of barrels per day, while tiny wells might produce only 10 barrels per day. The vast majority of economically successful wells are in the 200–900 bbl/d BOE range we classify as medium.

The third column is price. As we defined it earlier, price is the revenue per unit of production generated by selling the particular hydrocarbon product(s) per BOE. That means this measure of price is a weighted average of crude oil, natural gas, and NGLs, all converted to BOE to get the numbers to an apples-to-apples basis. A quick refresher, based on mid-2014 figures: Crude oil was going for the highest price, a number approaching \$100/bbl. NGLs were selling for less than half of the crude oil price, closer to \$40/bbl. Natural gas is sold in heating value units, dollars per millions of Btus or \$/MMBtu. Converting a typical natural gas price in mid-2014 of \$4.50/MMBtu to BOE (using the 5.8 gas to BOE factor), we get a price of only \$26/bbl. Those are big differences in price between the various commodities. Thus when there are big differences between commodity prices, the mix of commodities (the split between oil, gas, and NGLs) can make a significant difference in the price received at the wellhead. Using those mid-2014 prices, a well that produces mostly oil would have an average BOE price approaching \$100/bbl, while a well that produces mostly gas would have an average BOE price approaching \$26/bbl. That is what makes anything above \$70/bbl a high BOE price in our table, while numbers below \$50/bbl are classified as low prices.

The Shortcut Formula

Chapter 9 offered a relatively complex model for calculating production economics. This chapter identified the three most important variables that determine whether a given well will yield an attractive rate of return or turn out to be a bust. You might wonder if there is a quick-and-dirty rule of thumb that will allow you to judge whether a well is attractive by just knowing the values for the three big variables. Yes, such a rule of thumb can be proffered, referenced here as the **BOE payout**. That calculation is as follows:

$$\text{BOE Payout} = \frac{\text{Well Cost}}{[(\text{IP BOE}) \times (\text{BOE Price})] \times 365}$$

Basically, this calculation takes the IP rate times the price, converts it to an annual value, and then divides the well cost by the result. The BOE payout is the number of years it takes for revenues to equal the required investment in the well. If that number is less than two, the well will achieve a very attractive rate of return. Over seven, not so good. Somewhere in between, the BOE payout will probably be acceptable. This rule of thumb certainly does not replace well economics, but it does provide a simpified way, knowing very few pieces of information, to judge the economics of a well.

More than One Way to Skin a Cat

The point of all of this is that there is more than one way for a producer to win in the shale game. Triple-play, combined-commodity wells can work great in the Permian, while dry gas wells in the northeast Marcellus can achieve equally high returns. The outlook for the shale revolution is long and bright because there are so many ways to win. As market conditions change, producers can and will adapt their targeted plays and investment strategies to maintain attractive economics and keep drilling.

Hold that thought as we continue to drill down into a more comprehensive discussion of why shale has had such an impact in Chapter 11.

Chapter 11

Why Shale Changes Everything

WHAT IS IT ABOUT SHALE THAT HAS MADE SUCH A DIFFERENCE IN EN-ergy production? How could technologies that have been around for many decades transform the U.S. energy market from one of shortage to one of abundance, seemingly overnight? What are the implications for the future of energy in America?

The answers to these questions are directly tied to what you have learned so far about dominoes, the DBHs, and production economics, summarized in the following points:

- The application of shale technologies has had a huge, positive impact on production economics.

- A fortuitous combination of variables in the production economics equation for shale wells can yield extremely attractive returns for producers—when the price is right.

- This combination has driven high levels of investment in oil and gas production, generating record growth in production volumes.

- This surplus of energy resources has fundamentally changed the way oil, natural gas, and NGLs are transported, processed, and used in the United States.

- Even with lower prices, producers can still make more natural gas, NGLs, and certain grades of crude oil than the United States can use.

The implication is the potential for increasing exports—not just NGLs or gas, *but crude—a development that will be a common theme in chapters to come. It is not an overstatement to say, "shale changes everything." The United States is headed toward becoming a huge supplier of hydrocarbon commodities to the world, starting with NGLs and then moving to natural gas. The year 2014 saw global crude oil production exceed demand and crush global crude oil prices, which has broad implications for everything from foreign policy to the balance of payments to the economy at large. In other words, everything.*

High Returns Equal High Production Growth

In the last two chapters, we reviewed the big three variables driving production economics, pointing out that some plays have considerably better producer returns than others. *It is those economics that drive producers to drill in the areas with attractive returns and to back off drilling where returns are not so attractive.*

That higher level of drilling activity happened in a variety of basins across the United States, depending on the fortuitous combinations of our three big economic variables described in Chapter 9. For most of the shale revolution, crude oil has delivered better returns than gas because the price was higher. However, even at relatively lower prices, gas can also be good if the IP rate is high and the well cost is moderate. Gas plays can be good if the gas is very rich in liquids content and NGL prices are attractive, giving the producer the opportunity to make up for low gas prices with large volume NGL sales. The underlying theme is no surprise: bigger is better. The bigger the well—meaning the greater the production volume produced by the well—the better the economics (all other things being equal). The process is self-selecting, meaning that producers do their best to select drilling locations that are most likely to yield big wells. The implications are obvious and profound: when producers drill bigger wells, total production increases.

A New World for Transportation, Processing, and Demand

The increases in shale production have been happening in parts of the country that have never had big production volumes (Marcellus, Bakken, and Eagle Ford), or have not seen significant production growth in a very long time (Permian and Anadarko), which is reversing transportation flows. It has resulted in revolutionary developments in U.S. energy markets. Consider a few examples:

Since the early 1950s, the northeastern U.S. has received most of its natural gas via huge pipelines bringing supplies from the Gulf Coast, Midwest, Canada, and, more recently, the Rockies. Soon those pipelines will no longer be necessary in order to bring supplies to the Northeast, due to increases in production from the Marcellus and Utica. In fact, many of those pipelines are spending hundreds of millions of dollars to *reverse* their flow so they can send gas from Appalachia to Canada, the Midwest, and even the Gulf Coast. Much of these new supplies will be used to fire new power generation facilities, fuel new industrial plants, and provide supplies for the export of gas in the form of LNG. Combined, these developments completely reverse the behavior of pipeline flows, prices, and storage requirements for the natural gas industry across North America.

Until the shale revolution, the United States imported up to 70% of its crude oil. The largest volume of imports came into the Gulf Coast and moved up pipelines to Midcontinent and Midwest refineries. With increasing production from the Bakken and the Anadarko, plus growing imports from Canada, imports into the Gulf Coast are no longer necessary to supply Midcontinent and Midwest refineries. In fact, suppliers from areas north of the Gulf Coast now produce more crude oil than the refineries can use. This has stimulated huge investments in new pipelines and changes to existing crude oil pipelines to move those surpluses down to the Gulf Coast. As with gas, this completely changes flow patterns, prices, and storage requirements.

With producers moving to drill for more wet, high-Btu gas, NGL production grew astronomically, so much in fact that the United States already produces more than it can use. At the start of the shale revolution, there were not nearly enough natural gas processing facilities to handle all of the new NGL extraction. Since around 2011, more than 75 new processing plants have been built, and another 75 are slated to be built throughout the remainder of this decade. Twenty new pipeline projects have been built to bring the additional NGL volume to market, and another ten are being constructed. All of this increased NGL supply has stimulated investment in additional petrochemical plants for the NGL product that could experience the most growth: ethane. Several new olefin crackers are slated to be built. To reiterate the point, this results in changes in flow patterns, prices, and demand.

Imports Become Exports

Even with increased demand from gas-fired power generation, industrial plants, and petrochemical plants, producers have the potential to produce more drill-bit hydrocarbons than the United States can use. If prices remain high enough to encourage further increases in production, there is only one solution available to the market: exports. Natural gas surpluses will be exported in the form of liquefied natural gas, LNG. Several such facilities have been approved by the U.S. government and a number are being constructed. NGLs will be exported from a number of new facilities around the country, with new export docks and several expansions of existing docks being built just on the Gulf Coast. Crude oil exports have not been permitted by U.S. regulations for many decades, but this too may be changing. Crude has, for some time, been processed in refineries with its surplus gasoline and diesel fuel exported. One way or another, surpluses will leave U.S. shores.

Of course, the fact that the discussion here is about energy exports instead of energy imports is the most radical concept being driven by the shale revolution. It was not many years ago that the market, policy makers, and the public at large *absolutely knew* that the United States would be facing dwindling supplies of oil and gas for as far into the future as anyone cared to forecast. Ultimately, they predicted supplies would just run out, leaving the United States totally reliant on imports and renewables.

The shale revolution has turned that "absolutely known" fact on its head.

Why did so many miss this revolutionary turn in the market? Well, one reason is simple to understand: human nature. The belief in a hydrocarbon energy shortage had been pounded into us for many years. It was difficult to believe that, all of a sudden, something called fracking and drilling wells sideways could change everything about energy markets. The other reason was a lack of understanding about the production economics of shale.

As we've demonstrated in the past three chapters, it turns out the big three factors or variables of production economics come together in a number of different basins across the United States, but they do so in different ways. There is no one single formula or cookie-cutter approach that works for all shale drilling. In many ways, shale production remains as much art as it is science, with producers learning how to "break the code" in different basins and individual plays. That was an inconvenient truth for a lot of so-called experts who continually predicted the shale revolution was either an illusion or a flash in the pan. As you have seen again and again in this book, neither statement has any truth to it. Neither the *hows* nor the *whys* of the shale revolution are understandable in simple sound bites or bullet points. To understand what is going on today—and where this revolution is headed—you need to get into the details. We've just done that on the upstream side of the market. Now we turn to the midstream and downstream segments: where all these hydrocarbon products are heading.

Chapter 12

Movin' Things Around: Energy Logistical Networks

CERTAINLY SOME OF THE MOST IMPORTANT—AND VISIBLE—ASPECTS OF THE *domino effect are the changes underway in the transportation of the drill-bit hydrocarbons. The logistical infrastructure moving oil, NGLs, and gas from upstream production fields to downstream customers is complex and multidimensional. Each of the DBHs can move by pipeline, ship, barge, or truck. And all of them must be moved. You might think that is an obvious statement, but energy is worthless unless it can be moved to a location where it can be used. That simple assertion has huge implications for the drill-bit hydrocarbons markets and is the reason for this great irony of the domino effect:*

Surplus begets shortage.

Contemplate this fact for a minute. It means that an increase in supply can—and in the shale world frequently does—grow to the point where it exceeds the capacity of infrastructure (pipelines, rail facilities, loading docks, etc.) to accommodate that supply. The term used in the industry is takeaway capacity. *Increases in production (the surplus) can result in a shortage of takeaway capacity. Thus surplus of the commodity begets shortage of infrastructure. This great irony has been responsible for toppling more dominoes than any other aspect of the shale revolution.*

To understand how this great irony is rippling through the DBH transportation infrastructure, you need to know how the infrastructure works. There are solid, economic, and tangible reasons why different DBHs move as they do.

Which DBHs move by rail? What products can be moved by pipe, ship, or truck? Which transport mode is optimal for a particular commodity and why? These are some of the questions addressed in this chapter.

Location, Location, Location

For energy to have value, it must be in the right place—in other words, where it is needed—and at the right time. For example, energy needs to be on hand to provide heat for a city when cold weather hits, to fuel a jet when it lands at the airport, or to cook your BBQ at the next holiday gathering. If a DBH is delivered to a location where there is no demand, it must be stored, a costly proposition, and storage is not always available. Here are a few examples:

Natural gas prices in New Jersey during the polar vortex of the winter of 2014 spiked up to $123/MMBtu, while just 150 miles to the west in Pennsylvania the price of gas on the same day was one thirtieth of that price, about $4/MMBtu.

It was a similar story that same year when propane wholesale prices blasted up to nearly $5.00/gallon in the Midwest market, while down on the Gulf Coast the price was no higher than $1.55/gallon.

In the first half of 2014, crude oil was worth more than $100 per barrel in major Gulf Coast refinery centers, while theoretically it might be worth only a fraction of that amount in Cedar Rapids, Iowa. Why? There are no refineries there to process it, nor any infrastructure to store it. Remember, crude oil only has value once it is refined.

Ethane in North Dakota is sometimes flared, along with surplus natural gas, as a waste product because there are no pipelines to move it to market. But on the Gulf Coast, the very same hydrocarbon—ethane—is being used to make petrochemicals worth many times its feedstock value.

There is nothing atypical about these differences in value. In fact, such differences are an important feature of all three DBH markets every day. Understanding what makes these price differentials change over time is what much of the business of buying, selling, and trading the DBHs is all about.

Networks within Networks

The logistical systems used to move drill-bit hydrocarbons are networks, just like the Internet or the power grid. Individual pipelines, trucks, railcars, barges, and ships are all pieces of large, encompassing network systems. Cumulatively, these networks within networks represent the core energy market infrastructure. In Chapter 5, we examined the components of the natural gas network using the graphic in Figure 12.1 as a reference. In fact, this network structure is essentially the same for the other two DBHs, NGLs and crude oil. DBHs flow into a network at a point of production, move long distances along major long-line transportation systems, may be stored along the way, and then are distributed to refineries, petrochemical plants, factories, generation plants, businesses, and homes. These networks, connecting supply with demand, comprise the core mechanism determining the behavior of DBH energy markets.

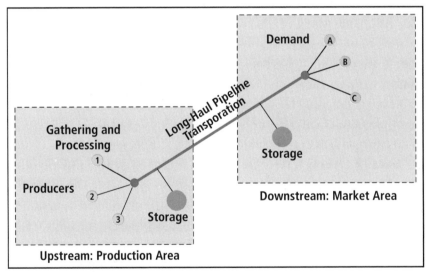

Figure 12.1. Natural gas network

Infrastructure

What kind of infrastructure is necessary for any of these networks to work? It depends on three primary factors:

1. the *physical characteristics* of what is being transported,
2. the *distance and terrain* over which the transport is required, and
3. the *volume* that needs to be moved.

Physical characteristics. Some DBHs are a lot easier to move around than others. The choice of transport for moving hydrocarbons is mostly based on two factors. One, can the DBH be stored at atmospheric pressures and temperatures, or must it be maintained under pressure or moved at very cold temperatures? This question deals with vapor pressure. That characteristic of DBHs is discussed in Chapter 6. Two, what is the most economical physical state in which to move the DBH (liquid or gas)? This question deals with a characteristic called density. Consider the following examples of how these physical characteristics determine how DBHs are transported.

Vapor pressure. You don't need a special tank to hold motor gasoline because its vapor pressure is low. It remains a liquid at atmospheric temperatures and pressures for an extended period of time. The gas can for your lawn mower is just a simple metal or plastic can. On the other hand, you need a specially constructed tank to hold the propane for your BBQ grill. Made of thick-walled steel with a special valve system, the tank must withstand the higher vapor pressure of propane that turns from a liquid into a gas at room temperature. It is the same with pipelines, trucks, ships, and railcars that store and transport propane. All such containers must be designed and constructed to handle the high vapor pressure of propane and, like the tank on your BBQ grill, are far more expensive than a container designed to hold gasoline.

Density. Density is the other key physical characteristic of DBHs that influences transportation. As a general rule, the less dense the DBH, the more important that pipeline transportation becomes for that commodity. For example, the least dense of the DBHs is natural gas. It comes out of the ground as a gas, it is used as a gas (for fuel, for heating, generating electricity, etc.), and in the United States almost all of it is transported as a gas. Compared to more dense liquid fuels, gases take up a lot of room. Let's put that in perspective. The United States uses about 26 trillion cubic feet of natural gas each year. That works out to about 71 billion cubic feet of gas each day. How big is one billion cubic feet? You will recall from our discussion in Chapter 6 describing the Mont Belvieu salt caverns capacity that the volume inside the Empire State Building is about 37 million cubic feet. So it would take 27 Empire State Buildings to hold one billion cubic feet of natural gas. And the United States uses 71 billion cubic feet each day! If you do the math, that works out to 1,917 Empire State Buildings full of gas each day. Now let's consider crude oil. Total crude oil consumed in the U.S. was about 16 million barrels per day in 2014, or 90 million cubic feet per day (5.61 cubic feet per barrel). That means that it takes only 2.4 Empire State Buildings of crude oil each day to supply U.S. refineries with all the crude they need. Clearly, the density of crude oil is much greater than the density of gas: 1,917 Empire State Buildings for U.S. gas versus only 2.4 Empire State Buildings for U.S. crude oil. Therefore, crude oil is much more energy-dense than natural gas. As you might expect, it takes a lot more pipelines, compressors, and other infrastructure to move around 1,917 Empire State Buildings worth of gas than it does 2.4 Empire State Buildings worth of crude oil. It should come as no surprise that moving crude oil is a lot cheaper than moving the equivalent (Btu value) of natural gas.

Consequently, moving and storing high-density hydrocarbons that are liquid at atmospheric temperatures and pressures, such as crude oil, motor gasoline, and the NGL natural gasoline, can be relatively cheap. Usually they are transported in pipelines, general-purpose rail tank cars, unpressurized trucks, or ships and barges; they are then stored in aboveground steel tanks at atmospheric pressures. When moving less dense, higher vapor pressure hydrocarbons like the NGLs propane and butane, pressurized vessels are required because if left exposed to atmospheric pressures and temperatures, the products would turn from a liquid into a gas with the result that the liquid would evaporate into the atmosphere. Thicker-walled pipelines and specially designed and pressurized railcars, trucks, ships, and barges move these higher-vapor-pressure fuels. When storing relatively smaller quantities, bullet tanks (oblong) or spheres (round)—which are thick-walled, aboveground steel tanks—are used. Alternately, for large quantities, huge underground caverns carved out of salt domes (discussed in Chapter 6) are used. Ethane, the other NGL, in its liquid state has a much higher vapor pressure than either propane or butane, so much so that it is rarely moved in trucks, rail cars, or barges because the steel walls of the vessels would have to be so thick that they would be cost-prohibitive to build. For that reason, almost all ethane is moved by pipeline with especially thick walls and is almost always stored in underground salt cavern storage.

Then there is natural gas. In the United States, only a tiny volume is transported in liquid form. Almost all U.S. gas is transported as a gas, and almost always by pipeline. Transporting it in its gaseous form by rail car, truck, or barge is simply not practical because of its low density: It is not possible to get enough natural gas into any one of those vessels to make economic sense. But there is another way to move natural gas in a much more dense form: as a liquid. Liquefied natural gas, or LNG, is natural gas cooled to minus 260° F, at which point it becomes a liquid (LNG) and can be stored at essentially atmospheric pressure.

Converting natural gas to LNG increases its density, a lot. The process reduces the volume of natural gas by about 600 times—think of reducing the volume of a 22-inch-diameter beach ball to the volume of a Ping-Pong ball—making transport possible when pipelines are not practical, like moving it in a cargo ship across thousands of miles of ocean.

Natural-gas-to-LNG conversion is a very expensive proposition from start to finish. It requires special cleansing prior to processing, the cost of a liquefaction plant (upwards of $5 billion), lowering its temperature, along with expensive LNG tankers and regasification at its destination terminal. The lower density of natural gas makes it a more expensive fuel in every respect, so pipelines are the first choice for transport. Unless, of course, it's moving on a tanker from an LNG-producing country like Australia to an LNG-consuming country like Japan. Then LNG is the only alternative.

Distance and terrain. These twin aspects of transportation comprise the second determining factor for how best to move DBHs across energy networks. Sometimes the choice is obvious, such as when moving product long distances over water: hands down, it's a tanker. Not only is it the cheapest, but it's really the only way. The difficulties and costs of laying pipelines on the ocean floor are prohibitive except for very unique circumstances. Ships carrying large quantities of liquid hydrocarbons provide the same economies of scale as pipelines on land. In most cases, the same holds true for river transport: barge transportation economics usually trump other ways to move hydrocarbon liquids.

For liquid hydrocarbon short-distance hauls (for example, moving crude oil from a well site to a receipt terminal on a long-haul pipeline or rail siding), there are typically two alternatives. The first is via a gathering system that collects crude from several well sites into a web of small-diameter pipelines that eventually collects larger volumes that can be piped or railed to market. The other is by truck, which can move crude oil when a gathering system is not available. This is frequently the case when a new crude oil play is being developed. On a per-barrel basis, truck transportation is expensive. A single truck will only hold about 200 barrels; then there is the cost of loading and unloading, paying the driver, and fuel for the truck. But when the distance is short and the quantity is small, truck transportation makes a lot of sense.

Natural gas, on the other hand, is an altogether different animal. If the transportation is by land, the only practical choice is pipeline no matter how short the distance. Gas is collected at the point of production by small-diameter pipeline gathering systems, similar to those described above for crude oil. Frequently, these gathering systems deliver the gas to natural gas processing plants for the extraction of NGLs. Then the gas is delivered into receipt points, sometimes called *injection points*, on long-haul pipelines. These pipelines move the gas to delivery points: local distribution companies (LDCs), power generators, and factories. To reiterate, pipeline is almost always the transportation mode used for U.S. natural gas, from the point of production all the way to the point the gas is used. This is because of the density of the product: you just can't get much natural gas in a truck or rail car.

In contrast, transportation networks for the liquid DBHs (crude oil and NGLs) are frequently amalgamations of several different transportation modes, selected to best accommodate distance and terrain. For example, crude oil from the Rockies frequently begins its journey from the well site via truck. Gathering systems through rocky terrain over large distances can be prohibitively expensive, so truck transportation is frequently the best economic alternative in the Rockies. In some cases, trucks bring those barrels to rail sidings where they are loaded onto railcars. Railcars can move the crude over long distances to refineries, but more often they will move to terminals where the barrels will be unloaded into tanks before moving on to refineries, either in pipelines or barges. As in this example, considerations for both distance and terrain determine the best transportation network for any movement of liquid DBH barrels.

Volume. It is pretty obvious that the larger the quantity of hydrocarbon that needs to be moved, the more infrastructure will be needed to move it. Almost all large-volume, long-distance transportation of DBHs in the United States is by pipeline—99.9% of natural gas, 90% of crude oil, and 85% of NGLs. There is an incredible distribution network for natural gas, composed of a mind-boggling 300,000 miles of pipelines. There are about 55,000 miles of crude oil pipelines confined to the middle part of the country, with no pipelines reaching to the East or West Coasts. Likewise, NGL pipeline systems are mostly located in the midsection of the country, comprising about 35,000 miles. These numbers do not include the thousands of miles of smaller-diameter gathering systems that bring products from the upstream to the midstream pipelines.

Differences between Liquids and Gas Pipelines

Although pipeline is the most common transportation mode for liquids (crude oil and NGLs) and is the almost exclusive transportation mode for transporting natural gas, the operation of liquids and gas pipelines is quite different. This is due to the physical characteristics of the products, primarily their density.

Natural gas. Natural gas is moved through pipe by compressors located all along the pipelines to boost the pressure of the gas. This is what keeps the gas moving downstream. There are more than 1,400 of these compressor stations in the United States on the major interstate pipeline network, shown in Figure 12.2. These compressor stations are generally located 50–150 miles apart and operate continuously. The average compressor station in the United States is capable of moving 700 MMcf/d, while the largest can move over 4.5 billion cubic feet (bcf/d).

As natural gas moves down a pipeline, the friction between the natural gas flow and the inside wall of the natural gas pipeline causes the pressure of the gas to fall; thus, the speed of the gas movement slows. A compressor station boosts the pressure of the natural gas back up, which effectively

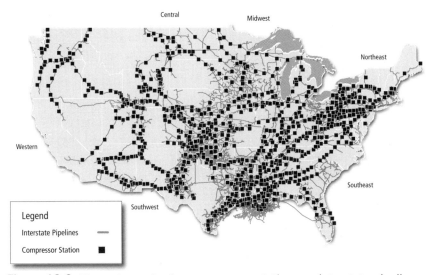

Figure 12.2. Natural gas pipeline compressor stations on interstate pipelines. Source: EIA

pushes the gas further downstream. A compressor station has equipment that removes any liquids that may have condensed out of the gas as it moved down the pipeline. Compressor engines run by either natural gas from the pipeline itself or by electric power and are usually unmanned, operated remotely via computer and telecommunication systems.

As discussed back in Chapter 5, from an operational perspective, natural gas pipelines work more like a bank than a UPS truck. A shipper delivers gas to a pipeline at a receipt point (a metered connection with a gas production facility or gathering system) and can get that gas delivered at some point hundreds or thousands of miles downstream the same day, regardless of the physical speed of the gas flow. That is because gas is said to be fungible, meaning gas moved on most interstate pipeline systems is of a like quality. Therefore, the pipeline can take a deposit (like a bank does dollars) and make a payment effective instantaneously. It is not necessary to move the shipper's molecules to effect delivery; whatever amount of gas is deposited is delivered by the gas that is already further up the pipe, nearest the delivery point. The inventory of gas which is held in the pipeline is called *linefill* and is almost always owned by the pipeline and considered in the asset base of the pipeline company, just like any other assets it owns.

Some Gas Is More Equal than Other Gas

Although natural gas is typically viewed as a fungible commodity in the interstate natural gas pipeline grid, this is really an oversimplification. Gas is anything but equal when it is produced at the wellhead. As discussed previously, gas from some fields is very dry (primarily methane, with low liquids content and low Btu) and requires little preparation to meet standard pipeline quality specifications. At the other extreme is very wet gas, containing significant quantities of NGLs that must be extracted before the gas can be delivered to a natural gas pipeline. Natural gas also requires treating (or conditioning) to remove various impurities before it can be delivered to a pipeline. Such conditioning may include an amine unit for the elimination of sulfur compounds and treatment to remove water, carbon dioxide, helium, nitrogen, oxygen, and other impurities. NGLs are removed in a processing plant, usually for their own stand-alone product value.

When gas is ready to be delivered into a pipeline, it must meet that pipeline's quality standards. Pipeline companies publish detailed quality standards in their tariffs, specifying the limits on heating value (Btu content), impurities, and NGLs for natural gas to be acceptable for receipt into the pipeline: that is, to be deemed pipeline-quality gas. Although pipeline quality standards are not exactly the same from pipeline to pipeline, generally they are close enough so that pipelines that interconnect can exchange gas supplies. Even when the Btu content for pipeline systems differs, gas can usually be exchanged because it is valued based on Btu content. In other words, since natural gas is priced on an MMBtu basis, a pipeline with a lower Btu content gas can deliver that gas to a pipeline with a higher Btu content and price will **true up**, or adjust the exchange from a value perspective. Thus natural gas tends to be **fungible enough**.

There is one other important feature of natural gas transportation. Natural gas is compressible: if more pressure is applied to a given quantity of natural gas, it takes up less room. This characteristic of gas transportation means that pipelines can be used as *long, skinny storage tanks*. If, on a given day, more gas is received by a pipeline than is delivered out of that pipeline, the difference can be accommodated by increasing the overall pressure of the pipeline. Of course, there are operational limits to how much pressure a pipeline is designed to take, but within those design limits and the capability of compressors on the pipeline system, the amount of gas contained within it on any day can vary considerably. Adding more pipeline compressor stations can increase the capacity or throughput of the gas pipeline, again within the pipeline's design limits.

Liquids. Liquids—both crude oil and NGLs—are moved in pipelines by pumps instead of the compressors used for natural gas. However, just as with natural gas, friction between the liquid and the wall of the pipeline slows the speed of flow over time. Instead of compressor stations, liquids pipelines have pump stations distributed every 30 to 60 miles along the length of the pipeline. Like compressors, the pumps usually run continuously and usually are controlled by remote computer systems. From a mechanical perspective, pumps are quite different from compressors. While natural gas is compressible and decreases in volume when subjected to pressure, liquids are not: the volume remains essentially constant when subjected to compressive forces. So, liquids are pumped using a mechanism similar to a water pump, while gas is moved by compression with a mechanism similar to an air compressor. Like gas pipelines, more

"WOOO—PIG—SOOIE!"

The **pig** is a sophisticated device critical to the safety and integrity of pipelines. In this case, the term has nothing to do with either the source of bacon, the Arkansas Razorbacks or the pig they throw around. This kind of pig can cost over $500,000 and does its work inside pipelines.

There are lots of stories out there about why these contraptions are called pigs. One that seems logical is the fact that pig is an acronym for **Pipeline Inspection Gauge** or **Pipeline Integrity Gauge**. But perhaps they got their name from the squealing sound they make when traveling through a pipeline or the fact that after traveling through a pipe, they look like a pig, covered in muck. Another story is how in the late 1800s, balls of pig leather (and other materials) were used to clean pipes. No one really knows for sure.

Pigs are used for pipeline cleaning and inspection. Over time, all kinds of debris can build up in a pipeline: sand, condensation, or salt water. All of this debris can impact product flow and ultimately cause corrosion. Pigs are inserted at one end of a pipeline and pushed along inside the pipe and recovered at the other end in a **pig trap**. In addition to cleaning, pigs are used for pipeline inspections. Over 90% of petroleum liquid pipeline inspections are done by pigs.

Pigs come in all shapes and sizes and are generally shaped like ... pigs. Well, not really. As shown in Figure 12.3, there are many designs for pigs, mostly shaped like plugs or barbells.

Figure 12.3. © Abdelmajidfahim | Dreamstime.com, Pipeline Pig Cleaner Photo

There are simple pigs (sometimes called **dumb pigs**), and there are complex high-tech pigs (a.k.a. **smart pigs**). The more sophisticated smart pigs are filled with electronic instruments and are the ones used as in-line inspection tools. Smart pigs are typically owned and operated by specialty services companies. Pipeline operators typically use dumb pigs for cleaning.

pipeline pump stations can increase the throughput of a liquids pipeline as long as it does not increase the pressure above design limitations.

Batching. One of the most important distinctions between gas and liquids pipelines is the need for, and the ability to, batch deliveries. A *batch* is a quantity of one NGL product or grade of crude that is delivered segregated and distinct from other products or grades. For natural gas pipelines, there is no need for batching since gas is essentially fungible. But there are big differences between the different NGL products and the different grades (qualities) of crude oil. For that reason, some liquids pipeline systems are designed to batch deliveries, with each product or batch distinct from the one preceding or following.

However, not all pipelines batch. Some pipelines are dedicated to a single NGL product or a single grade of crude oil, allowing them to operate similarly to natural gas pipelines with continuous flows of a fungible product. The operations of batch systems are quite different, with shipments accumulated in storage at the receipt end of a pipe, then pumped into the pipeline following the preceding batch, and followed by still another batch. Batch pipeline systems generally require much more *breakout storage* to accumulate batches at the receipt point and subsequently receive those batches at the delivery point. Most of the time, batches are separated at the delivery end by equipment that can detect if the quality of the NGL product or crude has changed as it moves by the sensor. Usually a small volume of *interface* liquid such as diesel fuel is used to separate batches and must be disposed of.

Quality banks. Another feature that applies primarily to liquids pipelines is the *quality bank*, a term that applies mainly to crude oil and mixed NGLs. Quality banks are typically not applicable to gas or purity NGL products. When liquids are transported via pipeline, different sources of liquids owned by different shippers will be mixed together into a *common stream*. In many such situations, the pipeline operator uses a quality bank to credit or debit shippers for differences in the quality between the liquids they put in and what they take out of the pipeline.

In a common stream system, different shippers can put in crudes of differing qualities as long as they stay within the pipeline's specifications. The problem is that differing qualities have different values in the market. This would be a big problem if there were not some way to equalize the value between some shippers putting in higher-value liquids and others putting in lower-value liquids.

Consider a crude oil example. Let's say you inject the highest quality light-sweet crude, but your neighbor puts in some half-baked blend they picked up on Craigslist. Chances are the quality of the crude you withdraw at the destination is going to be worse than what you injected. That means refiners wouldn't pay you as much as they would for the crude you originally put in, perhaps resulting in a significant financial penalty. The quality bank addresses this issue by accounting for the difference in the quality of the crudes that a shipper delivers to and receives from the pipeline. In effect, a quality bank is an accounting-allocation system. Across all shippers, theoretically the credits and debits net out to zero. Quality bank accounting is generally done on a monthly basis, in arrears.

Pipeline Regulation: Liquids Pipes Are from Mars, Gas Pipelines from Venus

Both gas and liquids pipelines are regulated by the Federal Energy Regulatory Commission (FERC). But the regulations are quite different. In fact, FERC's authority to regulate gas and liquids pipelines comes from two very different statutes. Gas is regulated under the Natural Gas Act (NGA) and liquids pipelines (crude oil and NGLs) under the Interstate Commerce Act (ICA). As a general rule, regulation under the NGA is much heavier than under the ICA. This fact has all sorts of implications for commodity markets, infrastructure development, and day-to-day pipeline operation.

On the gas side, FERC and the industry association NAESB (North American Energy Standards Board) prescribe detailed procedures for how pipelines operate, how they schedule their services, and how contracts with shippers work. Similar regulations for crude oil and NGL pipelines are much more general and light-handed.

The rules for the NGA versus ICA pipelines are even more different when it comes to building a new pipeline. According to the NGA, a company needs FERC authorization to begin or terminate service on an interstate natural gas pipeline. FERC must issue what is calls a Certificate of Public Convenience and Necessity, including details about the project such as the estimated rates it will charge. FERC determines whether the pipeline is *in the public interest* and if it considers the rates the pipeline will charge "reasonable."

With that Certificate of Public Convenience and Necessity comes a big benefit: *federal eminent domain authority*. That means the pipeline developer can force a landowner to allow the pipeline to cross the landholder's property. Federal rules trump state rules, so the eminent domain right is a very powerful tool for pipeline developers to navigate state and private objections to pipeline construction.

No such federal tool is available for liquids pipeline developers. FERC does not have jurisdiction over the construction of liquids pipelines. The ICA provides the FERC the authority to regulate the contract terms and conditions offered by a pipeline but does not provide authority to regulate a liquids pipeline entry or exit from any market. Since there is no corollary to the Certificate of Public Convenience and Necessity for liquids pipelines, there is no right of eminent domain. So it falls to the individual states to decide whether eminent domain is granted or not. That can be a big problem getting pipelines built, particularly if there is public resistance to their construction. If a pipeline crosses the border into another country (either Canada or Mexico), then the U.S. Department of State gets involved. That agency has been responsible for administering blockage of TransCanada's Keystone XL pipeline.

There is one other messy feature of liquids pipeline regulation. According to the ICA, liquids pipelines are *common carriers*, which poses all sorts of implications for the way a pipeline offers its services. Recall Chapter 7 covered how that happened in the Hepburn Act, passed by the U.S. Congress in 1906. As common carriers, liquids pipelines must—at least theoretically—take on all comers, which means providing transportation service to anyone who requests such service. Again, theoretically, if capacity on a liquids pipeline is maxed out and a new shipper asks for service, the pipeline must provide the service by allocating limited capacity between the existing customers and new customers. In practice, pipelines can get around some of this requirement by providing different levels of long-term transportation services. Nevertheless, it can be a problem when capacity gets constrained, which has happened frequently since the beginning of the shale revolution.

Under the NGA, natural gas pipelines are not common carriers. They provide service to shippers on a *contract-carriage* basis. Translated, that means if a pipeline's capacity is sold out, there is no requirement for that pipeline to provide any service to a prospective new customer. In this context, the term *sold out* means that all of the pipeline's firm capacity has been contracted to other shippers.

The key point is that the rules for gas pipelines and liquids pipelines are quite different, with each set of rules having its own advantages and disadvantages. When working in the pipeline world, it is important to check the fine print in order to make sure you understand the rules. Seemingly small variances in the rules can make big differences in the financial consequences for both pipelines and shippers.

Now that we have product moving to market, our task in Chapter 13 is to learn about what happens downstream with markets and prices.

Chapter 13

Interpreting Markets and Prices

HE MARKETS FOR THE DRILL-BIT HYDROCARBONS HAVE A LOT IN COMMON. *All are commodities. They trade in both physical and financial markets. The financial markets include futures exchanges that are quite similar to those for pork bellies, soybeans, and interest rates. Energy commodity markets are some of the most volatile commodity markets traded. Prices fluctuate due to factors like weather (such as the 2013–14 polar vortex), politics (the latest turmoil in the Middle East), supply (huge growth since the onset of the shale revolution), and rumors. Just as in all markets, buyers and sellers make purchase and sale decisions based on a combination of facts and the individual's gut feeling based on gossip, hearsay, or grapevine news.*

When trying to understand these freely traded energy markets, nothing is more important than price. It is the most reliable indicator of what is going on in energy markets. As with any commodity market, there is a lot of noise in daily action that cause prices to rise and fall. But over time, price is an extremely reliable indicator of the balance between supply and demand. A supply surplus drives price down. A demand surge pulls it up. Price may not be a perfect indicator of supply and demand, but there is no better bellwether in most commodity markets and certainly nothing better in the DBH markets.

Just a quick note for those less familiar with the workings of commodity markets like the DBHs: No individual, government agency, cartel, or commodity ex-

change sets U.S. energy prices. The market as a whole, seeking equilibrium, sets the price for energy resources. Buyers and sellers negotiate prices continually throughout each business day. If a seller perceives that the market is becoming tight—that is, more buyers than sellers—then the seller is inclined to raise his or her price. In contrast, if a buyer perceives that the market is becoming sloppy (oversupplied), he or she is inclined to reduce the price they are willing to pay. Thus there is a continuous tension between buyers and sellers, each trying to get the best price possible, but ultimately a deal gets done based on a freely-negotiated price. It is the accumulation of hundreds, if not thousands, of such deals each day that in aggregate gets reported as the price for that day, when averaged out. The bottom line is that price is set by the market's perception of demand and the supply available to satisfy that demand. Period. The resultant market price is dependent upon the relationship between these fundamental components.

DBHs were not always considered commodities; neither were they bought and sold on exchanges. But they are today, and it is essential that we understand how this seemingly simple, but really quite complex, relationship between supply and demand, pricing, and commodity markets works.

Physical Energy Markets

A market exists when there is a product, a seller, a buyer, and a transaction. It is really that simple. Remove any one from the mix and you have no market. A *commodity market* deals in products which for the most part are undifferentiated from one producer to the next. Commodities are typically the raw materials used to produce consumable goods. About fifty products trade in the most important global commodity markets, including pork bellies, cocoa, sugar, corn, soybeans, coffee, wheat, gold, iron, copper, and of course, the DBHs. One particular batch of a commodity may differ slightly from another, but as long as they meet the standard quality specifications for that commodity, they are generally treated—and priced—as if they are the same. Once a DBH commodity is produced (for example, refining crude oil into motor gasoline), it becomes a marketable product.

As discussed in Chapters 5, 6, and 7, there are two types of markets for energy commodities. The first is the physical market, which encompasses transactions for the purchase and sale of physical quantities of goods. The second is financial markets, which are used to either assume or lay off price risk.

In the markets for physical energy commodities, transactions usually involve transferring title of a specific, measured quantity of the particular energy commodity from a seller to a buyer. Title changes hands upon delivery, with documents (meter tickets, confirmations, bills of lading, etc.) providing evidence of the transaction. Transfer of custody and transporting the product may be an aspect of the deal. After title has been transferred, payment is made.

Physical energy markets can be characterized by three important features of those markets:

- **Deliverability.** Physical markets deal with the delivery and receipt of real physical goods. The enduring and unwavering premise is that the seller is truly going to deliver an energy commodity to the buyer for an agreed-upon price. Every effort will be expended to consummate the transaction, for satisfactory delivery to be made and dollars (or whatever currency is involved) to change hands.

- **Interruptibility.** In physical deals, things can go wrong. All parties to the transaction understand and accept that any number of things can happen which can change or disrupt deals. Physical energy markets must be flexible and adaptable to manage such disruptions, from a delayed rail shipment to the failure of a crude oil pipeline pump. The commercial arrangements between buyer and seller must accommodate a wide range of possible problems while at the same time insuring the integrity of the deal.

- **Disparity.** Physical energy commodities differ widely in value, based on their location, quality, market timing, and other often unpredictable factors. As commodities, they meet industry specifications as to quality. However, they cannot and should not be regarded as truly consistent manufactured products but rather as the raw materials that are used for other processes such as producing heat, power, or transportation fuels.

Financial Energy Markets

Financial energy markets are about risk management. Financial transactions can occur between two parties (called over-the-counter or OTC deals) or are conducted on futures exchanges. Today, in the aftermath of the 2009 crisis and ensuing Dodd-Frank Act legislation, most financial market transactions are conducted through exchanges, even if they have been arranged over-the-counter. A futures exchange is a centrally operated financial market where buyers and sellers can trade standardized contracts for commodities with delivery set at some point in the future. Rarely do futures deals actually result in the physical delivery of a product. Almost always, a futures trade is offset before delivery. For example, a buyer in January might buy 10 contracts for June natural gas. In May, that same individual sells 10 contracts for June natural gas. When June arrives, the two deals cancel out. No natural gas is ever delivered. However, if the buyer paid $4.00/MMBtu in January and sold for $4.50 in May, then the trade yielded a $0.50/MMBtu profit.

Similar to what occurs in physical markets, three features characterize financial markets:

- **Transparency.** When financial transactions are consummated via exchanges, it is easy to learn the price for those deals because various electronic information vendors such as Reuters or Bloomberg report the deals instantaneously based on information feeds from the exchanges. Traders know the numbers on their screens change from moment to moment, so they constantly monitor exchange transaction data.
- **Liquidity.** There are thousands of daily transactions on the commodity exchanges, so it is likely there is always a buyer for every seller and a seller for every buyer at a given moment in time. In this context, this is the meaning of the term liquidity. As a general rule, both buyer and seller seek the maximum liquidity possible.
- **Volatility.** Volatility is the tendency for market prices to move up and down rapidly and frequently. Since futures markets are so transparent and contracts so easily executed (by pushing a button on a computer keyboard or even programming a computerized trading model to transact based on an algorithm), they tend to react quickly to any new piece

of information that enters the market. Much of this volatility is the market noise mentioned earlier. Up-and-down price action can be an indication of a major supply-and-demand imbalance, or it may just be random fluctuations that have nothing to do with anything fundamental.

As mentioned previously, futures trading involves the purchase or sale of a standardized contract specifying the quantity, quality, and location of an energy commodity at a specified date in the future. All three DBHs have futures markets and are bought and sold with futures contracts, although futures trading volumes for crude and natural gas are much larger than NGLs. In futures transactions, the buyer is said to have *gone long*, meaning the holder of the position will profit if the price goes up. In contrast, *gone short* refers to the seller, meaning that the holder of the position will profit if the price goes down. In each futures trade there is a long position and a short position, someone betting the price goes one way while another has reason to bet it will go the other. That disparity between the perspectives of buyer and seller is what makes futures markets work.

The Evolution of DBH Commodity Trading

To some extent, DBHs have always been commodities. However, they began trading as physical commodities at different times and also started trading on exchanges at different times.

Crude oil came first. That DBH has traded in the physical market since the inception of the crude oil business. The first transaction mentioned in Chapter 7 between Colonel Edwin Drake and refiner Sam Kier counts as one of the first recorded crude trades. In the years from Drake's deal with Kier through the 1970s, most crude oil was sold based on refinery postings, also discussed in Chapter 7. The market functioned like an "old boys club" and was anything but transparent. But after 120 years operating this way, exchange trading changed all that. In early 1983, the New York Mercantile Exchange (NYMEX) instituted trading for West Texas Intermediate (WTI) crude oil delivered at the Cushing hub in Oklahoma, bringing real-time transparency to the world of crude oil pricing. Since then, the crude oil market has never been the same.

Natural gas has a much different history. Throughout the regulatory turmoil discussed in Chapter 5, physical gas did not trade as a commodity.

During much of its history, natural gas deals were for very long terms, sometimes up to 25 years, or for as long as a particular field continued to produce gas. Producers sold almost all of their production to pipelines. There were few other buyers. Pricing was set for the most part by the government; there were no negotiations, no commodity pricing, and certainly no futures market. As the natural gas market was restructured in the late 1980s and early 1990s, natural gas started to trade in an active commodity market, eventually developing into the physical natural gas market that exists today. In 1990, NYMEX introduced a futures market for natural gas with a delivery point at the Henry Hub in Louisiana. It took several years to become accepted, but eventually it evolved into an energy futures market second in size only to crude oil.

Like crude oil, NGLs have been traded as commodities in the physical markets since its products were first produced in the early part of the twentieth century. The NGL commodity markets became much more robust as the major trading hubs of Mont Belvieu and Conway developed. NYMEX tried introducing a futures contract for propane in the 1980s, but it was never accepted by the industry and trading halted in 2009. Even so, there has been electronic trading of NGLs since the mid-1990s. The electronic trading platform, Chalkboard, initially developed by The Williams Companies (a pipeline and trading firm), was acquired and popularized by Altra Energy Technologies[1]. This system changed hands in the early 2000s and was ultimately acquired by The Intercontinental Exchange (ICE). Today the ICE system is the primary trading system used for the purchase and sale of physical and financial NGL deals. Much of the NGL volume consummated on the ICE system is conducted as futures transactions.

Outright Prices, Benchmarks, Price Differentials, and Basis

Chapter 5 introduced outright prices, price differentials, and basis. Recall that in natural gas, some daily spot prices are negotiated outright at a fixed price (e.g., $3.50/MMBtu) agreed upon between buyer and seller. Others are based on a differential to the primary pricing location for natural gas in the United States, the Henry Hub, (e.g., $0.15 under the Henry Hub price). In the natural gas market, the Henry Hub is the pricing benchmark for all natural gas in the United States, which also extends to Canadian gas. As you recall, the term benchmark refers to the price of an energy commodity at a particular location that, by market convention, serves as a reference for the pricing of energy commodities at other locations. The Henry Hub is the natural gas benchmark for both physical and financial trading. The differential between the Henry Hub benchmark and other hubs is called the basis, basis spread, or more accurately, the location basis.

This same pricing structure exists for the other two DBHs. Crude oil typically uses the more complicated calendar month average mechanism, discussed in Chapter 7, but the basic structure is the same: the benchmark is WTI at the Cushing, Oklahoma hub. Other crudes are priced relative to WTI with price differentials reflecting differences both in location and quality.

The benchmark location for NGLs is the Mont Belvieu, Texas hub. Because there are five NGLs, there are five benchmarks: one each for ethane, propane, normal butane, isobutane, and natural gasoline. In fact, in some cases there is more than one benchmark per NGL due to quality and location differences. NGLs at other locations around the country are usually traded with reference to the Mont Belvieu benchmark price.

The prices you hear most about are these benchmarks. When a newspaper or TV anchor quotes prices, it is almost always the price of WTI at Cushing or the price of natural gas at the Henry Hub. In fact, the popular press rarely even explains what the prices are. More likely, there will just be some statement like, "The price of crude oil is up $1 to $81 per barrel." Of course, the level of these benchmark prices is incredibly important due to their role in influencing all other prices around the country. But they are not as important to the day-to-day business of the industry as you might think for two key reasons.

First, what really matters to a physical transaction is the price for that transaction, which is based on the pricing at the delivery point for that deal. For example, if the natural gas price at the Henry Hub is $4.00/MMBtu, but the basis for natural gas traded in northeastern Pennsylvania is $1.25/MMBtu then the price a producer gets for selling gas in Pennsylvania is not $4.00, it is $2.75 ($4.00 less $1.25). As discussed in Chapters 8 and 9, this makes a huge difference to the profitability of a producer's well. Location basis can be just as important, if not more important, than the level of the benchmark price.

Second, marketing and midstream companies tend to see a much bigger impact on their business from changes in price differentials than they do from changes in the benchmark price. Consider the following scenario of a physical trade on a natural gas pipeline that moves gas from that low priced market in Pennsylvania to an area where prices are much higher.

- Pipeline ABC transports gas from northeastern Pennsylvania to New York City for a transportation rate of $1.00/MMBtu.
- The price for gas in northeastern Pennsylvania is $2.75/MMBtu, while the price for gas in New York City is $4.00/MMBtu.
- A gas marketer can acquire gas at $2.75, pay $1.00 to move it to NYC for a total delivered cost of $3.75, and then sell it for $4.00. That results in a tidy profit of $0.25/MMBtu.

The economics of this trade do not change when the benchmark changes, as long as the price differentials do not change.

For example, if the Henry Hub price goes to $6.00/MMBtu (up $2.00), the price in Pennsylvania goes up to $4.75 (up $2.00), and the New York price goes to $6.00 (up $2.00), then that tidy profit is exactly the same amount, $0.25/MMBtu.

If there is no change in the benchmark (Henry Hub price) but the differentials change, the impact is huge. Say the price in New York goes up by only $1 but the price in Pennsylvania goes up $2.00. Now the shipper is acquiring gas at $4.75, paying $1.00 to move it to New York for a total delivered cost of $5.75, then selling it for $5.00. That is a loss of $0.75/MMBtu.

It is a similar situation for most midstream companies and many downstream markets. For example, a refiner makes money on the differential between the cost of crude oil and the cost of petroleum products that it sells. If crude oil prices increase, as long as refined products increase by the same amount, the refiner still makes the same margin.

This is the bottom line: price differentials can be much more important for most energy markets than outright benchmark prices. Few outside the energy industry understand this extremely important point. Price differentials are the most important variable driving profits for midstream companies.

Price differential trends are important market signals. When a price differential changes, it is a highly reliable indicator of a change in the supply-and-demand balance between any two locations. If a price differential widens significantly, it is almost always an indication of a lack of infrastructure. Recall the admonition in the previous chapter: *surplus begets shortage*. Most infrastructure investment—often billions of dollars—is a response to a change in a price differential. It is impossible to understand how and why midstream companies invest in infrastructure and thus make money (or not) without understanding what makes price differentials change.

One additional aspect of price differentials is critically important in understanding energy markets using the domino effect: *price differentials are considerably easier to predict than outright benchmark prices*. Those benchmarks are influenced by all sorts of factors; in the case of crude oil, things like geopolitics, the world economy, currency values, and the global supply and demand of crude. Obviously, such factors are notoriously difficult to predict and thwart most attempts at forecasting. Similarly complex factors impact the benchmarks for natural gas and NGLs. Fortunately, price differentials can be understood using far fewer variables and much simpler analysis. The behavior of any given price differential is primarily a function of the dynamics of local energy markets: supply, demand, flows, and infrastructure—all fundamental factors that can be measured and modeled. This notion will be explored in the remainder of this chapter and the next.

The Three Laws of Energy Markets

No matter which DBH is involved, price differentials are based on changes to market fundamentals, and those fundamentals are subject to what are described here as the *Three Laws of Energy Markets*. These three laws have not been passed by legislature or an industry body. Rather, they are natural market laws that have existed since each of the DBHs began trading as a commodity. These laws make energy prices behave as they do.

The First Law of Energy Markets: *energy wants to move from a lower-value market to a higher-value market*. That is pretty much true for any commodity. If you have a widget for sale at Location A, but it would be worth a lot more at Location B, you are economically motivated to move it there, as long as the cost for moving the widget is less than the difference in price between A and B. It is the same as the natural gas example above: If gas can be moved from Pennsylvania to New York City for a profit of $0.25/MMBtu, then some market participant will probably do so. Of course, the widget or natural gas only wants to move to that higher value market if it makes economic sense to do so; that is, if the price differential exceeds the cost of moving the energy commodity from the supply point to the demand point.

Three factors drive changes in price differentials: (a) the supply-and-demand balance at the source point, (b) the supply-and-demand balance at the destination point, and (c) economically available transportation capacity between the two points: specifically transportation costs and transportation capacity constraints.

The first two factors are pretty basic. Continuing with natural gas as the example, if supply goes way up at a particular point but demand does not go up at the same time, price is likely to go down.

Supply and demand impact the price of energy, just as they do in any other market. For example, consider the market for housing. If there are too many houses on the market and not enough buyers (the case in 2010 after the crash), house prices fall. Prices go back up only if houses are taken off the market or if buyers appear.

Likewise, if the supply of natural gas increases in Pennsylvania (which it did, due to the huge Marcellus Shale wells mentioned in previous chapters) and demand in that area stays about the same (which it has), then prices are going to come down (which they did). On the other hand, the demand for gas in NYC is higher, especially in the winter. So, the price in NYC is generally higher. The differential between the markets is nothing more than the price in NYC less the price in Pennsylvania. The behavior of that differential is simple math: The price in Pennsylvania is down, the price in NYC is up, and so the differential is wider. Sometimes that differential can be very wide, for example in 2014 when it was more than $100/MMBtu between Pennsylvania and NYC!

When a price differential increases, it is quite possible the market can respond and bring that differential back in line. In our example, if surplus natural gas in Pennsylvania could be transported by pipeline to NYC, it could be used to satisfy the demand in NYC while at the same time relieving some of the oversupply in Pennsylvania. More supply would bring down the price in NYC; more demand would increase the price in Pennsylvania, narrowing the differential between the two locations.

But what if no transportation capacity is available to move incremental gas supplies from Pennsylvania to NYC? There is capacity between the two markets, but it can be *filled up*, meaning it is 100% utilized. At that point, the amount of natural gas that could be moved from Pennsylvania to NYC is *constrained*. With no more transportation available to move natural gas between the two markets, there can be no more supply coming into NYC and no more relief to the surplus in Pennsylvania. At that point, the supply-and-demand dynamic of each operates totally independent of the other. If no transportation capacity is available between two points—either because a transportation capacity does not exist or because capacity is fully utilized so no more product can be moved—the two locations *might as well be on different planets!* One market cannot directly influence the other. Frigid cold weather can cause the price in NYC to skyrocket while the price in Pennsylvania remains low, which is exactly what happened to the price differential in these markets during the winter of 2013–14.

In this example, the Pennsylvania-to-NYC differential became very wide for a few days. Such a differential is said to have *blown out.* However, not all price differential changes are so large. Differentials between markets change continually. In some situations, the transportation capacity between the markets factors into the differential, and sometimes it does not. That gets us to the Second Law of Energy Markets.

The Second Law of Energy Markets: *if transportation capacity between any two points is unconstrained, the price differential between those points will narrow to equal transportation costs between the points.* Consider the market in Figure 13.1.

We have a supply point for a DBH at A. The demand point is at B. It might be the crude oil play in the Permian for supply and a Houston refinery for demand. Or, as before, it might be Pennsylvania natural gas for supply and New York City for demand. The market does not matter,

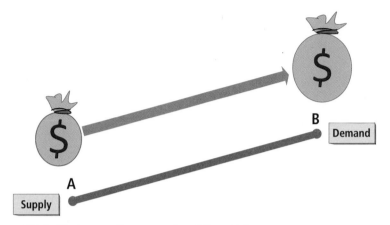

Figure 13.1. Understanding gas price differential

only the market structure. The price at B is much higher than at A (indicated by the size of the money bags), so the DBH wants to move from A to B, represented by the arrow. The pipeline (or any kind of energy transportation capacity) running from A to B is the blue line. In this example, assume that the only thing that changes is supply moving from A to B. Otherwise, there are no other changes that go on with either the supply or demand at A and B.

Let's say the price at A is $5, the price at B is $8, and the cost for getting from A to B is $2. Over time, we can expect enough of our DBH to flow from A to B such that the price at A increases (due to more demand from volumes moving to B) while the price at B decreases (due to more supply coming from A). Thus, the differential gets smaller, or narrower. Volume should continue to move between A and B until it no longer makes economic sense for it to do so. That occurs when the differential between A and B equals the cost of transportation between A and B.

In the real world, there are scores of factors that cause price differentials between any two market locations to change. But over time, particularly if one point is supply and the other demand, the differential between the points will tend to equalize around the cost of the transportation between the locations. Said simply, market participants will continue moving more and more supply to a point of demand until it no longer makes economic sense to do so.

But the third and final law is a critical exception to the Second Law.

The Third Law of Energy Markets: *lack of transportation capacity invalidates the Second Law.* If there is no way to move more supply from A to B, then A can have no impact on the price at B. Regardless of the difference in price between A and B, if the demand at A is not increased by moving volume to B, then the supply-and-demand balance at A does not change. Therefore, the *price* does not change. Figure 13.2 below is the same as Figure 13.1, except that a *capacity constraint* (the triangles) has been added between A and B. This signifies that no additional volume can be moved from A to B.

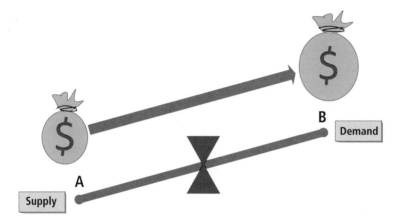

Figure 13.2. Impact of a capacity constraint

If there is no more supply coming into B, then the supply-and-demand balance at B does not change, so there is no change to the price at B. The price at B could go to the moon and it would not matter to A, because supply at A could not get to B to do anything about it.

This discussion about price differentials may at first seem abstruse if not irrelevant, but in fact there is no factor more important in the understanding of energy markets. Why? *Because price differentials encourage infrastructure investment.* When a transportation constraint results in a wide price differential, it suggests the market participants would be willing to pay for new transportation capacity between the markets. If a project to increase capacity were developed, market participants should be willing to make contractual commitments to pay the costs of getting the project built, just to move energy from A, where it is worth less to B, where it is worth more. That is the source of billions of dollars in energy infrastructure investment.

Kumquats and Energy Markets

Just in case this issue of market differentials is still a little murky for you, consider the following analogy comparing kumquats to energy commodities. The market mechanisms for kumquats and energy are more similar than you might think.

Imagine a highway bridge over a river in the middle of the land of kumquats. As long as the bridge is in place, goods (kumquats) can travel freely over the bridge. Even though kumquats are produced on the east side of the bridge but consumed in mass quantities on the west side, the price for kumquats on either side of the bridge should be about the same, with a slightly higher price in the west to account for the cost of shipping kumquats over the bridge.

But if the bridge were to go out, the east would be stuck with a bunch of kumquats it doesn't need, so the price of kumquats would go down. Simultaneously, the price of kumquats in the west would go up as the public responds to the kumquat shortage, bidding the price of kumquats higher in a market squeeze. Assuming there is no alternative transportation to the disabled bridge, nothing that happens on the east side would have any impact on the west side, and vice versa. Kumquats would be spoiling on the east side, while there would be kumquat riots on the west side. The prices of kumquats on the two sides of the bridge would be decoupled, responding only to supply-and-demand situations on one side of the bridge. Like natural gas in the example above, the two locations might as well be on different planets.

But the instant the bridge is repaired (infrastructure built to address the imbalance), the price differential between the two sides of the bridge should go right back to where it was before the bridge went out.

DBHs are just like kumquats. The implications for infrastructure developers are enormous.

Note

1. The author was a founder of Altra Energy Technologies and served as its CEO and chairman in the late 1990s.

Chapter 14

Bonfire of the
Price Differentials

THE PREVIOUS CHAPTER ESTABLISHED THE PRINCIPLE THAT PRICE DIFFER-
*ENtials can be just as important, if not more important, for most energy
markets than outright benchmark prices, particularly for midstream
companies. Price differentials between locations can be a key determinant of
profit margins for companies moving energy between those locations. Infrastructure investment by companies is almost always a response to a price differential. This is the case whether the infrastructure is our kumquat bridge, a
pipeline, or almost any other kind of midstream infrastructure, like processing
plants, rail terminals, or storage tanks. In all of these cases there is a gap between two or more market prices, and the infrastructure is intended to bridge
that gap.*

*But price differentials have a dirty little secret. A secret that has cost many
energy companies millions, if not billions, of dollars. That secret, and what it means
to the domino effect, is the topic of this chapter.*

*To reveal this secret, it is important to explore a more real-world example than
the kumquat market. Kumquats and bridges may be adequate to get some concepts across, but we need to review a sequence of actual market events to uncover
the secret of price differentials. The events in this example occurred in the mid- to
late 2000s in the Rockies natural gas market. But there is nothing unique about
either the location or the commodity market. The secret has always been a char-*

acteristic of energy markets, but in recent years it has become much more prevalent; since the inception of the shale revolution, the dirty little secret has reared its head time and time again.

King REX and the Rockies Natural Gas Market

Back in the late 1990s, the U.S. natural gas industry had a couple of problems. Production from the largest source of gas in the country—onshore and offshore production along the Gulf of Mexico—was in steep decline. Canadian imports were also falling. But the need for additional gas supplies was increasing, especially for power generation in the Northeast. Fortunately, there was an answer on the horizon: the Rockies. The region was exhibiting the fastest production growth in the country, causing problems of its own. Supply was coming on so quickly that it had become clear there would not be enough pipeline takeaway capacity out of the region to handle the supply growth. At the time, development of huge new natural gas plays in Ohio, Pennsylvania, and West Virginia was not possible in anyone's wildest imagination. So the answer was obvious: move all that surplus Rockies gas to the east.

The industry's response was a bold, dramatic stroke: a new, 1.8 bcf/d, $5-billion pipeline all the way from the Rocky Mountains to eastern Ohio. Named the Rockies Express, or REX, it would be constructed by Kinder Morgan with co-owners Sempra and ConocoPhillips. It would be the largest natural gas pipeline built in the United States in the previous 20 years and would ultimately span 1,698 miles, becoming one of the nation's longest interstate pipelines. The pipe would function as an escape valve to move gas from a region experiencing gas gluts to a region needing new supplies.

As REX was under construction in 2007, Rockies production was growing rapidly. As shown in Figure 14.1, production grew from about 7 bcf/d in early 2005 to almost 9 bcf/d by late 2007. The Rockies could not use nearly that much gas, so it had to be moved out of the region to the Midcontinent and the West. Unfortunately, pipeline capacity was inadequate to move that much gas. The result was a huge glut that could not be moved, creating dramatic consequences for natural gas prices. As shown in Figure 14.2, Rockies prices at the major Opal, Wyoming, hub collapsed. While prices at the Henry Hub were selling for $6–$7/MMBtu, prices in the Rockies dropped to $0.05/MMBtu on October 12, 2007. That's a nickel. Some gas changed hands at a penny. Sellers were essentially giving their gas away.

Fortunately, a major segment of REX came online in early 2008. As the price at the Opal hub in Figure 14.2 shows, it was an instant reprieve for the market. Like someone threw a switch (and they had), Rockies prices flew from only pennies up to $9.00/MMBtu, riding the new capacity out of the region and the mid-2008 commodity run-up that drove Henry Hub prices to $13.00 (dark blue line, Figure 14.2). REX had done its job. For a while.

But Rockies production kept on increasing, up to almost 10 bcf/d by the fall of 2008. Again, capacity constraints were limiting Rockies outflows. At the same time, the economic crisis was in full swing, evaporating the commodity inflation of earlier in the year and driving Henry Hub pricing down below $6/MMBtu. That double whammy slammed Rockies prices back down to levels below $0.50/MMBtu.

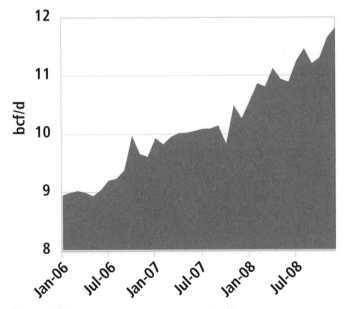

Figure 14.1. Rockies natural gas production

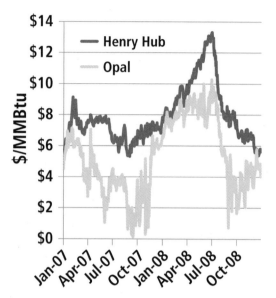

Figure 14.2. Rockies pricing

Finally, by the winter of 2008, REX was moving enough Rockies gas out of the region so that the pricing pressure was relieved. The price in the Rockies went back up to about the same level as the Henry Hub. The differential between the Rockies and Henry had all but disappeared. Rockies producers that had committed to decade-long transportation contracts to support the construction of the pipeline saw their prices increase. In the ensuing years, the differential between prices in the Rockies and the price in Ohio (the other end of the pipe) tended to gravitate around some number close to the marginal cost of transporting gas from the Rockies to Ohio, just like the Second Law of Energy Markets in the previous chapter predicted. Tallgrass Energy Partners purchased Kinder Morgan's share of REX in 2012.

But there is a huge "gotcha" in this happy story. The price differential did not narrow down to the *total cost* of moving gas from the Rockies to Ohio. It narrowed much further, down to the *marginal cost of moving* gas from the Rockies to Ohio. This point about marginal cost is extremely important, whether it is a gas pipeline or any other infrastructure. REX transportation rates—the cost to move gas—are structured the same way as most pipelines: by a *reservation fee*, payable whether or not any gas is shipped, and a *commodity fee*, paid only if gas is shipped. Most of the cost of the pipeline is paid in the reservation fee, which guarantees the developers a return on their capital. The commodity fee (and some other costs that also vary according to the volume of gas shipped) makes up a much smaller piece of the pie. The commodity fee is the marginal part of the cost for shipping gas and is paid by the shipper based on the volume shipped.

The other part of the cost to ship, the reservation fee, cannot be avoided by not shipping gas. It is called a sunk cost.

What It Means to Be Sunk

The concept of sunk cost is not unique to the energy market. It is an aspect of economic theory that basically says any cost already incurred or committed does not influence current commercial decisions. There are all sorts of economic arguments about the merits of the sunk cost concept that are far beyond the scope of this book. Here is the point: in the context of energy markets, *any cost to use an asset that must be paid, or has already been paid, has nothing to do with whether that asset will be used.*

Consider this example, again looking at a natural gas pipeline. Say Shipper XYZ reserves the pipeline capacity to move 1,000 MMBtu of gas from Texas to Chicago. The cost of that reservation is $0.30/MMBtu each day, so for 1,000 MMBtu that means that Shipper XYZ will pay Pipeline ABC $300 per day whether Shipper XYZ actually schedules any gas to move or not. This is the reservation fee. For every MMBtu that is actually moved, Pipeline ABC will charge Shipper XYZ another $0.10/MMBtu, over and above the $300 reservation fee. This is called the commodity fee. So, if Shipper XYZ elects to use all of its capacity, another $100 will be paid to Pipeline ABC. In total, Shipper XYZ will pay both the $300 reservation fee and the $100 commodity fee to move the gas, which is $400 or $0.40/MMBtu on the 100 MMBtu volume.

When will Shipper XYZ be economically motivated to move gas on this transportation contract? Let's say the price differential between Texas and Chicago is $0.50/MMBtu. Clearly, Shipper XYZ will use all of its capacity. The shipper can buy gas in Texas, move it to Chicago, and then sell it for $0.50, pocketing $0.10/MMBtu because it only costs $0.40 to transport the gas.

But what if the price differential between Texas and Chicago is only $0.25/MMBtu? Would Shipper XYZ use its capacity? Well, it will pay $0.40 to Pipeline ABC and only make $0.25 by moving the gas, therefore Shipper XYZ will lose $0.15/MMBtu on the deal. So Shipper XYZ will not ship, right? Wrong. Shipper XYZ has to pay the $0.30/MMBtu *no matter what*. Not shipping does not make that cost go away. So, if the shipper does *not* ship, the out of pocket cost is $0.30. But if Shipper XYZ *does* ship, the out of pocket cost is $0.15/MMBtu ($0.40 to the pipeline offset by the $0.25 on the trade). *Shipper XYZ ships as long as the price differential is higher than the marginal, or variable, cost of shipping.* The reservation fee is irrelevant to the decision to ship. That is what makes it "sunk." Shipper XYZ makes the same decision it would make if there were no reservation fee, and that is why it is a sunk cost.

Thus shippers will continue to use the capacity until the differential collapses below the marginal cost of transportation, which by definition ignores the sunk reservation fee. Any sunk cost has big implications for the holder of that sunk-cost asset or commitment.

It doesn't matter what form the sunk cost takes. In the example above, the sunk cost is a committed reservation fee on a pipeline, which must be paid whether the pipeline capacity is used or not. The construction of an asset can also result in a sunk cost. Consider a company building a gas processing plant. Say it takes $0.20/MMBtu to operate the plant, but the company would need to charge $0.40/MMBtu to make its target rate of return on its investment to build the plant in the first place. After the plant is built, the company would certainly like to charge $0.40/MMBtu. But if market conditions (the price differential between unprocessed natural gas and NGLs extracted by the plant) do not warrant that charge, the company may be stuck with charging anything over $0.20/MMBtu to earn some cash. And the company is economically incented to do so, even though it is not making its targeted return. This situation may look bad on the company's financial statements, but the company is still better off from a cash flow perspective running the plant and charging the lower price than shutting the plant down and making no revenue at all. In this situation, the cost of the investment in the plant is sunk. Thus a cost is sunk if it must be paid, or if it already has been paid.

Whether it is a pipeline, processing plant, or any other asset, users of the asset will have an economic incentive to use it as long as their revenue from its use exceeds the marginal cost of its use. The asset's sunk cost will be ignored in commodity transactional decisions. So a pipeline shipper will continue to move gas from A to B until the differential from A to B falls below the marginal cost of shipping, regardless of the reservation fee commitment. The owner of the processing plant will continue to operate the plant until the processing fee falls below the marginal cost of processing, regardless of the investment in the plant. To repeat this point one more time: a sunk cost is ignored in the economic decision to use an asset.

For investors in infrastructure to provide new capacity (pipelines, processing plants, or any other asset), there is a critically important implication. The price differential that justifies the construction of the infrastructure is likely to disappear when the infrastructure goes into service. The differential will narrow to marginal cost. The differential will not stay wide enough to cover sunk cost. *Essentially, it means the construction of new infrastructure to exploit wide price differentials works to make those differentials disappear.*

In effect, building a piece of infrastructure kills the goose that laid the golden egg. By relieving capacity constraints, the new energy infrastructure can, and frequently does, obliterate the price differentials that justified building the infrastructure in the first place. That is the meaning of this chapter's title, "Bonfire of the Price Differentials."

Do not get hung up on the natural gas pipeline or gas processing plant examples. The same principle applies for gathering systems, dock facilities, rail terminals, storage tanks, or refinery units: you name it.

The concept of price differentials justifying infrastructure, and then the infrastructure setting market decisions in motion which eliminate those differentials, is the dirty secret of price differentials. It means that those who invest in or commit to energy infrastructure are at risk of eliminating the economic underpinnings of their own projects unless they do things to protect themselves against that risk, such as structuring deals that lay the risk off on others.

Back to the REX example: the construction of that pipeline was backed by commitments from producers that wanted better prices for their Rockies gas. They had to make long-term commitments for lots of money, and they ended up with better prices. The infrastructure did exactly what it was advertised to do. Unfortunately, they also ended up paying those high transportation costs long after the differentials that had justified the construction of REX had gone away.

Free Ride

With REX, the price differentials would not have been eliminated unless the new pipeline infrastructure was built. Somebody—in the case of REX, the Rockies producers—made the commitments that got the pipe built and enjoyed higher Rockies prices as a result. So in our gas example, some but not all Rockies producers signed on to pay the reservation fees, or the sunk costs that provided the financial support for the pipeline construction project. But some producers elected not to make a commitment on the pipeline. And guess what? Since Rockies prices went up when the pipeline was completed, they went up for everyone, even those that had not made a commitment. Those free riders enjoyed the better prices and paid no reservation fee to do so. They simply rode on the backs of those who did.

That is the *really* dirty secret of price differentials. If you can get somebody else to make market commitments to get a piece of energy infrastructure built, sometimes you can enjoy the benefits while making no commitment yourself. It does not always work this way, but with the shale revolution making capacity constraints happen in different locales in all three DBH markets, the dirty little secret is coming up more and more often. The moral to this story: investing in energy infrastructure is not for the faint of heart.

Part IV

What's Goin' On: How the Energy Markets Are Changing and Why

"NATURAL GAS AND OIL LOW-PRICE FORECASTS ARE BASELESS ... CUR-rently, there appears to be no new transformative on-the-shelf technology that will significantly reduce the cost of extracting oil and natural gas," wrote Kurt Cobb in the *Christian Science Monitor* on January 14, 2013. Cobb is the author of the peak-oil-themed thriller *Prelude* and a columnist for the Paris-based science news site Scitizen. He concluded his article, "And so, barring a deep economic depression, we can look forward to prices for oil and natural gas that are consistently above the cost of production and therefore far above the bizarrely low forecasts in the air today."

It is now clear that the only thing bizarre in the air was Mr. Cobb's thesis. Production is way up and prices are way down. Yes, in the first half of 2015, lower crude oil prices slowed that growth. But production is holding up. As of this writing, production of the DBHs has tended to be relatively resilient.

If that level of resiliency holds up, it is quite possible that the United States is at the doorstep of that long sought-after goal of energy independence wherein the country can produce all the energy it uses. The goal may still be a few years away, and is surely fraught with every kind of uncertainty along the way, but it is a possibility.

In Part IV, we will examine the dominoes that have dropped since the Sweet Sixteen described in Chapters 2 and 3 and look forward to the dominoes likely to fall in the future. The Sweet Sixteen took the domino count through the end of 2012. In the subsequent two years from December 2012 through 2014, the shale revolution continued to accelerate for all three of the DBHs. U.S. natural gas production was up more than 4 billion cubic feet per day for an 8% increase. NGLs from natural gas processing plants ramped up about 500 Mbbl/d, or more than 20%. Crude oil production escalated the fastest of all, skyrocketing by 1.8 MMbbl/d, or about 25%.

With all this increased production, prices continue to fall. Then in late 2014 and 2015, the bottom fell out of the crude oil market. The world had changed.

Chapter 15

Crude Oil: Heavy, Light, Rail, and Exports

T
HE U.S. CRUDE OIL MARKET HAS SEEN A STEADY PACE OF FALLING DOMINOES *since 2012, and more of the same is on the way. The increase in crude oil production between 2011 and 2015 was dramatic and seems even more remarkable because the rapid growth was unforeseen by much of the market and certainly unanticipated by the general public. From a midstream perspective, the crude oil market has been a continual story of capacity constraints and new transportation infrastructure, followed by another cycle of capacity constraints with all of the price, commodity flow, and investment consequences predicted by the Three Laws of Energy Markets described in Chapter 13, with a few of the dirty secrets described in the previous chapter. Until 2015, U.S. crude oil was the most rapidly growing energy market on the planet and global crude oil prices have taken it on the chin. Who woulda thunk it?*

Much of that production growth has been coming from just three basins: the Bakken in North Dakota and Montana, the Eagle Ford in South Texas, and the Permian in West Texas and New Mexico. As shown in Figure 15.1, the production growth from these basins—the Big Three—was up from about 1.0 Mbbl/d in the late 2000s to almost 4.0 Mbbl/d by late 2014. Even more revealing, U.S. imports on the Gulf Coast (an area called PADD III in statistics from the Energy Information Administration) have declined almost barrel for barrel against increases from those three basins. The implication is that growing U.S. production has been

209

backing out waterborne imports. Unless low crude prices dramatically slow crude production growth, the displacement of imports by U.S. domestic production can be expected to continue until that Gulf Coast waterborne imports line in the graph has dropped to zero.

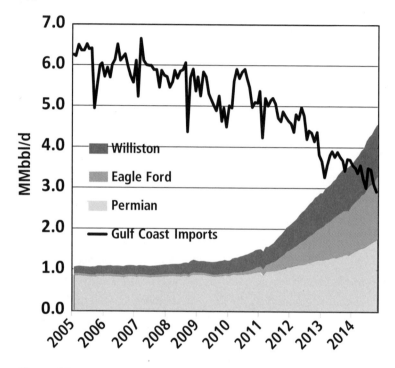

Figure 15.1. Big Three Basins vs. Gulf Coast (PADD III) imports

Over the past few years, these increases in production and the resulting decline in imports dropped several significant dominoes: crude by rail, the crude oil quality imbalance, and the export impediment. These dominoes set the stage for what has been one of the biggest dominoes to fall in recent years: a virtual collapse in crude prices not only in the United States, but across global crude oil markets. We start with rail.

The Bakken and Crude by Rail

The genesis of the shale revolution in crude oil came primarily in the Bakken. That hardy band of producers in the Williston Basin mentioned in Chapter 3 was the first to break the code for shale in the Bakken play, located mostly in North Dakota but also extending into parts of Montana. Here, crude production nearly quadrupled in four years, rising from 0.2 MMbbl/d in 2008 to 0.3 MMbbl/d in 2010 and then to 0.7 MMbbl/d in 2012. By the end of 2014, the Bakken was producing almost 1.3 MMbbl/d and accounting for more than 14% of U.S. crude production.

This magnitude of production was something new for the Bakken. As crude oil production ramped up, there was not nearly enough pipeline capacity to move crude out of the region. And there were certainly not enough refineries in the region—at the time only one in North Dakota—to use it locally. The result was the classic takeaway capacity-constraint, price-differential problem described in previous chapters.

Recall from Chapter 7 that Bakken crude transported by pipeline moves through two major hubs to market: east to Clearbrook, Minnesota and south to Guernsey, Wyoming. By early 2012, production in the region exceeded pipeline takeaway capacity from those hubs. The price differential between the hubs and Cushing *blew out* (an energy market euphemism for getting very wide). In this instance, it meant $28/bbl *below* Cushing. Previously, those hubs had traded at only a few dollars under Cushing price. Clearly, there was a big transport capacity problem and it needed to be resolved quickly. Unfortunately, it takes years to build a long-line pipeline. Several were announced at the time, but announcements by themselves do not resolve takeaway capacity constraints.

What *did* resolve the takeaway constraints was rail transportation. If pipelines could not be built soon enough to resolve the capacity problem, rail transportation was a viable alternative. Not only could rail facilities be built much faster, the up-front capital investment was cheaper, too.

Back in 2011, rail was a very small part of the crude oil transportation network, averaging just over 5,000 railcar deliveries per month in the United States. By early 2013, that number was up to more than 30,000. Scores of new Bakken rail terminals were built. In 2014, more than

> Increases in Bakken crude oil production resulted in takeaway constraints. The industry response was a huge buildout of crude by rail, which eventually expanded beyond the Bakken into the Gulf Coast, East Coast, West Coast, and Canada.

17

half the Bakken crude moved out of the region by rail. Just as predicted by the Three Laws of Energy Markets and those dirty secrets, the differential between Bakken and Cushing prices dropped back to a level below $10/bbl, sometimes even increasing above Cushing.

Crude by rail was Domino 17. From its beginnings as a stopgap solution driven by necessity, producers and refiners rapidly accepted crude by rail as a flexible and competitive complement to traditional pipeline transportation. One of the most important drivers was the ability of rail to transport crude to market from remote locations not adequately served by pipelines. But rail has been building several additional advantages that now makes it more competitive with pipelines. Consider:

Unit versus manifest. Until Domino 17 fell, most crude by rail moved by what are termed *manifest train shipments,* a small number of rail tank cars traveling as part of a larger freight train with assorted other cargo. Domino 17 brought on the widespread use of the *unit train,* a single train with 100 or more rail tank cars and at least two locomotives traveling nonstop from the point of origin to the destination. A crude oil unit train carries only crude oil, and there are no stops on the way to handle other cargo. These trains are given priority by railroads unlike manifest shipments that, combined with other freight, take longer to reach their destination and are subject to stopping and starting along the way. Most unit trains are loaded using sophisticated infrastructure to add crude to multiple rail tank cars simultaneously using overhead gantries. Due to its speed and efficiency, unit train transportation is considerably cheaper than manifest train shipment.

Multiple destination options. The rail system is already developed throughout North America; therefore, rail offers access to almost any location without the need to build significant new rail line infrastructure. That means shippers can send their trainloads to the point where the price is highest. For example, crude oil prices on the East and West Coasts are frequently higher than other parts of the country. Moreover, there are no crude oil pipelines from the shale basins to either of these coastal markets. Not only can rail shipments get to those markets, shippers can make decisions on the fly to deliver their crude to the best-priced markets. By contrast, pipelines can only move crude from a fixed point A to a fixed point B and thus do not provide the option to go to the best-priced market, called *destination optionality*.

Relatively lower cost of terminals. Unit trains require more extensive loading and unloading facilities to be built out than smaller manifest facilities. However, the cost of building a unit train rail loading facility is miniscule compared to the cost of a long-distance pipeline.

Shorter shipper terms. Most pipelines do not get built unless shippers make firm volume commitments to the project for 10 years or more, usually with penalty "take or pay" terms described earlier. Since rail terminals are less expensive, the commitment required of shippers is shorter, commonly one to two years.

Since 2012, more than 90 rail-loading terminals for crude oil have been built or significantly expanded in North America, not only in the Bakken but in all of the major shale basins. Another 70 destination terminals have been built or expanded elsewhere, mostly on the Gulf Coast, East Coast, and increasingly the West Coast. As mentioned, coastal markets previously received most of their crude by water, contributing to the teetering of another domino to be discussed later in this chapter.

Crude by rail has a secure future in the North American energy market. The rail terminal network will have a permanent role in the development and expansion of new crude plays. Whenever production exceeds pipeline capacity, the railroads can step in. Whenever new production has to wait for a pipe, it will travel by rail. Whenever markets are disrupted by pipeline congestion, rail will step in to bypass the tangle. In remote plays where there are no pipelines at all, rail will be the primary transportation mode.

Crude Oil Light and Heavy Imbalance: The Dumbbell

As the bounty of U.S. crude oil production works its way to its sole market—refineries—there is a small fly in the ointment. A quality problem. Most U.S. shale crude is very light. Most Canadian imports are very heavy. So the increases in U.S. crude oil supplies from domestic and Canadian sources are at opposite ends of the quality spectrum. Consequently, due to the growth in volumes of U.S. light shale crude and Canadian heavy crude, the mix of crudes available to the U.S. refining system—known as the *crude slate*—has been *dumbbelled*. Contrary to your likely first assumption, dumbbell is not a disparaging remark directed at any particular segment of the oil industry. Instead, it is a time-honored reference to a specific crude oil quality issue or, as most would say, a crude quality *problem*.

Chapter 7 introduced the concept of crude oil quality and the measurement of API crude gravity. We considered the fact that each type of crude oil yields a different mix of products, depending on the quality of the crude oil and the equipment the refinery uses to process it. Most light crude with an API gravity in the 40s is easier to refine and yields more gasoline. Heavier crudes with lower API gravity numbers are harder to refine and yield more fuel oil and asphalt, unless the refinery has the equipment to process, or crack, those products into more gasoline and diesel. Most crude oils as they come out of the ground are relatively balanced in the products they produce. So for example, an *intermediate-grade* crude might yield 5% NGLs, 35% gasoline, 25% diesel, 20% fuel oil, and 15% heavy fuel and asphalt. A *heavy* crude will have a lot less gasoline, more diesel, and a lot more fuel oil and asphalt.

Unfortunately, the crudes hitting U.S. refiners are more inclined to have a disproportionate share of NGLs and gasoline and at the same time more heavy fuel and asphalt. Not much diesel. Which is a bad thing, because diesel has been the highest-margin product for refiners over the past few years. The yield from this mix of light and heavy crude is big on one end of the yield curve, and big on the other end of the yield curve, and thus nothing in the middle. Like a dumbbell.

For decades, unscrupulous crude oil marketers have been buying batches of cheap heavy crude and very light crude. They blend the two together to make a crude with an API and sulfur specification that looks like West Texas Intermediate (WTI) then turn around and sell the resulting cocktail to unsuspecting refiners as WTI. Refiners dislike these artificial blends because their refinery processes are most likely balanced for real WTI, so the fake dumbbell grade throws operations off kilter. Further, because dumbbell crudes contain little diesel, which is typically priced attractively relative to gasoline and other refinery products, the refiner makes less money refining the dumbbell crude.

At one end of the dumbbell, the majority of new U.S. shale crude production discussed above is light-sweet crude, with a significant percentage consisting of super-lights and large volumes of super-light condensate. These super-lights and condensates, with their very high API gravity, are being produced from shale basin plays like the Eagle Ford and are increasing as a percentage of the total U.S. crude mix. The other end of the dumbbell has grown, too. That is because of increasing imports of Canadian crude, which is very heavy, creating one more quirk in the dumbbell problem. Very heavy Canadian crude extracted from oil sands (bitumen) is usually mixed with various diluents to enable the oil to flow in pipelines. The resultant mix known as *dilbit* is, by definition, a dumbbell crude. Most of this diluent is condensate or even lighter natural gasoline, so is still more super-light material for refineries to handle.

Put these developments together and you have a situation in which the entire U.S. crude slate is starting to look more like those dumbbell crudes the refineries do not like, with similar consequences. Refiners will either see their yields of diesel and other middle distillates decline, or they will find it necessary to invest in expensive upgrading equipment to maintain current levels of diesel production.

> Increases in the proportion of light-sweet crude from U.S. shale plays, combined with imports of heavy Canadian crude, are resulting in a dumbbelled crude slate for U.S. refiners.
>
> **18**

The entire crude quality imbalance situation is exacerbated due to limitations on the ability of many Gulf Coast refiners to run more super light crude and condensates. Many U.S. refiners simply do not have the capacity to run significant additional volumes of the light shale crudes without additional capital investments. Their refineries are not configured to process increasing quantities of light crudes due to physical plant and processing problems. Problems such as column limitations, compressor constraints, and overhead cooling issues can all limit how much total crude they can run. Put simply, that means refinery light crude handling processes overflow because the crude produces more light products than the refinery units were built to handle.

One way this imbalance could be resolved is by exporting some volume of the super light crude and replacing it with heavier crude. But as of this writing, that is a problem due to restrictions imposed by U.S. crude export regulations, discussed below.

To Export or Not to Export

Even with all the increases in U.S. crude oil production, as of this writing the U.S. still imports just under half of all of its crude supplies. Canada is the largest supplier of imported barrels into the United States, responsible for about 39% of all imported crude oil in 2014. Collectively, OPEC countries were the source of 41% of imports in that year, with various other countries making up the balance of 20%. With the United States still such a large importer of crude, you might wonder why there has been such a ruckus about exports. Well, for one thing, the issue has been politicized and generally blown out of proportion. But there is a legitimate issue associated with the quality imbalance mentioned above. Shale crude is light, super-light, or condensate. Up until the shale revolution, refiners had expected the only growth in crude oil supplies to come from Canada's very heavy crude. Refiners geared up to refine the heavy crude, only to get inundated with light crude from shale.

The regulatory prohibition on exporting crude oil from the United States to any country besides Canada constrains the market's ability to resolve this imbalance. The ban on crude exports goes back to 1979. That year, in response to the second oil shock following the Iranian Revolution (covered in Chapter 7), Congress passed the Export Administration Act (EAA) which gave the president authority to prohibit the export of most crude oil. The definition of crude oil specifically includes lease condensate, that very light material causing some of the quality imbalance. The law does not prohibit exports of many other hydrocarbon liquids such as gasoline, diesel, jet fuel, or NGLs. Even though the law expired in 1994, it has been extended each year thereafter by the administration. The Bureau of Industry and Security (BIS), a part of the U.S. Department of Commerce, administers the law.

A license from BIS is required for all crude oil exports. But in the spirit of Catch-22, in most cases you can't get one. The regulations stipulate that BIS will only approve oil exports from Alaska, transported to Canada for use within Canada, that are drawn from the Strategic Petroleum Reserve, or are California heavy crude (California producers must have had a good lobbyist).

The only other option was thought to be export volumes specifically permitted by the U.S. president. The situation changed somewhat on June 24, 2014, when the *Wall Street Journal* broke a story that Enterprise Products Partners and Pioneer Natural Resources had obtained permissions from BIS to export lease condensate—apparently because their condensate had been satisfactorily processed to bypass the export ban. Basically, this ruling stated if condensate is processed in a certain way—through a distillation column—and is segregated from other crudes and condensates that have not been processed in the same manner, it becomes processed condensate and is treated as a petroleum product which therefore can be exported, just like gasoline, diesel and NGLs.

Since then, a number of condensate cargos have been exported from the Gulf Coast to Asia and Europe. While this regulatory change will relieve some of the quality imbalance problem, it is unlikely there will be large volumes of condensate exports. In other words, it will not make much of a difference. Logistical decisions, transportation costs, and other issues are likely to keep the level of condensates down to a level that will not have a significant impact on the imbalances. Instead, investments in processing infrastructure on the part of refiners can be expected to resolve most of the problem, and the resulting products will contribute to the growth in U.S. petroleum product exports.

> The increasing volumes of light crude from shale plays are out of sync with the capacity of U.S. refiners to run the oil. Exports cannot be used to resolve the imbalance due to U.S. law, except for small volumes of processed condensate. Consequently, U.S. refiners are increasing exports of refined petroleum products.

If light crude oil is produced in the United States, it must be refined in the United States since crude oil (with few exceptions) cannot be exported. And it cannot be stored forever. Consequently, refineries are being adapted to run the lighter crudes and condensates, and additional smaller units called condensate splitters are being built to add still more capacity to handle the light crude and condensate. The net result is additional motor gasoline and motor gasoline component (naphtha) production. For most of the past few years, the demand for gasoline in the United States has not been increasing. There has been some growth recently, but the long-term outlook for gasoline demand is quite uncertain. If domestic U.S. demand does not absorb the barrels, the only other possible market for the surplus gasoline supplies will be overseas exports. This is Domino 19. The bottom line: it is likely that U.S. exports of gasoline into world markets will be increasing significantly. In effect, the U.S. surplus of light crude is being exported, not as crude oil, but as gasoline and gasoline components, plus some processed condensate.

The Surplus Bubble Moves to the Gulf Coast

In Domino 10 (Chapter 3), crude oil prices in the Midcontinent fell, relative to prices both in the rest of the United States and world markets. Up until that point, prices for the international benchmark, Brent Crude, and the U.S. domestic benchmark, West Texas Intermediate (WTI), traded within $1–2/bbl of each other. As the Midcontinent crude glut swelled, WTI began to trade at a discount to Brent that widened to as much as $28/bbl in November 2011. This price disparity was the direct result of a build-up of crude oil inventories at the Cushing, Oklahoma trading hub. Growing crude production in North Dakota and Western Canada overwhelmed Midwest refinery needs and before long got caught in Cushing because of inadequate pipeline transport capacity to Gulf Coast refineries. The result was much lower Midcontinent crude prices. There was a lack of pipeline capacity to move the oversupply of crude to other markets, particularly the Gulf Coast. So WTI crude oil prices responded by declining, relative to Brent.

As we have seen so many times before, it was a classic takeaway capacity constraint problem, resulting in a wide price differential between the Midcontinent and the Gulf Coast. And as usual, the industry responded. Over the next couple of years, more than 20 capacity expansions were completed on many of the pipelines mentioned in Chapter 7, including Magellan Longhorn, Energy Transfer/Sunoco Permian Express,

Occidental/Magellan BridgeTex, the Enterprise/Enbridge Seaway pipeline, and the TransCanada Marketlink system. This new capacity did exactly what it was intended to do: bring crude stranded in Cushing down to the Gulf Coast and shrink the differential between Cushing WTI and Brent.

All of this supply coming down to the Gulf Coast accomplished two more things. First, it continued to back out waterborne imports, a trend underway throughout the shale revolution. Second, the additional capacity provided attractively priced supplies, which encouraged refiners to crank up utilization and maximize output.

U.S. Net Surpluses Push World Crude Oil Markets over the Edge

From 2008 to 2014, U.S. imports of crude oil declined about 25%, from 9.8 MMbbl/d to 7.3 MMbbl/d, down 2.5 MMbbl/d. But not all imports fell. In fact, imports from Canada increased. Since 2008, imports

> As increasing volumes of crude oil move to the Gulf Coast, imports are being backed out and refiners are increasing refinery production and product exports. The net result is to push U.S. crude surpluses into the world market.

from Canada grew by 0.9 MMbbl/d, from 2.0 MMbbl/d to 2.9 MMbbl/d. That increase is shown in the leftmost graph of Figure 15.2.

Imports from other parts of the world had to decline to make up for growing U.S. production and increasing imports. The largest decline in import volumes was from OPEC countries, falling 2.4 MMbbl/d over the same period shown in the second graph of Figure 15.2. Imports from all other countries (bottom graph, Figure 15.2)—much of the volume from Mexico and West Africa—declined another 1 MMbbl/d, about 40%.

The net result was a decline in imports from overseas suppliers of 3.4 MMbbl/d that hit the global markets with essentially the same impact exports of U.S. crude oil might have had. This volume is more than the entire crude oil production of Venezuela.

But those are not the only barrels being thrust into global markets. In 2008, the United States had net imports of gasoline and gasoline components of almost 1 MMbbl/d. Yet by the fourth quarter of 2014 the U.S. was

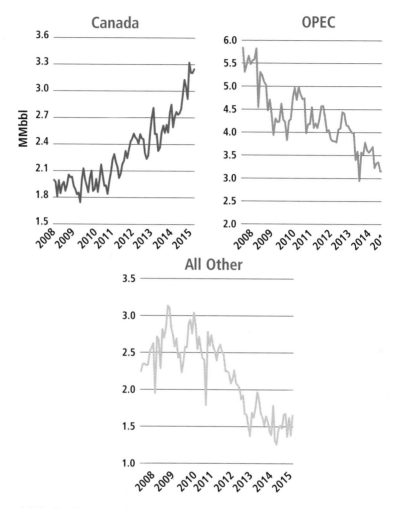

Figure 15.2. Declining crude imports in the U.S.

a net exporter, with the implication that these barrels too have been pushed into world markets. It is a similar story for diesel, with 2014 net exports also up over 0.5 MMbbl/d versus 2008. Consequently, product export volumes can be added to the 3.4 MMbbl/d of imports pushed back into world markets, indicating that a total of 4.9 Mbbl/d had been pushed out of the United States as of the end of 2014. Those volumes ultimately led to a dramatic realignment of world crude oil prices in late 2014 and early 2015.

In late 2014, demand growth mostly from the Asia/Pacific region had started to slow. At the same time, U.S. crude oil and product surpluses were taking market share from other crude-producing countries, either directly in the form of product exports or indirectly by forcing suppliers to find markets

> The combined impact of U.S. crude oil, product surpluses, and lower demand has led to a dramatic decline in world crude oil prices.

other than the United States for their crude oil barrels. The result was a collapse in crude prices over the 2014 Thanksgiving weekend, with WTI dropping $7.54/bbl that weekend to $66.15/bbl, which was down 38% since June of that year. Brent dropped to $70.02/bbl, lower by 39% in the same time frame. In the ensuing weeks, crude prices continued to fall. We will explore how the decline and fall of this huge domino is likely to play out in Chapter 20.

Chapter 16

NGLs: Rejection, Petrochemicals, and Exports

I N DOMINO 6, WE SAW THAT NGL PRODUCTION FROM NATURAL GAS PROCES-
*sors had increased from 1.6 MMbbl/d in 2009 to more than 2.4 MMbbl/d
by the end of 2012. The steady march of NGL production growth continued,
up to more than 3.0 MMbbl/d of NGLs from natural gas processing by early
2015. Although NGL prices fell in Domino 7, their value remained at least two
times the price of natural gas into 2015, even with much lower NGL prices due
to the crude price crash. Consequently, some producers continue to drill for natural gas in the higher liquids content NGL plays. Not only that, but the growth
in crude oil production that began in 2011 brought with it Domino 12's associated
gas, which also tends to have a high NGL content.*

*NGL production would be even higher if not for ethane rejection, the bane of
NGL production. With all of the production growth over the past few years, natural
gas processors can now make far more ethane than the U.S. petrochemical industry is able to use. As of the publication date of this book, ethane has yet to be exported to overseas markets due to lack of ethane export terminal capacity. That
infrastructure is coming soon, but until those docks and ships become available,
the only alternative disposition for surplus ethane is rejection (recall that ethane
rejection is the sale of ethane for its fuel value along with natural gas, rather than
being extracted and sold as a petrochemical feedstock). In 2014, about 260
Mbbl/d of ethane was rejected, about 20% of what could otherwise have been*

produced. In early 2015, that amount was up to more than 500 Mbbl/d, or 30%. Ethane rejection could continue for years. Even with several new large petrochemical plants slated for 2017–18, ethane rejection is likely to continue for the foreseeable future, based on the assumption that production growth continues to outpace demand growth. That has important implications for ethane prices and is a big economic driver for the NGL industry to find new markets for ethane.

Even with significant volumes of ethane being rejected, total NGL production is still growing fast. In order to process all of these liquids, an NGL infrastructure-building boom has been underway. During the period from 2013 through 2015, a number of new gas processing plants have come online, adding almost 16 bcf/d to U.S. gas processing plant capacity. These capacity increases have been split between the three highest NGL-volume growth regions: the Gulf Coast, the Appalachian region, and the Midcontinent/Rockies region. In addition, over the same time frame, several new large NGL pipeline projects have been developed, most of which bring mixed NGLs (y-grade) to the Gulf Coast. The number one destination for these pipelines is the major NGL storage and fractionation center at Mont Belvieu, Texas. New fractionators are also being built in Mont Belvieu, at other locations along the Gulf Coast, and in Appalachia.

As this infrastructure is completed and new NGL production flows into the market, the consequences for each of the NGL products are different, depending on demand and disposition alternatives for the specific products. But there is one overarching implication: the United States can now produce more NGLs than it can consume. The resulting outcome is most likely to be far more export volumes. In this chapter, we will explore both the near-term and long-term implications of that possibility.

Ethane and Rejection

Once produced, ethane has but one marketable use: as a petrochemical feedstock. Consequently, the petrochemical industry has the largest influence on ethane prices. However, sometimes the petrochemical industry cannot use all the produced ethane. This has been true during several periods in the past, it is true as this book goes to press, and is likely to remain true for the foreseeable future. During these periods of potential ethane abundance, the surplus is rejected, remains in the natural gas, and is sold as natural gas at natural gas prices. In the absence of a large-enough petrochemical market, the sale of ethane at gas value is usually not as high as the value of ethane sold into the petrochemical market on a Btu basis. Fortunately, since the natural gas market is much larger than the petrochemical market, there is effectively no limit on how much ethane can be sold as natural gas.

From a gas-quality perspective, however, there is a limit on how much ethane can be rejected or allowed to remain in the natural gas. Recall from Chapter 6 that if gas contains so much ethane that it exceeds a pipeline's quality specifications—the Btu specs, in particular—then the pipeline will not accept it for shipment. This is an important constraint on ethane rejection.

All the ethane not rejected is extracted at gas processing plants, fractionated into a purity product, and then moved to one of the 37 olefin crackers in the United States, almost all of which are located along the Texas and Louisiana Gulf Coast. Huge furnaces in these facilities crack, or break apart, the ethane molecules, which yields a number of petrochemical building blocks such as ethylene, propylene, benzene, and butadiene. These building-block chemicals are then used to make everyday products you use, from plastic trash bags to PVC pipe to antifreeze for your car. Unfortunately for ethane producers, these olefin crackers can only crack a finite volume of ethane, which is about 1,100 Mbbl/d as of early 2015. If more ethane than that is produced, it just goes into storage. When storage inventories get high, ethane prices drop and that triggers ethane rejection.

For the decades leading up to 2012, there had only been a few sporadic episodes of ethane rejection. But as the shale revolution drove NGL production ever higher, ethane prices dropped precipitously from about $0.75/gallon (Mont Belvieu pricing) in 2011 to an average of $0.40/gallon in 2012. By the end of that year, the price of ethane was less than $0.25/gallon. At the same time (December 2012), the price of natural gas at the Henry Hub in Louisiana was about $3.50/MMBtu, the equivalent of an ethane price of $0.2328/gallon. At that point, the price of ethane was almost down to the equivalent price of natural gas. How does that math work? Simply multiply $3.50 for a million Btus of gas by the number of Btus per gallon of ethane: 66,500. This gives you the price for a million gallons: $232,750. The price for natural gas converted to the equivalent price of one gallon of ethane is therefore $0.2328/gallon, slightly below the price of ethane. Thus you would think that the producer or gas processor would be better off selling the ethane as a liquid, rather than rejecting and selling it as natural gas.

But there is a catch: to get that price, the ethane must be transported to a fractionator, fractionated, and then moved on to a cracker. All of that costs money in the form of fees which, when grouped together, are called *transportation and fractionation*, or *T&F*. Thus the math for ethane rejection is a bit more complicated.

Assume T&F is $0.12/gallon. To compare the price of ethane to the equivalent price of natural gas, we need to subtract the T&F fee from the ethane price of $0.25/gallon. So the actual price the ethane producer receives would be $0.25 − $0.12 = $0.13/gallon, well below the equivalent price of gas. Based on those economics, the ethane would be rejected as long as it can go into the natural gas without violating the pipeline's Btu quality specifications or some other contractual requirement that mandates ethane recovery.

Here is the bottom line: ethane rejection is triggered by price. When ethane prices get cheap, producers and gas processors have an economic incentive to reject ethane.

Homes for Surplus Ethane: Petrochemicals and Exports

With all that cheap ethane being produced, it was inevitable that petrochemical companies would announce the construction of new olefin crackers. You will recall this was Domino 8: low NGL prices completely changed the economic environment for the U.S. ethylene cracker industry. Press releases at the time announced seven new olefin crackers designed to run on cheap ethane. Combined with upgrades to some of the existing crackers, new plants designed to run more than 600 Mbbl/d of additional ethane by 2018 have been announced, on top of the 1,100 Mbbl/d the industry was running in early 2015. That is a very significant increase in production.

But producers can make even more ethane than these new crackers can consume, perhaps as much as an additional 500 Mbbl/d, depending on the level of NGL prices. One contributing factor is that NGLs from shale gas tend to have a higher percentage of ethane. So *potential* ethane production is increasing faster than all other NGLs. Even so, not nearly that much ethane will actually be produced because so much will need to be rejected.

The fact is, even if all that ethane could be produced, it would still exceed the number of petrochemical plants being built by a half-million barrels per day. This is Domino 22. One scenario is continued rejection but an alternative is exporting it, which is one of the hottest potential markets for NGLs.

> Ethane production will likely continue to exceed the volume that can be absorbed by the U.S. petrochemical industry, even after several new petrochemical plants are built in the 2017-18 (and beyond) time frame.

Historically, ethane has been notoriously difficult to export because of its physical characteristics. Ethane must be held under very high pressure at ambient temperatures, or kept very cold in order to ship economic quantities overseas. With ethane surpluses continuing even after new olefin crackers come online, there are several ethane export initiatives underway, which is Domino 23.

The first project, announced in 2014, was a plan to move Utica/Marcellus-sourced ethane (from Range Resources and CONSOL Energy) through

> From the early years of the shale revolution and continuing into the 2020s, significant volumes of ethane will be exported from the United States, tightening the supply-and-demand balance for domestic ethane.

ETP Sunoco Logistics Partners' (SXL) Mariner East pipeline to an SXL ethane-loading terminal on the Delaware River in Marcus Hook, Pennsylvania. From there, the ethane would ship to INEOS, a petrochemical manufacturer in Northwest Europe. A few months later, Enterprise announced the construction of an ethane export terminal at Morgan's Point on the Houston Ship Channel to move Mont Belvieu ethane into the global market.

These projects and others being developed must deal with a number of complexities in moving U.S.-sourced liquid ethane into international petrochemical markets. Historically, the high cost and complexity of transporting ethane by ship has prevented such product movements. Now that is changing, but for ethane to move into overseas markets, the companies involved have had to remove four major barriers:

Loading and unloading terminal infrastructure. New facilities must be built to handle ethane. On the loading end, this includes a unit to chill the product down to a temperature near −127 degrees F. On the delivery end, this low temperature requires a special tank to hold the ethane.

Shipping. Because of the difficulty in shipping ethane, no ships designed to transport it are in service. Ships used for petrochemicals like ethylene can be used for ethane, but they are small and expensive. To move ethane in economic quantities over long distances, larger, more specialized vessels are required. Several new ships designed just to move ethane have been ordered and will be delivered starting in 2015.

Pricing. The third barrier is pricing. More specifically, pricing arrangements acceptable to both U.S. ethane sellers and overseas ethane buyers. The commodity price benchmark for U.S. ethane is the Mont Belvieu purity ethane price. When moved overseas, the ethane will be used in petrochemical crackers, just like in the United States. Currently, most overseas olefin crackers use naphtha as their primary feedstock, and the crackers would prefer to buy ethane at a guaranteed discount relative to naphtha. In contrast, most U.S. producers would prefer to sell ethane at a price tied to the Mont Belvieu ethane price. Various deal structures have been developed to address the differences in buyer and seller perspectives.

Petrochemical demand. Most international crackers are naphtha-based and require significant modifications to run ethane. These modifications cost hundreds of millions of dollars. Beyond the companies that have already announced plans to make ethane-related investments, it is unclear how many more international crackers will undertake such a significant investment to run U.S. ethane.

With Dominoes 22 and 23 dropping, the big question for ethane producers and U.S. ethane consumers is, "What happens next?" If enough was exported to tighten the U.S. market, the benefits of supplying cheap ethane for the new plants built by petrochemical companies could evaporate overnight. This would be a very big domino to fall and will be one of the most important NGL market developments to watch over the next five years.

Propane

Propane is the fastest growing product in the NGL family. In 2014, propane production from natural gas processing plants was responsible for more than half of the total growth in all NGL production. This is due to the combined impact of two factors:

- Propane makes up the second largest portion of the typical NGL barrel, second only to ethane.
- Propane does not have ethane's rejection issues. Since ethane became subject to rejection, it has held back ethane production growth.

U.S. propane production from natural gas processing plants grew about 260 Mbbl/d during the 2012–14 period, almost 35%. With lower crude prices in 2015, that pace of growth slowed, but would likely resume with only modest price increases. Refineries also produce propane, but their level of production is expected to be relatively constant.

With all the growth on the supply side, there has been no growth in U.S. demand, and only miniscule increases are anticipated. The only growth will come from the petrochemical sector. Several new petrochemical plants called *propane dehydrogenation units*, or *PDHs*, which produce propylene from propane, are scheduled for construction in the United States over the next few years. Declining propane demand from the residential and commercial market, where propane is used for fuel, will mostly offset this growth in petrochemical demand. The combined effect of conservation, more efficient appliances, and some propane customers shifting to natural gas or electricity for heating will likely keep a damper on overall propane demand.

So increasing supply and no new demand can only indicate one outcome: exports. Almost all propane volume will go to the export markets

Propane exports have increased dramatically and more growth is expected. In 2015, the United States could export more propane than is used in the entire U.S. residential and commercial propane market.

in Latin America, Europe, and the Asia-Pacific region.

As recently as 2009, propane exports were near zero and the United States was importing the product in significant volumes. But with production increasing and demand flat, by 2014 exports had increased to an average of more than 400 MMbl/d, and in early 2015 that number increased to more than 600 MMbl/d. That level is particularly significant since the entire volume of propane used by the residential and commercial propane market in the United States is only about 500 MMbl/d. The United States is now exporting as much volume as is used by all homes, businesses, and BBQ grills in the country. Domino 24 dropped. Propane exports have come into their own.

Normal Butane and Isobutane

Production of both normal butane and isobutane from natural gas processing plants has increased significantly over the past few years, getting pushed along with the growth in all NGL production from gas processing plants. Like propane, refineries also produce normal butane, in this case in the summer season when the demand for butane is low (due to the vapor pressure restrictions explained in Chapter 6). Not much change is expected in butanes supplies from refineries. As is the case with propane, the demand for butanes is stagnant.

The consequences of increasing supply and flat demand are exactly the same as those for propane: surpluses, mostly in the form of normal butane, will be exported.

LPG Exports and Dock Capacity

Liquefied petroleum gas (LPG) is the term used when referring to propane and butane in international markets. The rapid growth of U.S. LPG exports has radically changed the role of the United States in these markets. Figure 16.1 shows the major shift that has taken place. For decades, the United States has both imported and exported LPGs. Most of the imports have been propane for use in homes and businesses, through a number of terminals on the eastern seaboard. Most exports have been LPG surpluses from the Gulf Coast.

From the early 1980s until the early 2000s, waterborne imports (which excludes imports from Canada) were about equal in volume to total exports. In the mid-2000s, there was a brief surge of imports, just before NGL production started to ramp up due to the shale revolution. When the shale revolution took hold, exports skyrocketed.

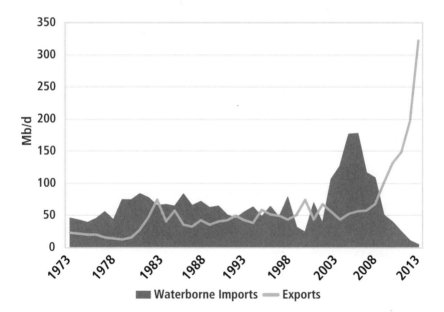

Figure 16.1. Imports and exports

The increases in export volumes happened not only because the surplus barrels were available for export but also because new export dock capacity was built. Prior to the shale revolution, the need for LPG export dock capacity was minimal, with most exports moving from the Gulf Coast over dock facilities owned by Enterprise Product Partners. Eventually, Targa developed competing dock facilities and both companies launched capacity expansion projects in the early 2010s. Another Gulf Coast LPG export facility from Energy Transfer Partners went into service in early 2015.

More expansions and new LPG docks are being developed and will be coming online in 2015 through 2018, mostly along the Gulf Coast, but also on the East and West Coasts. The Gulf Coast alone could have more than 1,200 Mbbl/d of LPG export facilities by 2017. Although there probably will not be enough propane and butane to take advantage of all that capacity, it still represents a huge opportunity for U.S. export volumes. The big question then is, "Where will all these exports go?" The answer could mean many more falling dominoes.

Where Will the LPG Exports Go?

LPGs trade in a robust international market, with transportation handled by hundreds of specially designed LPG seagoing tankers. Most of the major producers and exporters are in the Middle East, while most of the major consumers and importers of these waterborne LPG barrels are in the Asia-Pacific region. Figure 16.2 shows the major shipping routes for LPGs and the major market centers in the Middle East, Far East, Algeria, Northwest Europe, and the U.S.

The largest market for LPGs is Asia, where they are used both for heating and cooking, as well as transportation fuels and petrochemical feedstocks. Other significant markets are Europe, Latin America, to a lesser extent the Middle East (mostly for petrochemical feedstocks), and a few other countries.

Between 2012 and 2014, most of the increases in U.S. LPGs moved to Latin America, displacing volumes that region previously received from other parts of the world, such as Africa and the Middle East. Increasingly, U.S. volumes will be moving to Europe, also displacing quantities received from other producing regions. Those displaced barrels from Africa and the Middle East are destined for the Asia-Pacific region, which is the only LPG market where continued growth is anticipated. Much of the increase in demand is expected to come from China, where LPG is used to manufacture petrochemicals and for residential and commercial heating. India will also be a big market for LPGs displaced by U.S. exports, using it for heating and to power fleets of LPG-fueled vehicles. Japan, too, is looking to use more LPGs to manufacture petrochemicals, replacing naphtha in a portion of Japan's ethylene industry.

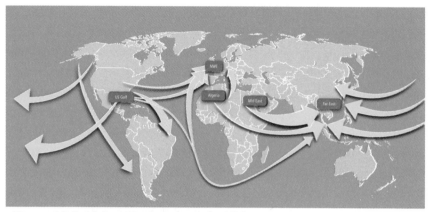

Figure 16.2. Major shipping routes for LPGs

Natural Gasoline

Production of natural gasoline increased (along with the surge in total NGL production) from about 270 Mbbl/d in the 2007-2010 time frame to almost 400 Mbbl/d in 2014.

As covered in Chapter 6, there are four traditional markets for U.S. natural gasoline. It is used:

- in blending for motor gasoline and into crude oil,
- as a feedstock for petrochemicals,
- as a diluent for bitumen crude, and
- as an exported product.

Natural gasoline has another use: as a denaturant in ethanol to make the alcohol unfit for human consumption. Regulations require ethanol producers to add this denaturant—about 2% by volume—to any ethanol destined to be blended into gasoline.

The fastest growing market for natural gasoline has been as a diluent. Natural gasoline, along with field condensate, is blended with heavy Canadian crude to liquefy it for transport in pipelines. Without a diluent, Canadian crude, or bitumen, is too viscous to be pumped through a pipeline. Diluent required for bitumen blending in 2013 (over and above Canadian domestic production of about 140 Mbbl/d) was about 300 Mbbl/d and could increase depending on what happens to Canadian heavy crude oil production over the next few years.

There is also considerable uncertainty about the demand for natural gasoline in other markets. For example, for most of the past five years, the use of natural gasoline as a petrochemical feedstock has been declining. The surge in NGL production has caused the price of ethane and propane—competing feedstocks for petrochemical crackers—to fall relative to crude oil, and natural gasoline prices have remained higher on a relative basis. Consequently most crackers have replaced natural gasoline feedstocks with ethane and propane to the extent possible.

The one final area of demand for natural gasoline is for blending into motor gasoline. Up until now, that demand has declined only slightly. However, over the next few years, using natural gasoline as a motor gasoline component could take a big hit due to increasing quantities of light crude, condensate, and diluent blended into Canadian heavy crudes arriving at refineries in significant volumes. These components could reduce refinery demand for additional natural gasoline, which again would force the surplus natural gasoline into the export market.

The bottom line for natural gasoline is the same as for the other NGL products. The United States can make more NGLs than it can use, which means the only other market is overseas exports. But just as the crude oil market has experienced, there is a big question as to how much of this surplus the overseas markets can absorb. Any NGLs displaced by U.S. volumes will need to go somewhere. And it is the same story for naphtha, displaced in the crackers around the world by U.S. NGLs. Watch out for those falling dominoes.

Chapter 17

Natural Gas: Marcellus, Utica, Flow Reversals, and Demand

A *"GAME CHANGER." THAT'S WHAT THE NEWSPAPERS AND ANALYSTS CALLED the huge natural gas ramp-up in 2010 and 2011. It was Domino 12, when Lower-48 U.S. natural gas production grew from 55 bcf/d to nearly 65 bcf/d, for an increase of about 18% over that two-year period. Even though much of the public and even some government officials were late to the party, by 2011 the shale revolution was finally being recognized for what it was. All this happened while natural gas prices languished around $4/MMBtu, considered quite low at the time. In fact, it became apparent that those low prices stayed low and eventually fell much lower because of all the production growth, which was Domino 13.*

However, by 2012–13, low prices started to take their toll. Production from conventional (non-shale) wells continued to fall. Even in some of the big, dry gas shale plays like the Haynesville and Fayetteville, drilling slowed significantly due to low prices. No surprise there, but a big surprise was coming: total natural gas production continued to increase! Much of that growth was driven by natural gas plays with a higher NGL content, as well as from crude oil plays that came along with associated natural gas. But the real surprise is that there was a dry gas play that was taking off like a skyrocket. Another domino was dropping, and it was a big one. The revolution had returned home. To Appalachia.

The Rebirth of Appalachia

As we saw in Chapter 5, the first 40 years of the U.S. natural gas market were dominated by Appalachia, the birthplace of the crude oil and natural gas industry. But by World War I, most of the easy-to-produce oil and gas was playing out. Production in the region had reached its peak and volumes in Texas, Louisiana, and Oklahoma were taking off. Eventually, Appalachian production fell into a long, slow decline, and the region became a backwater of the oil and gas markets. Only a few small wells were drilled, mainly for supplies across Pennsylvania, West Virginia, Ohio, and a few neighboring states.

Appalachia survived as a producing region mostly because it enjoyed relatively high prices. This was due to its proximity to some of the largest natural gas markets in North America, such as the cities of Philadelphia, New York City, Newark, Hartford, Boston, and Washington D.C. Another survival strategy for the region was conversion of many of the original oil and gas fields into natural gas storage facilities, receiving supply from the southwest in the summer and pumping it into storage formations for extraction during the winter heating season. By the 1970s, the Appalachian Basin, site of the iconic Drake well, had been relegated to the role of a huge storage tank for natural gas.

For much of the history of Appalachian oil and gas drilling, it was well known that the source rock for much of the region's production came from the Marcellus Shale formation. The Marcellus is big; it is one of the largest contiguous shale formations in the world. It extends from New York through Pennsylvania, Ohio, and West Virginia. Its thickness ranges from about 50 feet in eastern Ohio, western New York, western Pennsylvania, and northern West Virginia, to as much as 200–250 feet in northeastern Pennsylvania. Although the Marcellus Shale was always known to have a high organic content—meaning it contained lots of gas and liquids—its hydrocarbons were trapped by the low permeability of the formation, making it difficult to drill and essentially impossible to complete wells capable of producing enough oil and gas to be economically viable. As a result, producers just ignored the Marcellus Shale in favor of conventional Appalachian plays, which were easier to drill and produce, or avoided the region altogether.

Then in 2004, Range Resources decided to try shale drilling and fracturing techniques in the Appalachian Basin. The firm drilled what is recognized as the first *modern* Marcellus Shale well, the Renz #1, located southwest of Pittsburgh. The well began production in 2005, and the rest is history. Other producers followed Range into the region; more than 760 Marcellus wells were drilled in 2009 alone. Gas production from shale in Pennsylvania and West Virginia exploded, from less than 0.2 bcf/d in early 2009 to more than 2.0 bcf/d by late 2010. And it just kept on growing. By 2012, it was the fastest growing natural gas-producing basin in the United States.

The Renz Well #1

Drilling the Renz #1 was no accident. Most producers had the notion that the Appalachian Basin was played out. But in 2000, a geologist for Range Resources named Bill Zagorski, studying decades-old documentation, came upon records of another well, the Kelly-Sutherland, drilled on land owned by a farmer named Renz. There had been a blowout—a big one—and, upon further inspection and analysis, it gave Zagorski reason to believe there was oil and gas worth developing down in that Marcellus Shale. Seismic tests and studies confirmed his suspicions and, in 2003, drilling began. Almost at once, they hit gas. A lot of gas. Then it stopped. Zagorski was mortified; he had spent several million dollars of Range's limited drilling budget and appeared to have failed.

The ah-ha moment came in 2004. Zagorski got a call from some colleagues in Texas to come have a look at the well they were considering drilling in the Black Warrior Basin in Alabama. Part of the analysis included a comparison of the Black Warrior to the emerging Barnett Shale west of Fort Worth. "At that time I hardly knew what the Barnett Shale was," Zagorski later said. At some point in his review of the data, he realized that the Marcellus actually looked—from a geological perspective—strikingly similar to the Barnett Shale.

He convinced Jeff Ventura, Range president and CEO, to let him try again, and this time it worked. The following year a horizontal shaft was drilled, the shale was fracked, and the well produced commercial quantities of gas. The Renz yielded about 300 Mcf/d the first day. Then the rate doubled, and then tripled. The oil and gas industry in Appalachia had joined the shale revolution.

By 2012 as the Marcellus was hitting its stride, the Utica, another Appalachian shale play a few thousand feet below the Marcellus, started to kick in. It is about twice as big as the Marcellus, extending from Ohio, Pennsylvania, and West Virginia, into New York, Quebec, Ontario, and beneath Lake Erie and Lake Ontario. Like the Marcellus, the Utica was also known to be rich in hydrocarbons but was mostly ignored in the early days of the Marcellus because it was deeper and therefore more expensive to drill. Ohio producers were forced to go into the Utica to reach economically viable quantities of oil, gas, and NGLs because the productive part of the Marcellus does not extend into Ohio. Fortunately, the Utica gets shallower in Ohio (see Figure 17.1), which means Ohio is the center of Utica production.

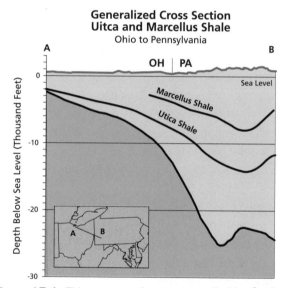

Figure 17.1. This cross section was compiled by Geology.com using data provided by the Energy Information Administration, the United States Geological Survey, the Pennsylvania Geological Survey, and the U.S. Department of Energy.

In 2014 the Utica represented only about 7% of total Appalachian production, but the play is growing very rapidly and is likely to make up more than 15% of total production by 2020. As will be examined in more detail below and with all due respect to Texas and Louisiana, the center of U.S. production growth has shifted to Appalachia.

Northeast Natural Gas Production Skyrockets and Some Prices Crater

The importance of Appalachia to the shale revolution quite simply cannot be overstated. Not only are the Marcellus and Utica plays responsible for most of the growth in total U.S. natural gas production, they are located adjacent to the Northeast, one of the U.S. regions of greatest natural gas heating demand. Figure 17.2 demonstrates the significance of this development. In this graph, total U.S. production has been split into two buckets. The dashed line (referencing the left volume scale) is production of natural gas from the Lower-48 United States in all other regions except Appalachia. The second series (solid line referencing the right scale) is production from Appalachia. Note that these numbers represent total Appalachian Basin production, which includes legacy production from wells that may have been drilled decades ago. Also, even though the two lines need to be read using different scales (dashed on the left, solid on the right), the interval from the bottom to the top is the same: 16 bcf. So the magnitude of decline shown by the *rest of the United States* is directly comparable to the growth in Appalachia.

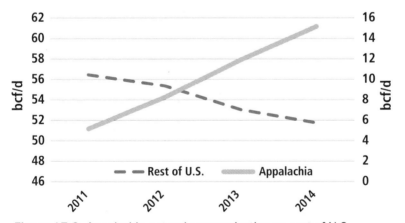

Figure 17.2. Appalachia natural gas production vs. rest of U.S.

The implications of this graph are striking. Over the period between 2011 and 2014, the rest of the Lower-48 United States saw production fall from about 56 bcf/d to about 52 bcf/d. During the same period, the Appalachian Region rose by an astonishing 10 bcf/d. This is Domino 25.

As natural gas production in the Marcellus and Utica plays has accelerated, the Northeast has become the fastest growing supply region in the United States.

There are two primary reasons why the Appalachian Region has been so much more prolific than the rest of the United States. First, the Marcellus has a dry gas window in northeastern Pennsylvania where wells have been coming in at huge volumes—single sites that would have been called fields a few years ago. For example, in December 2013, Cabot Oil & Gas brought a single-site, 10-well Marcellus pad online, which achieved a peak production rate of 201 MMcf/d and an average 30-day rate of 168 MMcf/d. That is about half as much gas as is produced from the entire Texas Offshore region, an area that 10 years ago provided 5% of Lower-48 United States gas supplies. As of mid-2015, other parts of Appalachia are starting to register equally large dry gas wells.

NGLs have been the second reason for the high growth in Appalachian production. The areas in southwestern Pennsylvania, West Virginia, and Ohio have a very high NGL content. Just like other plays that saw the impact of Domino 4 (when producers shifted to drilling for NGLs and crude oil after natural gas prices declined), this part of the Appalachian Basin has seen a huge increase in drilling for wet gas.

In a classic case of surplus begets shortage, the phenomenon introduced in Chapter 12, the pace of natural gas production growth overwhelmed pipeline takeaway capacity in some parts of the Marcellus and Utica. Although demand in the Northeast Region is huge, it is quite seasonal, spiking up in the coldest winter months (for heating) and hottest summer days (for power generation to meet the air conditioning load) and dropping to much lower levels in the spring and fall. The result has been very low natural gas prices for producers in several of the most prolific Marcellus/Utica producing regions, such as the dry gas area of northeastern Pennsylvania. Summer prices there for the past two years have been quite low, and are expected to continue to experience price pressure for several years to come. The west side of Appalachia, with more wet gas regions, has also experienced lower prices, though not quite as severe as northeastern Pennsylvania. As a general rule, the faster the production growth of a given area, the greater the price pressure it experiences. These lower regional gas prices are Domino 26.

> Increasing Appalachian production from the Marcellus/Utica has resulted in lower natural gas prices in the region.
>
> 26

The Great Flow Reversal

This dramatic increase in Northeast natural gas production is leading to radical changes in traditional natural gas flow patterns. Historically, natural gas flowed into the Northeast from four supply sources in North America: the Southeast/Gulf region, the Rockies, the Midcontinent, and Canada. The region also received some overseas imports in the form of LNG. As Northeast production continues to grow, the region is becoming increasingly self-sufficient. Figure 17.3 below compares Northeast natural gas production and demand. Back in 2010, Northeast production was less than 5 bcf/d, while demand averaged about 15 bcf/d, making the Northeast a *net-demand region*, which it had been ever since World War II. But that is changing. For the first time, in 2015, Northeast natural gas production will exceed demand, transitioning the Northeast from its traditional role as a demand region to a *net-supply region*.

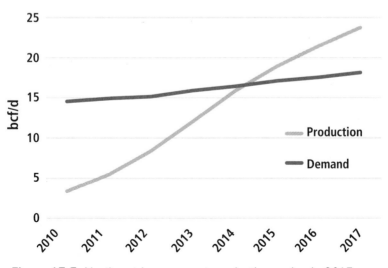

Figure 17.3. Northeast becomes net production region in 2015

This transition has significant implications for pipelines, which traditionally moved natural gas into the region. As explained earlier, prior to the emergence of the Marcellus, Appalachian natural gas supplies had declined steadily since World War II, while population growth—and demand—had grown just as steadily. That growing regional demand was met by gas shipped in from other parts of the United States, or overseas. Even all this gas was not enough to meet high winter demand swings, so storage (those depleted oil and gas fields mentioned earlier) was filled in the summer when pipeline capacity was available. In the winter, storage volumes were drawn down and supplemented with flows from those external sources of supply.

Many of the largest pipelines in North America have provided transportation capacity for this gas supply to the Northeast. Three of the most important of these pipelines are sometimes referenced by industry insiders as the *T-pipe systems* (because their names all start with a "T"): Kinder Morgan's Tennessee Gas Pipeline, Spectra's Texas Eastern Transmission (TETCO) pipeline, and the Williams Transco pipeline. Prior to 2010, these three pipelines brought almost 7 bcf/d into the Northeast on the coldest winter days. That volume was down to 5 bcf/d in 2011. During the polar vortex winter of 2013-14, the total volume bumped above 2 bcf/d for a few days. Several other pipelines, such as the TransCanada mainline system, Tallgrass Rockies Express, and the Columbia Gas system, have also been responsible for moving huge quantities of needed gas into the Northeast.

Now, with all the Marcellus and Utica growth in production, much of the gas coming from these pipelines is no longer needed. Flow volumes on all of these pipelines are down significantly and several are actually starting to reverse their direction, moving gas out of the Northeast to the Midwest, Southeast, and Canada.

As noted above, continued production growth will transition the Northeast into a net production region. Over time, the Northeast's need for gas from outside the region will disappear except for the coldest winter days, and the pipelines used to bring that gas to the market will no longer be required. New pipelines and projects to reverse existing pipelines will move natural gas from where there is supply to where there is demand. Recall this is the First Law of Energy Markets introduced back in Chapter 13: energy wants to move from a lower-value market to a higher-value market. As a consequence of that law and the changes brought about by the shale revolution, flows of natural gas across North America are reversing direction, which is Domino 27.

Billions of dollars in infrastructure investment will be required to make this transition happen. Between 2013 and 2020, over 70 pipeline expansions, modifications, or new *greenfield pipelines* have been or will be built in the Northeast or in adjacent regions on the receiving end of all this gas. Existing long-haul pipelines will make the necessary changes in their systems to reverse the flow toward other areas of the United States, as well as into northeast Canada and to LNG export facilities for shipment overseas. New gathering systems and pipelines will be needed to move the gas from the Marcellus and Utica producing regions to these long-haul pipelines. Other downstream pipelines will be required to shift their operations to accommodate this onslaught of gas coming from the Northeast.

> New pipeline takeaway capacity being built out of the Northeast is reversing the direction of gas flows across the United States. Since the 1930s, gas has flowed mostly north and east. Within a few years, the prevailing gas flow pattern in North America will be mostly south and west.

Where Is All That Gas Going to Go?

As Northeast gas rushes out of the region, the central question becomes "Where is all of that gas going to go?" Three sectors comprise the most demand for natural gas in the United States: residential and commercial, industrial, and power generation. The largest sector is residential and commercial, making up about 35% of total demand. Over the past several years, demand in this sector has been flat at best, with efficiency and conservation gains offsetting a gradual increase in the number of homes and businesses with gas heating. That trend is unlikely to change.

Thus any increase in demand will need to come from some combination of the industrial sector (which makes up about 31% of demand), the power sector (which today is about 34% of demand), and export markets. Included in the export markets is expanding gas demand in Mexico and the nascent liquefied natural gas (LNG) export market, which today is limited to tiny volumes from Alaska but is expected to grow significantly over the next few years. Can these demand sources absorb all of the new production expected to come into the market? Demand from the industrial and power sectors has certainly responded in the past. Between 2005 and 2014, natural gas industrial demand was up 2.9 bcf/d (16%), while demand for power generation was up 6.2 bcf/d (39%). Although those increases are significant, they are well below the rate of production growth over the same time frame, which was closer to 40%. The market balanced by backing out imports from Canada as well as LNG imports from overseas suppliers. A combination of demand and supply adjustments was required to balance the market. It is likely the same kind of adjustments will be needed over the next few years.

Part V

Break on Through to the Other Side: The New World of Energy Abundance

UP UNTIL THE EARLY 1990s, THE INTERNET WAS A RESOURCE FOR THE PRIV-
ileged few: computer science engineers and academics, the National Science Foundation, and government defense agencies. All that changed in
1991 when the English computer scientist Tim Berners-Lee introduced
several key technologies such as the Hypertext Transfer Protocol, plain
English domain names, and the World Wide Web. It was a revolution in
the use of online information.

That brings to mind another global revolution: representative democ-
racy. That one started about 240 years ago in the United States. It also
went global in relatively short order, spreading the concept first to Europe, then to Latin America, and eventually to many other parts of the
world. Both of these ideas changed the world. In between, other revolutions, from transportation to telecommunications, have gone global.

You might think that the shale revolution would also become a global
phenomenon. But not so. Even though the effects of the shale revolution
have certainly been felt globally, the revolution itself seems to be confined to the United States—in fact, just a few parts of the United States.
Is it because the U.S. has all the shale in the world? Hardly. Potentially
productive shale can be found underneath at least 10 million square
miles of the Earth's surface. To put that number in perspective, the entire
surface area of the United States, Canada, and Mexico combined cover

only 8 million square miles. U.S. shale makes up only about 9% of the world's total, and only a tiny fraction of U.S. shale acreage is actually producing hydrocarbons today. There must be good reasons why the shale revolution has remained bottled up in the United States for the past decade, and there are.

These final chapters are about how the shale revolution will play out in the future, and how the domino effect can help make sense of the upcoming market developments. To understand these dynamics, it is important to start with the reasons why the shale revolution has been confined to the United States. That is the subject of Chapter 18. Chapter 19 examines how the effects of the shale revolution are playing out on the world stage. Then in Chapter 20 we get to the bottom line: which dominoes can be expected to fall next, and why. Finally, Chapter 21 steps back and looks at the big picture: how the domino effect will drive energy markets for decades—if not centuries—to come.

Chapter 18

Does the United States Have a Monopoly on Shale?

S INCE SHALE HYDROCARBONS CAN BE FOUND ACROSS THE WORLD, IT SEEMS *like there should be no good reason why the benefits of the revolution should not extend to any country with shale resources. And yet, the pace of shale development in countries other than the United States is proceeding very slowly, and often not at all. The goal of this chapter is to provide an understanding of both the scientific and the human factors which contribute to the ease or difficulty of shale exploration and production in any country. In light of these factors, what follows is a summary of the current state of shale production in several notable regions where shale development, at least theoretically, could occur. As we do so, we will compare and contrast conditions in these regions with those in the United States, which has made the successful exploitation of its shale resources a reality.*

There are a variety of factors that contribute to the success of shale production, which we can separate roughly into two categories: below-ground factors and above-ground factors.

- **Below-ground factors** *are directly related to the physical geology of a particular shale formation or the costs of drilling and completing a well. Formation depth, production decline curve, and exploration costs are all below-ground factors.*

- **Above-ground factors** *are the legal, political, and business conditions ex-*

isting in the country where a physical resource play is located. For example, mineral rights, existing infrastructure, macroeconomic policy, and social attitudes regarding the environment are all above-ground factors.

Successful shale development requires positive alignment of both below-ground and above-ground factors. Unfortunately, this rarely occurs. For example, there may be shale rock in the right place geologically and development of the resource may be economically viable. But if a region's legal, political, or business institutions stand in the way of shale production, it will not happen. Let us take a closer look at each.

Below-Ground Factors

Below-ground factors have everything to do with the physical configuration of the shale gas formation and the associated costs of exploration, drilling, and well completion. If the shale formation is not favorably situated, these factors can make shale development extremely challenging, if not economically unviable, to drill and produce. Below-ground obstacles to drilling exist everywhere, in the United States as well as the rest of the world. For example, the Marcellus Shale spans five states in the Northeast. But today, only about 10% of that entire area is seeing any serious drilling activity. Much of the shale in the region is not suitable for economic drilling and production for a variety of reasons associated with the rock itself, at least using today's technologies. Across the rest of the world, shale development has many of the same problems as the noneconomic portions of the Marcellus. There are several significant below-ground factors which account for this.

Geology

The unique challenges producers face when trying to explore and develop a shale formation into a commercially viable resource stem from its distinctive geology. These challenges arise primarily from three sources: formation depth, formation composition, and formation complexity.

Formation depth. Shale formations can be found anywhere, from outcrops at the earth's surface to 15,000 feet or more below. Deep shales (at depths greater than 15,000 feet) can be very difficult to produce.

Their depth alone makes them quite expensive to drill, and they tend to be under very high pressures, which results in difficult drilling conditions. Shallow shales (with a depth of less than 3,000 feet) also have problems. Much of the hydrocarbon content may have percolated out of the formation over millions of years, leaving nothing but rock. Only shale at the "right depth" will actually provide economically viable wells.

Formation composition. As mentioned earlier, no two shale formations are alike. Many are difficult to drill because the formation's composition creates conditions that make it difficult for hydrocarbons to flow through the fractures in the rock (the result of fracking) and into the well. For example, shale with a high clay content can cause the fractures to close up soon after fracking. Worse yet, the formation may be susceptible to what production engineers call *borehole instability*. Put simply, the shale's composition can result in mechanical problems such as hole closure, hole enlargement, and possibly the complete collapse of the well. All of these conditions are bad for the driller; sometimes they can be worked around, sometimes not.

Formation complexity. Shale may start out as a large, flat sedimentary formation, but over its millions of years of geological life it will be subjected to varying amounts of tectonic and seismic activity that can break it up. Imagine the beginning of a shale formation as a large glass pane sandwiched between two layers of sand in a plastic tub. Now imagine a car drives over the tub, compressing the sand and breaking the glass. This is the effect when faults ripple through the shale. Next, pick that tub up and shake it a bit. This is similar to seismic activity. At the end of this process, we can imagine there are a lot of disconnected glass shards mixed in with the sand. This analogy is similar to the structure of shale deep underground, where a large, flat formation has quite possibly been broken and deformed into a number of disconnected pieces. The greater the tectonic and seismic activity, the more complex or disorganized the shale formation becomes.

Production from a shale well depends on drilling so the wellbore has the largest amount of contact possible with the shale formation. Trying to hit several pieces with a single well is a bit like playing connect-the-dots in the dark. Every shale formation is different, as it is subject to varying amounts of seismic and tectonic activity. Obviously, the more broken up, the more difficult to drill successfully. Producers must learn from the use of sophisticated seismic data, steerable downhole motors that allow the wellbore to change direction as the formation changes, and a bit of trial and error to determine the best way to drill into the formation in order to maximize contact and obtain the highest productivity.

Total Organic Carbon or TOC. This is a measure of the quantity of hydrocarbons in the rock, expressed as a percentage. For example, 4% is considered an excellent TOC number for shale, while anything below 0.5% is considered poor. A good number is typically between 1% and 2%. As a general rule, the higher the TOC, the more economically attractive the shale play. Not only does TOC vary greatly from one region to the next, there can be a huge range within a given shale play. The high TOC content areas are considered the sweet spots and are usually the best candidates for drilling. Low TOC areas are usually not drilled. Although the low TOC shale may be at the right depth, with the right geology, it simply does not contain enough hydrocarbons to justify the cost of drilling and developing a well with current technologies and market conditions.

Part Science, Part Art

Getting a viable well drilled is the end result of what drillers call *breaking the code* of a shale formation. Since every shale formation is unique in its depth, composition, and geological complexity, each time a producer moves from one shale to another the process of learning what it takes to break the code begins all over again. As George Mitchell (see Chapter 2) learned from 15 years of experimentation in the Barnett Shale, it involves a great deal of money, time, and uncertainty to, hopefully, drill a commercially viable production well. By definition, exploration is trial and error and thus expensive. Often, this trial-and-error process is marked by technological breakthroughs based on the unique, innovative, and creative ways drilling problems are solved. Consequently, the code-breaking process for each new shale play is as much art as it is science.

Due to the combination of below-ground factors, the exploration and development of shale resources carries with it a great deal of uncertainty. In practice, oil and gas companies exploring for shale hydrocarbons have no idea how much time, money, or technology it will take to break a shale formation's code—or if it is possible at all. This distinction is necessary, for in the discussion of above-ground factors it becomes apparent that some producing organizations are quite averse to ambiguity in decision-making and uncertainty in drilling projects, which affects their willingness to explore new, undeveloped shale formations. In other words, the science may be used for factual assessment, but it's still up to the humans to make the artful decisions. A prime example of this was the story of the Renz #1 well, related in Chapter 17: the left-brain side may have said, "No, don't drill again," but the right-brain side said, "Let's give it another go with one last tweak to the process, just in case this one might work." It did. Some producers have the risk tolerance to deal with that level of uncertainly and ambiguity. Many do not. We will explore this issue further at the end of the next section covering above-ground factors.

Above-Ground Factors

Arguably, the most important factors affecting the production of shale gas resources are those above ground. They govern the incentives of producing shale resources and also the decisions companies make to engage in exploration and production—or not.

Mineral Rights

One of the most important above-ground factors associated with the production of hydrocarbons in the United States is securing the *mineral rights* for the underground resource. In the United States, mineral rights characterize an owner's prerogative to exploit his or her property for any or all resources it harbors. Legally it is a *mineral estate*, which means an interest in real property. It is something that can be *owned* by an individual or any other entity. In the United States, these rights are owned either by the owner of the surface rights or some other person or entity. In some cases federal or state governments may own mineral rights, but individuals own most rights to shale formations being produced today in the United States.

For example, a farmer in West Texas may own the rights to produce all of the hydrocarbons underneath his property and can lease the right to produce those hydrocarbons to any third party he chooses. Or that farmer may have purchased the land without the mineral rights (said to have been severed from the surface rights) and those mineral rights might be owned by descendants of a former owner of the land and mineral rights a century ago. Regardless, the owner of the mineral rights can lease the rights to produce those minerals, and the company leasing those rights obtains the legal authority to produce and sell those minerals, almost always providing some percentage of the proceeds back to the mineral rights owner.

In most of the rest of the world, individuals do not usually own similar mineral rights; they belong to the state instead. This means that owning a plot of land does not give the owner any rights to the minerals underneath it, and neither can those rights be leased by that surface owner to any other individual or company.

Typically, if a company wants to develop a shale play in most countries outside of the United States, it must first petition the government for a license to begin exploration on plots of land that have been designated for drilling activity. Next, if commercially viable reserves are found, the company must again petition to convert the exploration license into a production license. Typically, these petitions include a development plan, environmental impact statements, and additional plans for buildings and plants. Licensing procedures vary from country to country. In some, the process is relatively straightforward; an exploration license can be converted to a production license quickly and easily. But in many other countries, there are no guarantees the production license will not simply be sold to the highest bidder. Production licenses may be awarded by competitive tender, regardless of which company performed the exploration. The effect of this process of acquiring property rights is fourfold:

- First, the process of acquiring and converting licenses can result in significant delays. Often, months and years go by between license application and approval.
- Second, in many countries this process is rife with extortion by government officials, which increases the costs of exploration.
- Third, state-owned mineral rights allow the government to exclude any or all independent companies from exploration and production. This was historically the case in Mexico, where until recently private participation in hydrocarbon production was banned under constitutional law.

■ Fourth, the process significantly increases the uncertainty that the right to produce oil and gas will be granted or whether an exploration license will ever be converted to a production license. It is quite possible that one company will spend the money to prove out the play and then another company is granted the right to produce that play.

Due to its mineral rights laws, such a thing cannot happen in the United States, where gaining the right to explore and produce on a plot of land can be as easy as leasing a farmer's mineral rights on the property he owns. The producer pays a lease-signing bonus up front, agreeing to give the farmer a cut of the revenues (termed royalties, discussed in Chapter 9) followed by filing the signed lease document at the county courthouse. In contrast, obtaining the rights to explore and produce outside the United States can be a nightmare of bureaucratic red tape, delays, complex applications, and graft, any or all of which significantly increase the costs of resource development.

Government Policies: Price Controls

In the United States, market forces determine the production and sale of hydrocarbons. Hydrocarbon owners can sell at any price they wish, provided there is a buyer willing to pay that amount. On the other hand, in some countries hydrocarbon pricing is severely restricted by government decree, sometimes at prices below cost. Being unable to sell produced hydrocarbons at market prices clearly reduces incentives for production. For example, in an extreme case in 2012, Repsol (the large Spanish integrated energy company) was accused by the Argentinian government of failing to sufficiently invest in domestic production, which led to an energy crunch. Repsol blamed government price controls that kept prices low, which resulted in their limited investment in production. The situation ultimately led to the forced nationalization of Repsol's Argentinian assets.

Macroeconomic Policy

Shale exploration, as we have seen, is an expensive process requiring a significant amount of capital. Independent producers in a country with a weak banking sector caused by poor monetary policy, high levels of debt, or even sovereign default find it very difficult to secure sufficient amounts of credit for exploration and production activities. For these and other reasons, many additional countries often have a difficult time attracting large experienced multinational corporations to invest in drilling. For example, as of August 2014, following the Repsol settlement, Argentina went into technical default on its debt obligations. Such economic difficulties increase the risk of investment, discouraging shale development.

Existing Infrastructure

Once a company has developed a shale play to the point where it is producing commercially, there must be infrastructure in place to move the production to market. Certainly, the most preferable way to do so is by pipeline, but what if none exist? Pipelines are expensive (averaging over $1.5 million per mile) and take two to five years to build, depending on length. Due to its long history of oil and gas production, the United States is fortunate to have had a significant amount of midstream infrastructure (gathering systems, processing facilities, and pipelines) in place before the shale revolution. That is simply not the case in many other countries with shale development potential. The need to build out production and transport infrastructure from scratch vastly increases the cost of developing and marketing shale resources. For example, the Canning Basin in Western Australia has 235 Tcf of technically recoverable shale gas, but it is literally in the middle of the country's outback and will require billions in infrastructure investment before it becomes commercially viable.

Access to Water

The process of hydraulically fracturing a shale gas well requires 500,000 to as much as 10 million gallons of water, a huge amount. Clearly, access to a cheap source of nearby water is of crucial importance to successful well completion. Difficulty getting water can quickly add to the cost of shale development. In China, for example, some of the notable shale formations are in areas where surface water is very scarce and any available water is already dedicated to human needs.

Environmental Attitudes

In recent years, public concern surrounding the environmental consequences of hydraulic fracturing has increased significantly. Both within and outside the United States, there is an ongoing political duel between environmental groups and the oil and gas industry regarding if, where, and how much fracking should be allowed. For example, as of this writing, the state of New York bans fracking. So do Germany, France, and several other countries.

Success of Independent Producers and Big Company Problems

The shale gas revolution in the United States was pioneered by waves of small, independent companies willing to accept the uncertainties of shale exploration and production. Most oil and gas majors active in U.S. shale bought their way into the shale production business by purchasing one or more of these independents rather than developing the resource themselves. Yet even after such acquisitions, some large producers have been unsuccessful in shale and a few have even divested their holdings. Why? Let us explore why most large corporations seem to be culturally ill-equipped to pioneer shale resource development. Principally, there are two reasons: a low tolerance for uncertainty and an equally low tolerance for repeated failures.

Tolerance for Uncertainty. Large energy companies are expert at taking large risks. They will pour billions of dollars into a risky investment if the expected cash flow and rate of return justifies it. However, calculating an expected rate of return requires the ability to quantify the probability of a successful investment. As discussed in the below-ground factors section, developing a new shale play can defy efforts to quantify or even estimate the probability of successful development. Every shale formation is unique, and previous experience developing one may be of little help in breaking the code in a different formation. As good as large energy companies are at managing risk, they are usually poorly suited to taking on *ambiguous uncertainty*, the kind of uncertainty which does not fit well into structured risk analysis and decision-making. In other words, big oil and gas companies are good at managing the uncertainties they know about. They are not so good at managing the unknown. This is where small independent producers come in: historically, they have a much higher tolerance for ambiguity. Think about it this way: the payoff to developing a commercially successful shale well is something like winning the lottery.

If the risk is split between a small number of hard-working entrepreneurs and they win, each of them can buy a fleet of boats and a marina to go with it. They are comfortable taking on more ambiguous uncertainty because the reward—if they are successful—is so huge.. On the other hand, if you are a manager of exploration and development at a large corporation, there are two possible outcomes to the development of a pioneering shale well: one, your efforts are an expensive failure and your career is tarnished, or two, the well is a success and your company makes money. But if the latter, those huge profits accrue to the company while you might get a bonus or raise that is small in comparison to the level of risk you took on. The disparity in risks and rewards in big companies encourages conservative investing and decision-making, while the independent invests aggressively.

Tolerance for Repeated Failure. This is another and even more important dimension to the issue of risk tolerance. It is generally associated with the source of investment capital. How much risk is the *money* willing to take? Private equity investors with large appetites for risk provide funding for many smaller U.S. independent producers. They, too, understand the lottery economics of early shale development and may invest in several companies, each with a huge upside potential if they happen to score a success. Here's how that can play out in shale development. Company #1 tries to break the code in a new play and fails, and they depart for greener pastures. But Company #2 thinks they are smarter and tries again. Perhaps they also fail and fade from the scene. The process may repeat itself over and over again until some lucky or highly talented producer breaks the code and wins the lottery for themselves and their financial backers. Or not. Sometimes the shale play has such a complex code that it simply cannot be cracked. At least not with technologies available today.

The point is, tolerance for repeated failure is built into the mindset of the U.S. small independent producers often pioneering early shale plays. The culture of large companies can rarely stomach so much failure. It is almost impossible to imagine government-owned companies with huge political overtones making such a system work. Outside the United States, such tolerance for failure—which is absolutely necessary for the trial-and-error nature of shale development—is rare.

The U.S. Monopoly on Shale

Consequently, the U.S. advantage in shale production is baked into the country's legal, political, and economic systems. Those systems came together in a crucible of technological advances and investment incentives in a way that has radically shifted the cost curve for the production of natural gas, NGLs, and crude oil. And of course, the shale revolution happened in the United States because it *needed* to happen in the United States. The fiscal and political consequences of a huge shift to much more imported energy could have had dire implications for the U.S. economy.

But there is a lot of shale outside U.S. borders, and the need for indigenous energy sources is just as great in many other countries. It is only a matter of time before they develop their own approaches to shale development, which are likely to be quite different from the systems and structures that have worked in the United States The question is: how much time will it take until that happens? How much longer can the United States expect to enjoy a virtual shale monopoly?

The reality is that, if all the pieces were in place tomorrow, it would take at least a decade before any other country could develop enough shale production to have a material impact on the market. This is not to say that it will take a decade for non-U.S. shale to happen. Even so, it will not grow to a level great enough to have an impact on world markets for at least a decade, and probably longer. There is just too much technology to be adapted, too much infrastructure to be built, and too many processes to be developed for it to happen any faster than that. And the reality is that all the pieces will not be in place tomorrow. So significant shale development outside the United States is even further down the road.

In the interim, the United States will enjoy an energy advantage relative to most of the rest of the world. That advantage has been quite unexpected both within the United States, as well as across the globe. The implications of that advantage are the subject of the next chapter.

Chapter 19

The Big Picture:
Economic and
Political Fallout

HIS IS A BOOK ABOUT ENERGY MARKETS. AS SUCH, UP UNTIL NOW WE
*have avoided straying into the domain of policy and politics. These issues
can be contentious and ambiguous and are certainly not within the do-
minion of facts and statistics, which are the foundations of this work. However,
the shale revolution has already had huge political, economic, and national defense implications on the global stage. Its impact will only grow in the coming
years. So it would not be right to go through 21 chapters about the shale revolution without briefly examining its political and policy ramifications.*

*These two spheres, policy and politics, are undergoing a radical shift in their per-
ception of energy markets, not only in the United States but also around the globe,
because of the newfound abundance of DBHs in the United States. Previous chapters
have covered how, prior to the shale revolution, the United States was gearing up
for huge increases in natural gas imports in the form of LNG and continuing increases in crude oil production. NGLs had been viewed as a backwater of the energy
markets, no more than a byproduct of gas production. Now that outlook has been
turned on its head by the expectation of LNG exports, the elevation of NGLs to a
key role in energy markets, and a global crude oil surplus that crushed prices in late
2014 and early 2015, inciting calls for changes in U.S. law to allow crude oil exports.*

*These developments have been responsible for equally significant shifts in ex-
pectations across the globe. Both friend and foe alike have become aware that the*

United States is no longer very dependent on overseas sources of energy. In fact, the U.S. can and will be an important source of energy for others. One important implication is that the United States might be a little less likely to go to war to protect a crude oil-producing regime. Beyond that, the United States might be in a position to replace an energy source previously used by one country as political leverage over another.

Such perceptions are out there, and they are influencing the behavior of all producers and consumers of energy—which means pretty much everyone. In this chapter, we will examine several of the most important economic and political is-sues happening now and how they may play out in the near future for seven of the most important global energy market segments: OPEC, Europe, Russia, China, Japan, Latin America, and the United States.

OPEC

Since 2008, U.S. imports of crude oil from OPEC have been cut almost in half. OPEC now provides less than 20% of U.S. crude oil supplies, with Saudi Arabia making up less than half of that number. Clearly, that fact was front and center when on Thursday, November 27, 2014—the U.S. Thanksgiving holiday—OPEC members attending their Vienna meeting announced they would keep their current production ceiling in place. OPEC would not cut production in response to a growing surplus of world crude oil supplies, coming mostly from U.S. shale. The market response was fierce. Brent prices fell from $78/bbl on November 26 to $60/bbl by mid-December. Since then, many tomes have been written on OPEC's apparent strategy to retain market share at the expense of price. After all, several of the key OPEC members can produce oil at prices well below U.S. shale and Canadian bitumen producers. So the logic goes, OPEC (or at least the key OPEC decision-makers) have concluded that retaining mar-ket share at the expense of current revenue is the best way to handle a growing global surplus of crude oil. After all, the alternative is cutting back production, which also forgoes some revenue, theoretically to be offset by rising prices due to lower supplies. But the unintended consequence would be to yield market share to higher-cost producers in North America who would also enjoy those higher prices and continue to increase their pro-duction, displacing OPEC production in world markets.

While OPEC's strategy may be subject to debate, there is no dispute about the fact that OPEC has been losing crude oil market share to North America. As discussed in Chapter 15, from 2008 to 2014, U.S. crude oil imports decreased 2.4 MMbbl/d, Canadian imports increased 0.9 MMbbl/d, and U.S. net petroleum product exports increased by 1.5 MMbbl/d. Thus almost 5.0 MMbbl/d of barrels that previously satisfied these imports now must find other markets around the globe. Most of these barrels can be viewed as loss of market share for OPEC.

This dramatic reduction in U.S. dependence on overseas imports has important implications for U.S. energy policy, and OPEC countries have seen the handwriting on the wall. The United States is simply not as worried about dependence on OPEC as it was in the past. Arab countries historically friendly to the United States now fear U.S. disengagement, based on a concern that the Middle East now is not nearly as important to U.S. strategic interests as it was in past decades. Of course, Saudi Arabia is the country with the most to worry about; about one-third of OPEC production and most of the country's revenues come from sales of its crude and petroleum products. Not only must the Saudis be concerned about a declining reliance on imported crude, but at the same time the United States has pulled back from Iraq and Afghanistan and is facing more toward domestic issues. Put this all together and it is not surprising that Saudi Arabia might sense the U.S. commitment to the region is on the wane.

On the other hand, Iran appears to be slightly more amenable, and seemingly more willing to negotiate the nuclear issue than in years past. Some have speculated that this is because Iran has concluded the United States no longer fears the possibility of oil production cutbacks and may be more willing to take military action if Iran gets too aggressive with its nuclear program. Of course, it is impossible to know if such thinking goes on in Iran, but it is certainly a possibility.

Europe

The U.S. shale revolution is a good-news-and-bad-news story for Europe. On the good-news side of the ledger, Europe has historically been highly dependent on imports from Russia and OPEC. Russia provides about one-third of Europe's crude oil and a quarter of its natural gas. Another

40% of its oil, along with a smaller percentage of its gas, comes from OPEC. With the United States moving toward the certainty of natural gas exports (in the form of LNG), U.S. crude oil supplies driving global crude prices lower, and increasing U.S petroleum exports in one form or another—gasoline, diesel, condensate, or perhaps even crude oil itself—Europe can look forward to lower oil and gas prices. The prospects are good for Europe to diversify its supply sources and therefore diminish the leverage Russia and OPEC have over its economies.

Unfortunately, the bad news is threefold. First, the dramatic decline in world crude oil prices has killed off much of Europe's fledgling shale development. Until late 2014, high crude oil prices provided the economic incentive for a few companies to break the U.S. monopoly on shale described in Chapter 18. But the combination of poor well performance across much of Europe, plus the impact of low crude oil prices,

Shale development in countries other than the United States has been virtually killed off by lower crude oil prices.

was too much for producers to take. Majors including Exxon, Chevron, and Shell halted or dramatically cut shale spending in Poland, Hungary, Germany, Romania, and Ukraine. Other than the U.S., other parts of the world are also seeing cutbacks. This is Domino 28.

The second piece of bad news for Europe is that cheap natural gas in the United States gives U.S. industrials, petrochemical plants, and refineries a significant cost advantage over European competitors that pay at least twice as much for their gas. For economies which must rely on exports for a big portion of their GNP, this translates into difficulties for European countries in global markets.

Third, European petrochemical plants and refineries are at particular risk from the U.S. shale revolution. In the petrochemical sector, cheap NGL feedstocks—in particular ethane—are driving investments in new steam crackers. You recall that was Domino 8. U.S. petrochemical demand is not increasing, which means most of the ethylene, in the form of derivative products like polyethylene, will be pushed into the global market, using a lower price as the primary leverage. U.S. petrochemical producers can afford the price competition because of their cheaper NGL feedstock costs. Most European petrochemical producers are stuck with higher-priced feedstocks and thus may be elbowed out of the market.

The situation is even worse for European refineries, which have been in decline for decades due to lack of investment, difficult regulatory regimes, and a weak European economy. As long as the United States continues its ban on crude oil exports, the only choice to relieve crude oil surplus supplies on the Gulf Coast (Dominoes 19 and 20) is for U.S. refineries to produce more refined petroleum products for export. Due to the oversupply of Gulf Coast crude—and the fact that the Gulf Coast is the largest, most sophisticated center of refinery capacity in the world—U.S. refiners will be able to produce petroleum products at a significant cost advantage versus European refiners. Fear has gripped not only European refiners but their host countries as well. U.S. cost advantages are likely to put many European refineries out of business and throw thousands of people out of work, meanwhile increasing Europe's dependence on imports for its transportation fuels. Clearly, the bad news aspects of this scenario portend difficult market conditions for Europe.

Russia

The U.S. shale revolution creates even more difficulties for Russia. That changed in 2014: it is now the United States. Just a few short years ago, Russia was planning on the United States becoming a major new customer for its LNG exports. That is no longer in the cards. In fact, Russia must face the prospect that its exports will have to compete with LNG from the United States, particularly in Asia. Of course, that problem pales in comparison with the much more difficult issue resulting from the U.S. shale revolution: prices. As crude oil prices crashed in 2014–15 and LNG prices also dropped (since the pricing in many LNG contracts is tied to crude prices), there have been dire implications for Russia's economy. That is because over 60% of Russia's exports are oil and gas, and the funds from those exports make up about 30% of the country's GDP. Consequently, as crude prices dropped, the value of the ruble was slammed and inflation soared. Some of these economic woes may have come from sanctions imposed by the United States and other countries due to the Ukrainian situation, but lower crude prices are a big contributor to Russia's economic problems.

Russia's problems from the shale revolution go beyond the economic realm. Russia's energy exports have provided clout in the world economy, but lower prices and market share competition from the United States weaken that clout. Russia controls about one-third of Europe's oil supply and a quarter of its gas supply; it was planning to increase its European market share. Although most European countries did not welcome those prospects—particularly in light of the Ukrainian developments—they were also facing continuing declines in their own oil and gas production. So the situation from Europe's perspective looked grim: having to accept Russia's supplies on Russia's terms. But now with lower prices and the potential for U.S. gas, petroleum products, and perhaps even crude oil exports, Europe can afford to be more assertive in negotiating terms and pricing.

Russian Warnings

As an interesting aside, back in 2012 Gazprom executives were actively trying to talk down shale. The Wall Street Journal reported that Gazprom Deputy Chief Executive Alexander Medvedev said that shale drilling, which requires fracking, poses "significant environmental risks, particularly the hazard of surface and underground water contamination with chemicals applied in the process." Somehow, these environmental concerns coming from Russia did not ring true to many observers. In fact, it has since been reported[1] that Russia has begun fracking in Western Siberia, using Western technologies.

It is clear the U.S. shale revolution has convinced Russia to make a strategic shift toward the East. In May 2014, Russia took a big step in that direction by inking a reported $400-billion deal to sell natural gas from Siberia to China. It is a 30-year arrangement that, presumably, will divert gas to China that otherwise would have gone to Europe. This deal provides a new market for Russia and a new source of a clean fuel for China, a good thing for both countries. Even though it is a significant volume of gas, it still will not make China materially more dependent on Russia for its energy supplies. China's appetite for energy resources is much too big for that.

China

In 2010, China became the largest energy-consuming country in the world. The EIA has estimated that China accounted for one-third of the world's growth in oil consumption in 2013. However, in 2014 and 2015, China's crude oil demand growth slowed along with other parts of the Asia/Pacific market, a development which has been blamed as a factor in the crude oil price crash. China's demand is still growing, but apparently not quite fast enough to absorb enough of the barrels displaced by production increases from North America. Whether or not that continues to be the case will depend in part on the outlook for coal.

Coal is by far the largest energy source used in China, making up about 70% of the total. Oil is approximately 18%, with natural gas only about 5%. That much coal consumption has resulted in significant air pollution problems for China. The Chinese government announced plans to reduce coal use to no more than 65% of the country's total energy mix by 2017, thus one of the drivers of the deal with Russia described above.

Buying natural gas from Russia is simply an extension of China's strategic goal of energy supply diversity. Even as recently as 2013, China purchased roughly half (about 3.0 MMbbl/d) of its total crude oil imports from the Middle East. It is apparent that the Chinese wish to change the state of their dependence on that volatile region. One way of addressing that goal has been investing in U.S. shale through its state-owned oil companies. In 2010, China National Offshore Oil Corporation (CNOOC) did a $2-billion joint venture with Chesapeake Energy in the Eagle Ford Basin. Two years later, in 2012, China Petroleum & Chemical Corporation (Sinopec) did a similar $2.5-billion deal with Devon Energy focused in the Tuscaloosa Marine Shale in Alabama and Mississippi, the Niobrara Shale in Colorado, and the Utica Shale in Ohio. The next year, Pioneer Natural Resources did a deal in the Permian Basin with Sinochem for $1.7 billion to sell a 40% stake in the southern half of its Wolfcamp acreage. All of these deals benefit the Chinese by providing access to U.S. shale production, whether or not the volumes will actually be exported to China. In addition, presumably the Chinese get the benefit of an education in shale production techniques, which is no doubt one of their most important long-term motivations behind these deals.

Japan

Japan's dependence on Middle East energy is far more problematic than China's. The country imports 85% of its energy, with most of its oil imports coming from the Middle East. Japan is the largest importer of LNG, with most of those supplies sourced both from the Middle East and Southeast Asia (Malaysia and Indonesia).

For several decades, an important component of Japan's strategy to diversify its energy supplies was nuclear power. Beginning in 1966, and for more than forty years thereafter, 54 nuclear reactors were built across the country and at one point provided more than 30% of its electric power. That all came to an end on March 11, 2011, when a massive earthquake and tsunami devastated the northeastern part of the country, severely damaging three reactors at the Fukushima Daiichi Nuclear Power Plant, which eventually resulted in a shutdown of Japan's nuclear industry.

With its nuclear power generation either in limbo or permanently shut down, Japan has been aggressively pursuing supplies of both LNG and LPG from producers around the world, including North America. Japan's U.S. energy supply strategy includes investment deals similar to the Chinese, such as Tokyo Gas's investment of about $0.5 billion in 25% of Quicksilver Resources' Barnett shale-producing assets. It also includes long-term purchase arrangements from U.S. LNG export terminals.

Those LNG export deals are not only intended for fuel-generating capacity to replace nuclear plants. Japan is using lower-U.S. natural gas commodity prices as leverage in negotiations with Middle East and Southeast Asia LNG suppliers that have held on, at least in part, to LNG contracts with prices indexed to crude oil. The so-called JCC or "Japanese Crude Cocktail" price represents the average price of crude imported into Japan and is the pricing basis for most of Japan's LNG imports. With crude oil prices lower and the prospects of U.S. imports on the horizon, Japan is whittling away at some of the JCC pricing, diversifying its price mix as well as the sources of its supplies. Japan is replacing a portion of its supply with LNG prices based on the value of gas at its production source, such as the Henry Hub in the United States, thus providing protection against some future escalation of crude prices.

Latin America

All three of the major oil-producing countries south of the U.S. border—Mexico, Brazil, and Venezuela—have been hit hard by the decline in crude prices, but each in its own way. Mexico is in the process of major reforms in its oil industry, opening investment to companies from outside the country for the first time since 1938, when its oil industry was nationalized. The timing of much lower crude prices could not have been worse for those promising a huge economic boost from a more open Mexican energy market.

Brazil's problems are of a different nature. Just a few years ago, Brazil was getting geared up to exploit what are known as the *pre-salt oil deposits*, a huge group of potential oil fields off the coast of Brazil in deep water under a thick layer of salt below the ocean floor. Recently, a series of corruption scandals threw a wrench into pre-salt development plans, and the situation has been made much worse by lower oil prices. Most estimates show that $100/bbl oil prices will be needed to produce the pre-salt oil. Many of the projects to produce the pre-salt were put on hold when prices declined.

And then there is Venezuela. Oil makes up most of Venezuela's exports, and since Hugo Chavez came to power in 1999 (into the regime of his successor, Nicolás Maduro), most of that revenue has been used for a combination of popular social programs, infrastructure, subsidized gasoline, free oil to its Caribbean neighbors, and corruption. With oil prices lower, the money to pay for all of this has been cut severely. Consequently, the country is in serious trouble, with reported shortages of basic goods, failures in medical services, and the distinct threat of Venezuela defaulting on its national debt.

If all of these economic and social consequences of lower crude prices were not problems enough, these countries must also deal with the same market share competition threatening other producers around the world. Historically, Mexico and Venezuela have exported about one-third of their production to the United States (Brazil exports a much smaller volume to the United States). With U.S. crude production increasing and Canadian imports also growing, there is no doubt that the United States will need far less supply from either Mexico or Venezuela.

The problem for both of these countries is exacerbated by the fact that most of the oil imported from Mexico and Venezuela is heavy crude, which the refinery system on the U.S. Gulf Coast is ideally suited to process. If Canadian heavy crude displaces imports from Mexico and Venezuela, then the crude from those two countries must find markets that are both farther away (thus incurring higher cost transportation) and less compatible with the quality of the crude (thus reducing the value of refined products produced from the crude). Consequently, the netback prices received by the two countries to the south could be several dollars per barrel lower than historical values based on U.S. yields. That will compound problems that both countries are already experiencing with declining prices and production volumes.

United States

The economic and political implications of the shale revolution in the United States could fill volumes and certainly cannot be addressed here in just a few paragraphs. But we can touch on a few general issues, which may provide some insight into the rapidly changing energy policy dynamics in the United States.

At the most basic level, the country is struggling with a massive transformation from a market of shortage to one of abundance, which has happened, in political terms, almost overnight. Many still have doubts that this transformation is real. How could such a huge shift have occurred when U.S. industry leaders and policy makers had been warning of, and preparing for, declining production for decades?

Some wonder if it *should* be real. If the shale revolution is dependent on fracking, which some believe is an environmental disaster waiting to happen, shouldn't the government nip this thing in the bud? If that is not true and the shale revolution can continue to yield abundant quantities of cheap, domestic hydrocarbon energy, what does that mean for renewable energy sources which were counting on high-cost energy imports to justify their economics? And finally, if the shale revolution is a good thing, then how does the U.S. government reverse decades of geopolitical policy without throwing both allies and foes into a tizzy? Only time will tell. We leave it to the policy makers and politicians to answer those questions.

But for our purposes, let's assume the shale revolution is in fact a good thing, that prudent government regulation will address fracking concerns and other environmental issues, and that the combination of policy reforms and investment dollars will result in a U.S. market truly integrated with the global markets for crude oil, natural gas, and natural gas liquids. This would mean imports and exports of natural gas, NGLs, crude oil, and petroleum products would be based on market dynamics, not government policy. Admittedly, all this might be seeing through rose-colored glasses (or blinders, depending on your politics), but stay with the concept and let's see where it leads us.

The most profound result would be that the United States would likely achieve energy independence, or at minimum, independence from all except our northern neighbor, Canada, a country unlikely to hold the U.S economy hostage for political purposes. Until the rest of the world catches up with shale—a development many years, if not decades, away, as pointed out in the previous chapter—the United States would enjoy a competitive advantage in the global energy market unmatched by all but a few (Middle East) countries. Such a development would stimulate exports, which would fuel economic growth, which would in turn encourage increases in employment and bring with it the long-sought goal of America's energy independence. It would also be an extraordinary development for the U.S. balance of payments and the trade deficit. By exporting significant volumes of natural gas, NGLs, petroleum products, and perhaps even crude oil, the U.S. economy could dig out of deficits and see the surplus side of the ledger for the first time since the Bill Clinton presidency.

Perhaps most significantly, the days of panic when another country threatens to cut oil supplies to the U.S. are quickly becoming ancient history. In a world where the sum total of United States energy *could* come from North America—whether it actually does so or not—means that economic blackmail using energy as the cudgel would no longer have national security repercussions for the United States. If you buy even part of that logic, the shale revolution could be one of the most important developments for the United States since that last revolution 240 years ago. And that one worked out pretty well for the United States.

Political Fallout

The shale revolution is shifting the political landscape. OPEC may be abdicating the role of swing crude producer. Japan is enjoying far cheaper energy prices. Weak oil-producing countries are in chaos. The United States has reclaimed its role as a major energy exporter. This is Domino 29.

Lower crude oil prices have changed the political landscape in countries across the globe.

Note

1. www.corpwatch.org/article.php?id=15931

Chapter 20

You Ain't Seen Nothin' Yet: The Next Dominoes to Fall

D*OMINOES ARE TOPPLING FASTER AND FASTER. THE PACE OF GROWTH IS accelerating. Revolutionary changes are just around the corner. Yes, all of these statements are true. But the irony is that the most significant transformations in energy markets are still a few years in the future. **You ain't seen nothin' yet**.*

In 2020, the United States could be exporting far more LNG than it ever imported, providing the largest single outlet for surplus natural gas supplies. But it will take a few years for those LNG liquefaction plants to be completed. In the same time frame, all crude imports, except for those from Canada, may have vanished. But it won't happen overnight. There are a lot of wells that need to be drilled between now and 2020. Similarly, new petrochemical plants and export facilities could eliminate the current surplus of NGLs. But it will take several more years for most of those assets to be built and placed into service. In the interim, U.S. energy markets are in a bit of a limbo period, with the potential for production growth expected to outstrip demand growth in all three of the DBHs. This potential supply-and-demand imbalance has profound implications for energy markets, both in the United States and around the world.

In this penultimate chapter, we pull together everything that has happened in energy markets over the past decade as a foundation for looking forward. What dominoes will be dropping next? What could go wrong? If things go right, how good could it get? What do you need to watch for in order to anticipate which way the dominoes are tipping? Those are the questions we will address here.

The First 30 Dominoes

There are a lot of moving parts to the domino effect. So to put the projections of this chapter in the proper perspective, it is important that we step back one more time for a very brief refresher on the first 30 dominoes that have already dropped.

In Chapters 2 and 3 we reviewed the Sweet Sixteen, the first dominoes to fall from inception of the shale revolution through 2012. The following are sound bites for those first dominoes: (1) shale technologies hit the natural gas markets, driving new efficiencies and productivity throughout the industry; (2) this productivity stimulated natural gas production, resulting in a supply overhang and (3) falling gas prices, (4) but crude oil prices stayed strong, supported by global markets, resulting in diverging crude and gas prices; (5) to avoid low returns for dry gas wells, producers shifted drilling budgets to wet (high Btu) gas and crude oil plays; (6) consequently, NGL production increased, (7) driving down prices for NGLs, particularly ethane and propane (8) with very positive consequences for petrochemical manufacturers. In the crude oil markets, (9) production in the Bakken and Midcontinent plus Canadian imports increased dramatically, well beyond the ability of the pipeline infrastructure to move the barrels to market, (10) resulting in wide Cushing-vs.-U.S. Gulf price differentials, (11) with very positive consequences for Midcontinent refiners. Meanwhile in the gas sector, (12) wet and associated gas kept production strong, (13) so natural gas prices remained weak, resulting in (14) a massive shift by power companies to gas-fired generation in 2012; low gas prices drove (15) a decline in the use of coal for power generation and (16) a resurgence in the use of gas for new industrial capacity.

Since 2012, 14 more big dominoes have toppled, which we reviewed in Chapters 15, 16, 17, and 18. In the crude oil market, (17) most of the growth in U.S. crude oil production turned out to be light-sweet crude and condensate that overwhelmed the capacity of Midcontinent refineries to use it; (18) the additional light crude, combined with imports of heavy Canadian crude, resulted in a dumbbelled (quality imbalanced) crude slate for U.S. refiners; (19) surplus Midcontinent inventories encouraged development of new pipeline capacity to the Gulf Coast; (20) as increasing volumes of crude oil moved to the Gulf Coast, imports were backed out and refiners maximized runs. The net result was to push U.S. crude surpluses into the world market; (21) the combined impact of U.S. crude oil, product surpluses, and lower demand led to a dramatic decline in world crude oil prices.

NGL markets have also been characterized by growing surpluses: (22) ethane production will continue to exceed the volume that can be absorbed by the U.S. petrochemical industry, even after several new petrochemical plants are built; (23) consequently, for the first time, infrastructure is being developed for significant volumes of overseas exports of ethane; (24) similarly, propane exports have increased dramatically, and more exports of propane, butane, and natural gasoline are probably on the way.

Like NGLs, natural gas surpluses are targeting export markets; (25) there have been huge increases in Northeast natural gas production from the Marcellus and Utica plays, with (26) increasing Appalachian production resulting in much lower natural gas prices in the region, (27) and as a result, new pipeline takeaway capacity being built out of the Northeast is reversing the direction of gas flows across the United States.

Following the decline in world crude prices, three other big dominoes fell. Those lower crude oil prices had (28) a negative impact on prospective returns for international shale projects, and (29) those low prices shifted the political landscape for crude producers. The decline and fall of Domino 30 is coming up later in this chapter.

The next dominoes will be toppled by the 30 that came before but will not do so randomly. Instead, they will drop based on the relationships between the DBHs that were described in Chapter 4 as the six domino principles.

Looking Into the Future—The Domino Principles

So we need one final refresher to have a clear view into the future. Dominoes have toppled the way they have due to the influence of the six domino principles. The bottom line on these principles is that the DBHs come from the same source but go to different markets and have different values depending on how they are used. As we have covered throughout the chapters of this book, DBH's are linked at their source—the well—but are diverse in their market destinations. Here is a recap of the six domino principles:

1. **All three DBHs are produced by drilling a well.** Because of that common source of supply, one DBH domino can knock over one of the other DBHs' dominoes.
2. **All three DBHs compete for the same investment dollar.** Producers will allocate their drilling budgets to the DBH that makes the most money.
3. **The price drivers for each DBH are unique.** The market response of each DBH to changes in supply and price can be quite varied because the downstream uses for the DBHs are very different from each other.
4. **All of the DBHs are subject to the same laws of energy markets regarding flow, capacity, and price differentials.** Each of the DBH markets will experience the full wrath of transportation capacity constraints and resulting negative price consequences.
5. **The production of one DBH influences the production of the others.** The impact of this principle will continue to grow and has the potential to relegate natural gas to the role of a byproduct across much of the U.S. market.
6. **Supply-and-demand dynamics in the DBH markets are both distinct and interrelated.** Oversupply in one DBH has the potential to influence supply and demand in other DBHs.

As we look to the future, each of the six principles is primed to impact the tumbling of more dominoes. Some of the most significant of those dominoes are already wobbling in the natural gas market.

Collision of Natural Gas Surpluses

In Chapter 17 we saw how rapidly growing natural gas production in the Northeast will soon exceed demand in that region. Regional oversupply has already depressed natural gas prices across much of Appalachia, and that development is driving scores of new pipeline projects to increase takeaway capacity. That buildout will soon result in a reversal of gas flows across the United States, with most gas moving south and west rather than in its traditional flow patterns to the north and east.

Over the next few years, these gas supplies will move into several demand sectors that are expected to grow, including new gas-fired power generation, industrial demand, and exports. These new demand sources can eventually absorb a significant portion of the surplus. Since much of that demand growth is in areas outside the Northeast, the pipeline capacity being added to the region is not only necessary to relieve takeaway constraints, it is equally needed to move gas supplies to growing markets, many of which are in the southeastern portion of the United States. However, it will take several years for that new demand to develop. In the meantime, Northeast gas surpluses will take market share from other producing regions in North America. Over the next few years, these Appalachian supplies will displace gas that previously moved into the Northeast from producers in Canada, the Rockies, the Midcontinent, and the Gulf Coast. As new pipeline expansions and reversals provide routes to physically move gas into those markets, Northeast gas will be able to capture market share from what were, in the past, secure local markets for these producers.

But there is a problem in that competition for market share. The Northeast is not the only supply region that has been experiencing growth. Producing regions in the middle part of the United States—the Eagle Ford, Permian, Oklahoma region, and the greater Rockies (Williston/Niobrara) have also increased, primarily from gas associated with crude oil production and wet gas containing large quantities of NGLs.

Future production in these basins will be heavily influenced by the level of crude oil prices. But if this growth continues, the stylized map below suggests the implications. Most of the production growth from the Northeast will be moving west, but those flows will encounter significant market competition—in effect, a *wall* of increasing supply from those four producing regions, all of which are being driven by the economics of oil and NGLs to produce more gas supplies, so much so that natural gas is frequently relegated to byproduct status (principle #5). Natural gas is produced because it comes along with the oil, not because of the value of the natural gas itself. But that does not mean natural gas production is not increasing rapidly. In fact, pipeline capacity and markets to absorb gas from those regions are nearing maximum capacity, with limited outlets going to the West or the Midwest. That leaves only one outlet for those supplies: the Gulf Coast. The implication is that Northeast supplies bearing down on the Gulf Coast will run directly into supplies from western basins, with the collision of gas flows occurring primarily in the states of the Southeast and centered in Louisiana. Such a collision would be a big domino.

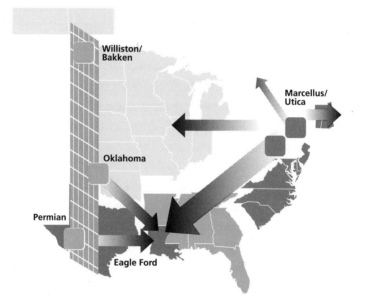

Figure 20.1. Possible natural gas flows

We've Seen This Kind of Gas-on-Gas Competition Before

As this book goes to press, market conditions are somewhat similar to the market share competition described in Chapter 14 between Rockies gas and the shale plays a decade ago. Back then, Rockies supply had grown beyond the ability of pipelines to move surpluses out of the region. The lack of takeaway capacity resulted in a price collapse within the region. But the rest of the national market, represented by Henry Hub prices, was protected from this impact by the same constraints that made the local impact so severe—in essence, the oversupply monster was fenced in.

Eventually the capacity constraints were relieved, primarily by the completion of the Rockies Express (REX) pipeline from the Rockies to Ohio. The oversupply monster got out. The local Rockies market prices saw immediate relief as its prices approached Henry Hub price levels, but the freeing up of the supply surge hit national markets, causing prices across the country to feel the impact and begin falling. At almost the same time the Rockies supply surge reached the market, it was joined by simultaneous and competing natural gas supply growth from new shale plays, from the Haynesville, Fayetteville, and Barnett coming into Louisiana on new pipeline capacity from Texas and Oklahoma.

All of this supply eventually converged on the Henry Hub, and prices fell to a threshold price low enough to discourage drilling in both the Rockies and those new shale plays. That threshold price turned out to be an economic breakeven price of about $4.00/MMBtu. Not coincidentally, the national price at the Henry Hub declined to about $4.00/MMBtu.

This Time, Natural Gas Price Implications Are Different

But this time it is Northeast gas versus the western shale basins. With supply possibly pouring into the Southeast market from the east and west, significant increases in demand will be necessary to balance the market. As described in Chapter 17, eventually this new demand will help balance the market. But the problem is one of timing. Only one LNG export facility—Sabine Pass, Louisiana—will be online in the 2015–16 time frame. The rest are not planned until 2018–2020, at best. In the ensuing years of 2015 through early 2018, natural gas production will be growing dramatically while LNG export capacity is under construction. The timing problem is further exacerbated by long lead times for industrial and power demand. The bottom line is, if all that gas gets produced, there is nowhere for it to go until new demand in the form of industrial plants, natural gas-fired generation, and export capacity are in operation, which is a few years out.

The implication is that, just like a decade ago, the supply half of the equation must help balance the supply-and-demand equation. But backing out imports will be extremely difficult. LNG imports are at zero while imports from Canada have nowhere else to go besides the United States. That suggests for the medium term, the only way the glut of supply can be relieved is for producers to cut back drilling activity in response to a decline in gas prices below their breakeven price levels. This would be another big domino.

Consequently, just like in the earlier market share competition between Rockies gas and the early shale gas plays, gas-on-gas competition between the Northeast and the western shale plays will likewise be concentrated in the Southeast, with much of the surplus gas flowing into Louisiana. But there is a significant difference between the earlier market situation and that of 2015. In the Rockies conflict, the breakeven price level for most dry gas was about $4.00/MMBtu. When oversupply required producer cutbacks, the price fell to a level at or below breakeven price, discouraging drilling activity in the marginal plays, which turned out to be dry gas-producing regions like the Haynesville and Barnett.

In the 2015–2020 time frame, the breakeven price situation looks to be quite different. Due to productivity improvements and other technological advances, breakeven prices are much lower. Thus the supply-and-demand balance scenario is similar to that of the Rockies dry gas conflict of 2009–10, but the implied floor to which natural gas prices could fall is much lower. If the average breakeven price was $4.00 in that earlier competition, in mid-2015 it is closer to $2.50/MMBtu. As increasing natural gas production volumes descend on the Louisiana area over the next few years, there would seem to be little besides the curtailment of producer drilling activity due to lower prices that could balance the market. If this scenario plays out, the domino of dramatically declining natural gas prices would have the potential to topple many other dominoes down the road.

Crude Oil: The Shale Revolution Hits Global Crude Oil Markets

In late 2014, the combined impact of U.S. crude oil and product surpluses, along with lower demand, led to a dramatic decline in world crude oil prices. That was Domino 21. This is a huge domino, not only because of its implications for global energy markets but also because of its potential impact on the other DBHs. The Great Divide, Domino 4, where crude prices diverged from natural gas prices, was a driving force throughout the most important early years of the shale revolution beginning in 2009. Could crude prices decline to a level where The Great Divide fades to obscurity? If so, what would it mean for each of the DBH markets?

The full impact of Domino 21 has yet to play out. We know that global crude oil prices have succumbed to the shale revolution and that this is a big breakaway from market conditions over the previous few years. From 2011 through Fall 2014, the price of the international benchmark Brent Crude remained rock stable, plus or minus a few dollars around $110/bbl. During that period, prices in the United States were being bounced around by the shale revolution and consequent infrastructure constraints, but international crude markets seemed relatively immune. Then in late 2014, the bottom seemed to drop out from under the price of Brent in reaction to increasing production from the United States and stagnant worldwide crude oil demand. The tipping point was reached over the Thanksgiving 2014 weekend, when OPEC failed to take any significant action to reduce production at a meeting in Vienna. The market perceived that a global crude surplus had developed and that prices could fall precipitously. It became a self-fulfilling prophecy on the Friday after Thanksgiving when Brent dropped to about $70/bbl, $40/bbl below its previous three-year average.

That development set up what amounts to a battle between U.S. producers and OPEC for market share. If the pain of lower prices eventually were to cause OPEC to cut production and thus increase prices, U.S. producers will continue to flood the market with additional barrels, meeting the demand that OPEC would have otherwise filled had production not been cut. If OPEC does not take action, or if that action turns out to be only superficial, then U.S. crude oil producers are in exactly the same situation as described above for natural gas producers. It will take a supply-side response to balance the market. This means the price must fall low enough for U.S. producers to meaningfully reduce the rate of production growth.

If OPEC never takes substantive action and demand stays tepid, then prices will theoretically fall to the point where the marginal producer—presumably the producer in North America—reduces drilling activity to the point where production growth grinds to a halt and eventually begins to decline.

Lower Prices and Crude Oil Production

The first phase of that theory played out over six months following the November 2014 crude price crash. U.S. producers hacked their drilling budgets in half, cutting the rig count by more than 50%. This is Domino 30, and it is significant. From November 2014 to mid-2015, the U.S. rig count fell from more than 1,900 to less than 860.

 Lower crude oil prices resulted in a dramatic decline in U.S. shale drilling activity.

With the decline in drilling activity, the theory then tells us that production should drop, eventually re-balancing the market. And to know when that domino will fall, theoretically *all* you need to know is that price threshold: the price below which producers cut drilling enough to impact production volumes. At least that is what theory would tell you. But the theory has three complicating factors: (1) It will probably take some time for any change in producer behavior to have a material impact on production, (2) it is not at all clear what price is necessary to result in meaningful declines in production, and (3) something we call the loop-back principle.

First, the complicating factor of timing. While producers have responded to lower prices by drilling fewer wells, to the surprise of some, the production response has, as of the publication date of this book, been quite muted. This is because the cause-and-effect relationship between drilling activity and production is quite abstruse. When producers cut back drilling budgets, they often focus their remaining investments on the very best "sweet spot" plays, which are likely to yield higher hydrocarbon output for each dollar of development cost, thus mitigating the impact of less drilling. Furthermore, as prices change, costs can also change. With lower prices come lower costs as service providers become considerably more willing to negotiate attractive prices for their services. As costs come down, so does the impact of lower crude prices on producer revenues. Finally, productivity keeps improving. The technology of shale development has steadily reduced the per-unit cost of production and will continue to do so, especially in the face of financial pressure. Put these factors together and it can take a considerable length of time for changes in price to have a material impact on the actual volume of hydrocarbons produced.

The second complicating factor is the determination of the price that will actually result in a significant change in producer returns. That gets us all the way back to Chapters 8–10 covering production economics, specifically Chapter 9 where we examined the data used in calculations and the math used to compute the rates of return. In that chapter we examined one representative Wolfcamp well and came up with a return of 31% based on a crude oil price of $70/bbl. While that may be a representative outcome for the basin, it is by no means the result you would obtain for any specific well. In fact, the variability around many of the key model inputs, such as well cost, initial production rate and decline rate, can be substantial, resulting in a high degree of variability of the financial outcomes. For a particular change in price to have a meaningful effect on the market, it must be sufficient enough to alter investment campaigns across a wide swath of producers over an extended period of time. While it is quite possible to analyze a representative well in a given basin for crude prices on a given day, how all of the input factors change over time can make a huge difference in producer returns and thus the level of production.

There is a third complicating factor: the loop-back principle. The calculation of returns includes a forecast of prices. But if the price used in the analysis is low enough to discourage drilling across a wide range of basins, and thus production growth is curtailed, would that not likely result in increasing prices and higher returns?

The implication of all of these complicating factors is that, if OPEC does not act to balance the crude oil market, there is a price level that over time will do so. But it is nearly impossible to determine in advance exactly what that price level will be. Beware of consultants bearing price forecasts.

So Where Will Crude Prices Land?

The most likely scenario is that crude oil prices will not be *landing* anywhere, anytime soon, at least if the definition of *landing* means stabilizing at a given level for an extended period of time. Consider the scenario where OPEC eventually cuts production and ratchets world crude prices back above $100/bbl. In that case, it is very likely that both U.S. and Canadian crude oil production will continue to increase, and over the next several years the remaining overseas imports into the United States will decline into oblivion.

Based on the numbers discussed in Chapter 15, when U.S. imports from overseas go to zero, the result will be another 5.5 MMbbl/d of crude jammed into the world crude market. Continued increases in product exports (gasoline and diesel) could add another 1.0 to 2.0 Mbbl/d over the next few years. Thus if crude oil prices return to their previously lofty levels through the good graces of OPEC, then OPEC will continue to lose market share to U.S. producers. This production potential will not simply go away. It will either be produced or it will hang over the market like the sword of Damocles. In the likely scenario where OPEC abdicates its role as price setter to U.S. producers, then the market price will be a constantly evolving value, based on an unpredictable interaction of economic, technological, and logistical factors. One way or the other, about the only certainty the crude oil market has in the future is uncertainty.

Dominoes in All Directions

Even though the future of crude oil prices may be fraught with uncertainty, the impact of lower crude oil prices is a bit more predictable, but no less momentous. For example, recall *principle five: the production of one DBH influences the production of the others*. If low crude oil prices result in significant cutbacks to oil production, not only will crude volumes be affected—associated natural gas production will decline as well. And with lower crude oil prices, NGL prices will also be lower, shrinking the economics for drilling for wet gas, thus reducing the production of gas produced along with NGLs. Lower natural gas production would tend to reduce natural gas supplies and tighten that market. So it is possible that a domino of lower crude prices leading to a lower crude production domino could lead to a domino of lower gas production and higher natural gas prices—a very ironic domino sequence indeed, if it were to play out that way.

A similar development is possible in the NGL market. The domino of higher natural gas prices could crash into a domino of lower NGL prices, pushed down due to the relationship of heavy NGLs (primarily butanes and natural gasoline) to lower priced crude oil. That would mean a lower frac spread, a domino that could tumble directly into low processing margins and poor processing economics. The possible ramifications of that domino will be addressed below.

Infrastructure dominoes could tumble as the geography of crude oil production shifts. Lower crude prices will impact the economics of each basin differently. For a corollary, we only need to look at the natural gas market when its prices declined in 2009. Gas production in some dry gas basins like the Haynesville, Fayetteville, and several Rockies basins declined. But production in the dry portion of the Marcellus in northeastern Pennsylvania took off like a skyrocket. More pipelines were needed in the Marcellus. Pipelines out of the Haynesville were vastly underutilized. The same economic impact is likely to selectively impact crude oil basins, depending on the level of crude oil prices.

These are only a few examples of the dominoes that could fall, depending on what happens to crude oil prices over the longer term. Many more secondary effects are down the road as the U.S. shale revolution forces more realignments across the drill-bit hydrocarbon markets.

Natural Gas Liquids: Multiple Domino Collisions

Chapter 16 explored the NGL dominoes that have dropped since 2012. Production volume from all five of the NGLs has increased, and the result is oversupply in each of the individual markets. But *principle three: the price drivers for each DBH are unique* is particularly pertinent to NGLs. Not only are NGL markets quite different from the other DBHs; the price drivers differ for each member of the NGL family.

Consider the following NGL market factors. In today's oversupplied marketplace, the petrochemical industry has little impact on the price for ethane, even though almost all produced ethane is consumed in the manufacture of petrochemicals. Instead, the ethane price is primarily dependent on rejection economics, which translates to the equivalent value of natural gas, adjusted for transportation and other cost differentials. Propane also moves to the petrochemical industry, but its prices are mostly buffeted by weather. Cold weather will usually boost prices due to spikes in demand. On the other hand, if there is too much propane for U.S. domestic markets the only other alternative is export markets, which become the primary factors influencing prices. Normal butane and isobutane get bounced around primarily by the value of motor gasoline and the gasoline blending season. Motor gasoline also has a big influence on natural gasoline prices, and natural gasoline will also be affected by the economics of oil sands bitumen production.

Even though today's NGL prices are influenced by a wide range of market factors, this disparate world of NGL price drivers looks to be converging, or at least trending toward convergence. It is an extremely complex and little understood trend, and it goes back to exports. To understand what may make NGL prices change over time, we need to consider the market outlook for each of the NGL products. This market outlook assumes that crude oil prices will be high enough (and production costs low enough) for NGL production volumes to continue increasing:

- Because ethane supplies exceed U.S. petrochemical demand, some portion of ethane surpluses will be exported. Almost all exported ethane is destined for the global petrochemical market, moving to steam crackers located in coastal regions of Europe and the Asia-Pacific region. These crackers will be converted from running their current feedstock to running ethane. For the most part, that current feedstock being replaced is naphtha.
- Gas processing plants will produce more propane than the United States can use for residential and commercial needs and for petrochemical demand. The balance will be exported. Most of those exports will go to feed steam crackers modified to run more propane. As with ethane, the feedstock displaced by propane will primarily be naphtha.
- It is a similar story for normal butane. Surpluses will move overseas, some into petrochemical markets where naphtha will be displaced

and some into the gasoline blend pool for refiners, effectively competing with naphtha-range materials in that market.

- Increasing production of natural gasoline from gas processing plants (itself a naphtha-range product), combined with lower demand for natural gasoline into refineries, will likely result in surplus barrels moving overseas. These barrels will compete with naphtha-range materials in the petrochemical and gasoline blending sectors.

Obviously, what all of the NGLs have in common is an outlook for overseas exports that will primarily compete with naphtha in world markets. Demand for naphtha-range material is not increasing. In fact, naphthas displaced by NGLs will compete directly with condensates that will be exported from the United States under the more liberal BIS rules, plus increasing motor gasoline exports from the United States as refiners invest in capacity to run more light-sweet shale crudes. Consequently, almost every road leading from U.S. surpluses of NGLs, condensate, and crude oil ultimately leads to surpluses of naphtha on the global market.

For NGLs, It All Comes Down to Naphtha

Unfortunately, the impact of naphtha surpluses cannot be easily gauged. World naphtha markets are a fragmented, opaque corner of the liquids hydrocarbon markets where there are few statistics available to provide insight as to how supply-and-demand balance. Even the term itself is ambiguous, sometimes referring to plant condensate (natural gasoline), field condensate, a mix of the two, and refinery naphthas. These naphthas come in a wide range of qualities as measured by API gravity, sulfur content, and other components. These qualities effectively determine the best market for any particular naphtha stream.

There is one more very important naphtha characteristic: whether it is paraffinic or naphthenic. Paraffinic naphthas and condensates contain a high percentage of paraffin compounds, making them best suited for use in steam crackers. Other condensates may contain higher percentages of naphthenes and aromatics, which are better suited for producing high-octane gasoline components or as a feedstock for petrochemical plants that produce aromatic chemicals like benzene. As a general rule, naphthenic condensates are priced higher than paraffinic condensates. To make matters even more complicated, condensates from different basins, even different parts of the same basins, can be more or less paraffinic or naphthenic.

It certainly appears likely that global naphtha supplies will be growing while at the same time naphtha demand will be displaced by U.S. NGLs and condensates. At this writing, it is quite uncertain as to which segments of the naphtha market will see the biggest impact from oversupply.

Since naphtha is rarely in the spotlight, an imbalance in the naphtha market may seem like an obscure imbalance in a distant market. Nothing could be further from the truth. The primary ingredient of motor gasoline is naphtha. As goes naphtha, so goes motor gasoline. So if there is a supply overhang of naphtha, it has the potential to translate directly into an oversupply of motor gasoline. In such an oversupply situation, refiners need to run less crude. Reduced crude purchases result directly in downward pressure on crude oil prices. Already, naphtha oversupply has contributed to weak crude oil prices. The more naphtha is pushed into a surplus position, the weaker crude oil prices are likely to become, all other things being equal. How the naphtha imbalance plays out will be an important factor in overall crude markets and so will be an important market to watch in coming years.

The Biggest Domino

We have identified 30 dominoes that have dropped between the onset of the shale revolution and the publication of this book. Each is important in its own right and even more significant in the linkages between events that define the domino effect. As we look back over how the domino effect has played out in the three DBH markets, there is a clear common theme: technology creates a surplus of supply, that surplus of supply creates infrastructure bottlenecks, and eventually the oversupply results in declining prices. It happened first to natural gas, then to NGLs, and finally to crude oil.

All three DBH markets are now moving toward the exact same market solution to rebalance supply and demand and to relieve downward pressure on prices. That solution is exports. The United States is undergoing a massive shift from shortage to surplus, which is transitioning the

U.S. role from the largest importer of energy to a major energy exporter. There is no bigger domino than this.

Swelling export volumes have huge political, economic, and national defense implications. In the political arena, energy exports will mean greater U.S. influence in growing economies in need of energy to fuel their growth. From an economic perspective, growth in energy exports translates directly into improvements in the balance of payments equation. And just as significantly, the era when a foreign producer can threaten the United States with production cuts has drawn to a close. In a world where most of the United States' energy supplies come from North America, threats from overseas oil-producing countries no longer have the same national economic or security implications they have had over the past four decades.

This is truly a revolution in energy markets, but it is also much more than that. The shale revolution is changing some of the most important drivers of the world economy. And that transformation will go far beyond energy.

Chapter 21

Over the Horizon: Assessment of the Opportunities

I believe in intuition and inspiration.... At times I feel certain I am right while not knowing the reason. When the eclipse of 1919 confirmed my intuition, I was not in the least surprised. In fact, I would have been astonished had it turned out otherwise. Imagination is more important than knowledge. For knowledge is limited, whereas imagination embraces the entire world, stimulating progress, giving birth to evolution.

> —Albert Einstein,
> *Cosmic Religion: With Other Opinions and Aphorisms* (1931), p. 97

You say you want a revolution ...

S HALE HAS BEEN A REVOLUTION. DOMINOES HAVE TOPPLED AND WILL *continue to fall. But what does this really mean for your business, for your career, and for the way energy will impact your life in the future? Even though shale has caused an energy revolution, all revolutions eventually culminate and things settle back into more sustainable patterns and processes. Sometimes the revolutionary changes are permanent. Other times they are quickly and violently reversed.*

So what about shale? Has the shale revolution brought a permanent change to the energy markets, creating opportunities for all who learn how those markets are likely to behave in the future? Or is shale a flash in the pan, destined to play

out in a few years, eventually consigning energy markets back to the world of
scarcity and the price shocks energy markets have faced in past decades?

These are reasonable concerns, because the U.S. energy industry has been
known for its boom-and-bust cycles. From those early days in Pennsylvania, to
Spindletop in Texas, and through the flourishing of offshore production in the
1960s and 70s, the icon for energy production was the gusher. When hydrocar-
bons pour out of a well, muddy wildcatters become wealthy oil barons. But inter-
spersed between these well-known booms and many others there were the busts,
characterized by crashing prices, devastated businesses, and massive layoffs.

Is This Just Another Cycle?

What about the shale revolution? Is it just another cycle? The shale revolution took off when technologies came along that radically changed the
cost structure for producing oil and gas. This is typical for the launch of a
boom cycle in the oil and gas patch: a new field gets discovered, a new
drill bit is invented, or a new way to drill shales with horizontal drilling
and hydraulic fracking is developed. One way or the other, it gets a lot
more profitable to produce a barrel of oil or a cubic foot of gas. Profits go
way up. Drilling rigs pop up like mushrooms. But inevitably, it seems, the
market goes awry. Producers become too successful for their own good.
Too many wells are drilled, surpluses develop, prices collapse, and companies fail. The weak players are weeded out of the market, demand re-
acts positively to lower prices, and gradually the supply-and-demand
equation comes back into balance. Then a few years later, the cycle starts
all over again.

Before shale, prevailing wisdom was that the United States had seen
the last such cycle within its borders, and that an increasing portion of
the country's hydrocarbon needs would be met by imports. The shale
revolution exposed the folly of that logic. But does that mean shale is
just one more boom doomed to turn into a devastating bust? There appears to be some evidence to that effect as a series of price collapses has
characterized the shale revolution. Natural gas production increased and
prices dropped in 2009. It happened to Midcontinent crude oil and
NGLs in 2011–12 and then again to global crude oil at the end of 2014.
Do these price declines signify the shale revolution is destined to repeat

boom and bust cycles? Perhaps not.

When the price collapse hit natural gas, most of the market reacted by becoming more efficient, lowering costs, and moving their drill rigs to more prolific plays. The result was not a production decline that would have characterized a bust, but continued production *increases* while prices remained low. The boom transformed itself into a sustainable market environment. It was the same story later for NGLs and Midcontinent crude oil; in both cases, lower prices changed the market but did not change the production growth trajectory. The market simply morphed in ways to handle the supply-and-demand imbalance, which did not result in market devastation. In late 2014, world crude oil prices collapsed, triggering predictions of a bust in U.S. crude oil production. As of this writing, the curtain has not fallen on this act. Perhaps it is another of those midcourse corrections that simply rebalance supply and demand just enough to maintain a healthy environment for producers and consumers alike.

For this to be true, it would mean shale must be quite different from a new play or a new drill bit. Shale would need to represent a fundamental change in the way energy markets work: a sustainable, self-correcting engine based on a technological shift permeating oil and gas production not only in the United States, but ultimately around the globe.

This is not only possible but probable. We could well be experiencing a very long-lived transformation of energy markets. The following three pillars support this hypothesis:

- **We are in the very early years of the shale revolution.** Producers continue to achieve significant improvements in productivity and learn how to replicate their success from one basin to the next. This productivity improvement suggests the possibility of continuing production growth, even in a lower-price environment.
- **As of mid-2015, the shale revolution has been confined to the United States. That will change.** It will take a decade or two, but obstacles to material shale production outside the United States (examined in Chapter 18) will eventually be overcome. There is a lot of shale out there. The benefits of shale technologies will eventually be applied and adapted to exploit the many different types of shale formations throughout the world.

■ **The various price collapses of the first shale decade were neither booms nor busts.** Granted, a few companies did not fare all that well when prices fell, with the industry experiencing layoffs following the decline of crude prices. But even after such a price correction, some wells continue to be drilled. Infrastructure continued to be developed. In hindsight, it is quite possible that these price corrections will be seen as growing pains and mid-course adjustments in the supply-and-demand equation.

This hypothesis of a long-term, technology-driven transformation is not at all certain. But consider the impact of a few other fundamental technological shifts: railroads, automobiles, airplanes, telephones, television, and the Internet. Each had their own booms and busts, but every one permanently changed the world. Could the shale revolution be a player in this league, or has it been just another boom in the long record of oil and gas cycles?

The Biggest Domino

We will not know the answer to that question for many years. But even if it is a cycle, it is a really big, important cycle. So either way, the permanent shortage mentality that has marked most of the past 40 years of oil and gas markets is a dead notion. The problem confronting most of today's oil and gas markets is abundance—as remarkable as it is to use that word. What to do with all this oversupply? Certainly that is the biggest domino of all.

The implications are profound at both the business and personal level. It is a whole new game in which, as Einstein said at the beginning of this chapter, "Imagination is more important than knowledge." Since the early 1970s, everyone who has grown up in the U.S. energy markets has done so in the context of shortage. There may have been occasional episodes of surplus, but they were always viewed simply as blips along the way toward the day when hydrocarbon supplies would run out. This time around, it is quite possible a market of abundance may be around for quite some time. That is a whole new world for everyone involved in the energy business. Success in navigating abundant energy markets will be far more dependent on the ability to think creatively and imaginatively than on relying on past experience from those bygone days of shortage. If there was ever a time to begin a career in the energy business, this is it. The opportunities just ahead are staggering.

But along with great opportunity comes great risk. It is very early in this new marketplace of abundance. The future offers high reward, along with high risk. The mistakes will be colossal. Most will miss the major turns in the market. But some will get it right, and a few will make fortunes.

Whether you end up making a fortune, building a career in the energy industry, or simply becoming more informed about one of the most significant economic developments in decades, this is certain: the future of energy markets will not be boring. Dominoes will continue dropping relentlessly. We are entering one of the most dynamic periods in an industry with a rich history of innovation, upheaval, and renewal. Welcome to the revolution.

We all want to change the world.
—John Lennon, "Revolution"

Index